# Fire and Gold

# Fire and Gold

## Benefiting from Life's Tests

compiled from the teachings of the Bahá'í Faith

*by Brian Kurzius*

GEORGE RONALD
OXFORD

GEORGE RONALD, Publisher
46 High Street, Kidlington, Oxford OX5 2DN


© This compilation Brian Kurzius 1995
Reprinted 1997
All Rights Reserved


British Library Cataloguing in Publication Data
A catalogue record for this book is available
from the British Library


ISBN 0-85398-402-6

Cover painting 'For Christine' and jacket design by Brian Kurzius
Typesetting by ComputerCraft, Knoxville, Tennessee
Printed and bound in Great Britain by
Redwood Books, Trowbridge, Wiltshire

To the memory of my spiritual father

*Richard Gowan*

without whose enthusiasm, deep devotion
and love for Bahá'u'lláh
this compilation would neither have been
started nor completed

# Contents

# Acknowledgements

This compilation has received much assistance during its development.

Particular thanks are due to Diane Iverson for her invaluable encouragement, advice and knowledge of the Bahá'í writings. Her enthusiasm was instrumental in bringing this book to completion.

To Wendi Momen, at George Ronald, I would like to express my sincere appreciation for her insightful editing of this compilation as well as her encouragement and patience during the long and, at times, arduous journey to publish this book.

To my sister and brother – Hope Zelinkski and Matthew Kurzius – and to the memories of my parents, Doris and Charles Kurzius, I give my deepest thanks and love.

I would also like to express my most heartfelt appreciation to the following people for their friendship and support during the years it took to complete this project: Jane Gowan, Geoffrey Boeckel, Michelle Walker, Teresa Gowan, Collen Gowan; Moin, Rajan and Ramin Burney; Rosamond Lincoln-Day; Ron PeaceTree; Peter Bornn and Millie Hezari.

Finally, this compilation would have been impossible had it not been for the efforts of countless others who have compiled and published the books quoted in this volume. It is upon their foundation that this book has been built.

# Introduction

Perhaps no greater gift exists than to be given comfort in a time of trial, hope in a time of suffering, guidance in a time of confusion and despair. It is in this spirit that this book is offered. In it are contained innumerable gems of guidance, comfort and hope drawn from the sacred writings and other literature of the Bahá'í Faith. It not only answers the age-old question of why suffering exists on this earth but, most importantly, explains how we can face and overcome the trials that beset us from time to time.

Basic to an understanding of the subject of tests and trials is an understanding of the nature and purpose of life. Bahá'u'lláh, the Prophet-Founder of the Bahá'í Faith, explained:

> The purpose of God in creating man hath been, and will ever be, to enable him to know his Creator and to attain His Presence.[1]

> All men have been created to carry forward an ever-advancing civilization. The Almighty beareth Me witness: To act like the beasts of the field is unworthy of man. Those virtues that befit his dignity are forbearance, mercy, compassion and loving-kindness towards all the peoples and kindreds of the earth.[2]

Bahá'u'lláh tells us that our purpose on earth is to know God and draw closer to Him, as well as to develop virtues and to 'carry forward an ever-advancing civilization'.

Bahá'u'lláh also explained that our soul is our true reality, not the physical body that we occupy for a few dozen years on this earth. This soul will continue to exist long after our body has returned to dust.

The time we spend on this earth is a period of preparation for our souls, a time to develop virtues and perfections in order better to know and draw closer to our Creator. For it is only by acquiring qualities such as love, mercy, patience and fortitude that we are able to understand the Creator who is the source of these virtues and their highest expression. These virtues are also the spiritual faculties we need in order to exist in the next world. 'Abdu'l-Bahá, the son of Bahá'u'lláh and the interpreter of His writings, explained:

> In the beginning of his human life man was embryonic in the world of the matrix. There he received capacity and endowment for the reality of human existence. The forces and powers necessary for this world were bestowed upon him in that limited condition. In this world he needed eyes; he received them potentially in the other. He needed ears; he obtained them there in readiness and preparation for his new existence . . .
>
> Therefore, in this world he must prepare himself for the life beyond. That which he needs in the world of the Kingdom must be obtained here. Just as he prepared himself in the world of the matrix by acquiring forces necessary in this sphere of existence, so, likewise, the indispensable forces of the divine existence must be potentially attained in this world.
>
> . . . In that world there is need of spirituality, faith, assurance, the knowledge and love of God. These he must attain in this world so that after his ascension from the earthly to the heavenly Kingdom he shall find all that is needful in that eternal life ready for him.
>
> . . . It is a world of perfections; virtues, or perfections, must be acquired.[3]

This physical world is thus a place for preparation and growth; a 'workshop' in which to develop virtues such as kindness, mercy, patience and fortitude – qualities which by their very nature exalt not only the individual but have a great effect on the growth and progress of civilization. Throughout our lives we are faced by many challenges and tests, and although we cannot control most of the experiences that come to us, we *can* choose how we respond to them. Contrary to the belief that we cannot control our emotions, the Bahá'í Faith teaches that through the exercise of free will we can choose most of our responses to the world around us. We choose to be patient or frustrated, accepting or angry, loving or dejected. The more we strive to exhibit virtues, the more we develop spiritually. And even when we fail to respond appropriately to a test, we can use our failures to learn more constructive ways of coping with our trials. As Shoghi Effendi, the great grandson of Bahá'u'lláh, explained:

> We must always look ahead and seek to accomplish in the future what we may have failed to do in the past. Failures, tests, and trials, if we use them correctly, can become the means of purifying our spirit, strengthening our characters, and enable us to rise to greater heights of service.[4]

The challenge of tests is to use them to grow rather than complaining about their appearance. For if we look upon our suffering as an opportunity to grow, we transform our negative experiences into positive ones and can develop capacities and strengths that we never knew existed.

All of us can remember a particular test which, at the time, was the worst catastrophe we could imagine, and yet when we look back on it we realize that it left us with greater fortitude, a stronger character or a better understanding of life.

We can also find countless examples of humans throughout history who, despite – and perhaps because of – tremendous personal crises, went on to make exceptional contributions to the progress of civilization. As Shoghi Effendi said:

> Suffering is both a reminder and a guide. It stimulates us better to adapt ourselves to our environmental conditions, and thus leads the way to self improvement. In every

suffering one can find a meaning and a wisdom. But it is not always easy to find the secret of that wisdom. It is sometimes only when all our suffering has passed that we become aware of its usefulness.[5]

\* \* \*

This compilation has been designed to explain the subject of trials and tribulations and to give us a better understanding of this mysterious and dynamic process. A few of the quotations are published here for the first time and some may not be familiar even to well-read Bahá'ís. This book is intended to bring comfort and hope to us all in our times of trial and to help us to understand the purpose of tests. Most importantly, it will help us deal with tests and enable us to make them the means of our growth and ultimate happiness.

The first section of the book is concerned with the purpose of tests: why we face them and the qualities they help us to develop. The second section describes the sources of the trials we face in life. The third section, and perhaps the most important, provides solutions to the tests and challenges facing us. The fourth section offers readings of comfort in times of illness, while the fifth section provides words of comfort to the bereaved.

Let there be no mistake, however. There is no quick and easy path when one is faced with tests. No matter how specific the guidance or clear the answer, the road can still be exhausting and difficult. The best that we can do is to struggle, be patient with ourselves and with others, and know that no matter how afflictive our suffering may be, no matter how or why this trial came to us, God's love for us, His care and protection, are strong and unending.

*Brian Kurzius*
*October 1995*

# The Purpose of Tests

*The Purpose of Tests:*

## To Draw Us Closer to God

# To Draw Us Closer to God

### The story of a lover and his beloved

There was once a lover who had sighed for long years in separation from his beloved, and wasted in the fire of remoteness. From the rule of love, his heart was empty of patience, and his body weary of his spirit; he reckoned life without her as a mockery, and time consumed him away. How many a day he found no rest in longing for her; how many a night the pain of her kept him from sleep; his body was worn to a sigh, his heart's wound had turned him to a cry of sorrow. He had given a thousand lives for one taste of the cup of her presence, but it availed him not. The doctors knew no cure for him, and companions avoided his company; yea, physicians have no medicine for one sick of love, unless the favour of the beloved one deliver him.

At last, the tree of his longing yielded the fruit of despair, and the fire of his hope fell to ashes. Then one night he could live no more, and he went out of his house and made for the marketplace. On a sudden, a watchman followed after him. He broke into a run, with the watchman following; then other watchmen came together, and barred every passage to the weary one. And the wretched one cried from his heart, and ran here and there, and moaned to himself: 'Surely this watchman is 'Izrá'íl, my angel of death, following so fast upon me; or he is a tyrant of men, seeking to harm me.' His feet carried him on, the one bleeding with the arrow of love, and his heart lamented. Then he came to a garden wall, and with untold pain he scaled it, for it proved very high; and forgetting his life, he threw himself down to the garden.

And there he beheld his beloved with a lamp in her hand, searching for a ring she had lost. When the heart-surrendered lover looked on his ravishing love, he drew a great breath and raised up his hands in prayer, crying: 'O God! Give Thou glory to the watchman, and riches and long life. For the watchman was Gabriel, guiding this poor one; or he was Isráfíl, bringing life to this wretched one!'

Indeed, his words were true, for he had found many a secret justice in this seeming tyranny of the watchman, and seen how many a mercy lay hid behind the veil. Out of wrath, the guard had led him who was athirst in love's desert to the sea of his loved one, and lit up the dark night of absence with the light of reunion. He had driven one who was afar, into the garden of nearness, had guided an ailing soul to the heart's physician.

Now if the lover could have looked ahead, he would have blessed the watchman at the start, and prayed on his behalf, and he would have seen that tyranny as justice; but since the end was veiled to him, he moaned and made his plaint in the beginning. Yet those who journey in the garden land of knowledge, because they see the end in the beginning, see peace in war and friendliness in anger.[6]

*Bahá'u'lláh*

## We achieve perfection through suffering

While a man is happy he may forget his God; but when grief comes and sorrows overwhelm him, then will he remember his Father who is in Heaven, and who is able to deliver him from his humiliations.

Men who suffer not, attain no perfection. The plant most pruned by the gardeners is that one which, when the summer comes, will have the most beautiful blossoms and the most abundant fruit.[7]

*'Abdu'l-Bahá*

Many a time a calamity leads to a bounty. Not until a man has endured hardship on account of a thing will he appreciate the full value of that thing. The more one suffers because of something or other, the better will one understand the worth of it. As the Qur'án says: 'Never will they attain (unto Divine bounty), except through severe trials.' . . . For the people of faith, trials and disasters and tribulations lead to spiritual progress, that is, if one bears them with patience and detachment from all save God. It is said in the Qur'án: 'Think ye to enter Paradise, when no such things have come upon you as on those who flourish before you? Ills and troubles tried them . . .' Man can never be intoxicated, unless he drink of these. Never can he feel the bliss of those who are drunk with the wine of loving God, unless he too has a draught from calamity's cup. The more you beat upon the steel, the sharper is your sword. The longer you leave gold in red-hot fire, the purer it will be.[8]

*Attributed to 'Abdu'l-Bahá*

## . . . *no matter what our minds and bodies go through*

. . . as we suffer these misfortunes we must remember that the Prophets of God Themselves were not immune from these things which men suffer. They knew sorrow, illness and pain too. They rose above these things through Their spirits, and that is what we must try and do too, when afflicted. The troubles of this world pass, and what we have left is what we have made of our souls, so it is to this we must look – to becoming more spiritual, drawing nearer to God, no matter what our human minds and bodies go through.[9]

*Written on behalf of Shoghi Effendi*

## *To enable humankind to draw closer to God*

The suffering of mankind, we know, must ultimately prepare it to turn to Bahá'u'lláh and His life-giving message – but how soon this process will be accomplished we cannot say. We can only strive to show forth the example which will attract men's hearts, and to busy ourselves day and night in spreading the Teachings.[10]

*Written on behalf of Shoghi Effendi*

Your letter . . . in which you share the anguish of your heart and express deep concern for the fate of the suffering masses of mankind has been received by the Universal House of Justice . . .

The world is clearly beset by ills and is groaning under the burden of appalling suffering. The trials of the innocent are indeed heart-rending and constitute a mystery that the mind of man cannot fathom. Even the Prophets of God Themselves have borne Their share of grievous afflictions in every age. Yet in spite of the evidence for all this suffering, God's Manifestations, Whose lives and wisdom show Them to have been far above human beings in understanding, unitedly bear testimony to the justice, love and mercy of God.

To understand the condition of the world it is necessary to step back, so to speak, to gain a clearer view of the panorama of God's great redemptive Major Plan, which is shaping the destiny of mankind according to the operation of the divine Will. It should not be surmised that the calamitous events transpiring in all corners of the globe are random and lack purpose, though individually they may be difficult to comprehend. According to the words of our beloved Guardian: 'The invisible hand is at work and the convulsions taking place on earth are a prelude to the proclamation of the Cause of God.' We can confidently anticipate therefore, the arrival of the 'new life-giving spring' once the destructive icy blasts of winter's tempests have run their course.

As Bahá'ís, we know that the 'sovereign remedy' for each and every one of these ills lies in turning and submitting to the 'skilled', the 'all-powerful' and 'inspired Physician'. Bahá'u'lláh has assured us in His writings that God has not forsaken us. He is the all-Seeing and All-Knowing, the 'prayer-hearing, prayer-answering God' to those who turn to Him in supplication, and He intervenes actively in human history by sending His Manifestations, Sources of knowledge and spiritual truth, to 'liberate the children of men from the darkness of ignorance' and to 'ensure the peace and tranquillity of mankind'. In this Age, God has determined to establish His everlasting

Kingdom among men, and so, to this end, He sent us the spirit
and message of the New Day through two successive Manifestations, Who alas, were rejected by the generality of people.[11]

*Written on behalf of the Universal House of Justice*

*The Purpose of Tests:*

*Moral and Spiritual Development*

# Moral and Spiritual Development

O Son of Man! For everything there is a sign. The sign of love is fortitude under My decree and patience under My trials.[12]

*Bahá'u'lláh*

## Spiritual development

The more difficulties one sees in the world the more perfect one becomes. The more you plough and dig the ground the more fertile it becomes. The more you put the gold in the fire the purer it becomes. The more you sharpen the steel by grinding the better it cuts. Therefore, the more sorrows one sees the more perfect one becomes. That is why, in all times, the Prophets of God have had tribulations and difficulties to withstand. The more often the captain of a ship is in the tempest and difficult sailing the greater his knowledge becomes. Therefore I am happy that you have had great tribulations and difficulties. For this I am very happy – that you have had many sorrows. Strange it is that I love you and still I am happy that you have sorrows.[13]

*'Abdu'l-Bahá*

The labourer cuts up the earth with his plough, and from that earth comes the rich and plentiful harvest. The more a man is chastened, the greater is the harvest of spiritual virtues shown forth by him. A soldier is no good General until he has been in the front of the fiercest battle and has received the deepest wounds.[14]

*'Abdu'l-Bahá*

13

O thou maid-servant of the Blessed Perfection! Be thou not sad, neither be thou unhappy; although the divine tests are violent, yet are they conducive to the life of the soul and the heart. The more often the pure gold is thrown into the furnace of test, the greater will become its purity and brilliancy and it will acquire a new splendour and brightness. I hope that thou art thyself in such a position.

Consider thou the lives of the former sanctified souls; what tests have they not withstood and what persecutions have they not beheld; while they were surrounded with calamities they increased their firmness and while they were overwhelmed with tests they manifested more zeal and courage. Be thou also like unto them.[15]

*'Abdu'l-Bahá*

## To cleanse the self

These tests, even as thou didst write, do but cleanse the spotting of self from off the mirror of the heart, till the Sun of Truth can cast its rays thereon; for there is no veil more obstructive than the self, and however tenuous that veil may be, at the last it will completely shut a person out, and deprive him of his portion of eternal grace.[16]

*'Abdu'l-Bahá*

## To change weakness to strength

The more one is severed from the world, from desires, from human affairs, and conditions, the more impervious does one become to the tests of God. Tests are a means by which a soul is measured as to its fitness, and proven out by its own acts. God knows its fitness beforehand, and also its unpreparedness, but man, with an ego, would not believe himself unfit unless proof were given him. Consequently his susceptibility to evil is proven to him when he falls into the tests, and the tests are continued until the soul realizes its own unfitness, then remorse and regret tend to root out the weakness.

The same tests comes again in greater degree, until it is shown that a former weakness has become a strength, and the power to overcome evil has been established.[17]

*Attributed to 'Abdu'l-Bahá*

## To prepare us for our mission in life

... how often we seem to forget the clear and repeated warnings of our beloved Master, who, in particular during the concluding years of His mission on earth, laid stress on the 'severe mental tests' that would inevitably sweep over His loved ones of the West – tests that would purge, purify and prepare them for their noble mission in life.[18]

*Shoghi Effendi*

## To purify our spirit

We must always look ahead and seek to accomplish in the future what we may have failed to do in the past. Failures, tests, and trials, if we use them correctly, can become the means of purifying our spirit, strengthening our characters, and enable us to rise to greater heights of service.[19]

*Written on behalf of Shoghi Effendi*

... Suffering, of one kind or another, seems to be the portion of man in this world. Even the Beloved ones, the Prophets of God, have never been exempt from the ills that are to be found in our world; poverty, disease, bereavement, – they seem to be part of the polish God employs to make us finer, and enable us to reflect more of His attributes! No doubt in the future, when the foundation of society is laid according to the Divine plan, and men become truly spiritualized, a vast amount of our present ills and problems will be remedied. We who toil now are paving the way for a far better world, and this knowledge must uphold and strengthen us through every trial.[20]

*Written on behalf of Shoghi Effendi*

## To develop morally and spiritually

Every believer needs to remember that an essential characteristic of this physical world is that we are constantly faced with trials, tribulations, hardships and sufferings and that by overcoming them we achieve our moral and spiritual development; that we must seek to accomplish in the future what we may have failed to do in the past; that this is the way God tests His servants and we should look upon every failure or shortcoming as an opportunity to try again and to acquire a fuller consciousness of the Divine Will and purpose.[21]

*Written on behalf of the Universal House of Justice*

Naturally there will be periods of distress and difficulty, and even severe tests; but if that person turns firmly towards the Divine Manifestation, studies carefully His spiritual teachings and receives the blessings of the Holy Spirit, he will find that in reality these tests and difficulties have been the gifts of God to enable him to grow and develop.

Thus you might look upon your own difficulties in the path of service. They are the means of your spirit growing and developing. You will suddenly find that you have conquered many of the problems which upset you, and then you will wonder why they should have troubled you at all.[22]

*Written on behalf of Shoghi Effendi*

The Guardian urges you not to be discouraged by any setbacks you may have. Life is a process of trials and testings, and these are – contrary to what we are prone to thinking – good for us, and give us stamina, and teach us to rely on God. Knowing He will help us, we can help ourselves more.[23]

*Written on behalf of Shoghi Effendi*

### Sufferings as blessings in disguise

Has not Bahá'u'lláh assured us that sufferings and privations are blessings in disguise, that through them our inner spiritual forces become stimulated, purified and ennobled? Remain, therefore, confident that your material hardships will, far from hindering your activities for the Cause, impart to your heart a powerful impetus to better serve and promote its interests.[24]

*Written on behalf of Shoghi Effendi*

*The Purpose of Tests:*

*To Detach Us from the World*

# To Detach Us from the World

I know of a certainty, by virtue of my love for Thee, that Thou wilt never cause tribulations to befall any soul unless Thou desirest to exalt his station in Thy celestial Paradise and to buttress his heart in this earthly life with the bulwark of Thine all-compelling power, that it may not become inclined toward the vanities of this world.[25]

*The Báb*

. . . He will send down from the heaven of His mercy that which will benefit you, and whatever is graciously vouchsafed by Him shall enable you to dispense with all mankind.[26]

*The Báb*

## . . . so that we may spurn this mortal world

O thou servant of God! Do not grieve at the afflictions and calamities that have befallen thee. All calamities and afflictions have been created for man so that he may spurn this mortal world – a world to which he is much attached. When he experienceth severe trials and hardships, then his nature will recoil and he will desire the eternal realm – a realm which is sanctified from all afflictions and calamities. Such is the case with the man who is wise. He shall never drink from a cup which is at the end distasteful, but, on the contrary, he will seek the cup of pure and limpid water. He will not taste of the honey that is mixed with poison.[27]

*'Abdu'l-Bahá*

21

Just as the plough furrows the earth deeply, purifying it of weeds and thistles, so suffering and tribulation free man from the petty affairs of this worldly life until he arrives at a state of complete detachment. His attitude in this world will be that of divine happiness.[28]

*'Abdu'l-Bahá*

## All sorrow and grief come from the world

There is no human being untouched by these two influences [joy and pain]; but all the sorrow and the grief that exist come from the world of matter – the spiritual world bestows only the joy!

If we suffer it is the outcome of material things, and all the trials and troubles come from this world of illusion.

For instance, a merchant may lose his trade and depression ensues. A workman is dismissed and starvation stares him in the face. A farmer has a bad harvest, anxiety fills his mind. A man builds a house which is burnt to the ground and he is straightway homeless, ruined, and in despair.

All these examples are to show you that the trials which beset our every step, all our sorrow, pain, shame and grief, are born in the world of matter; whereas the spiritual Kingdom never causes sadness. A man living with his thoughts in this Kingdom knows perpetual joy. The ills all flesh is heir to do not pass him by, but they only touch the surface of his life, the depths are calm and serene.[29]

*'Abdu'l-Bahá*

Disasters of this kind [San Francisco earthquake of 1906] should serve to awaken the people, and diminish the love of their hearts for this inconstant world. It is in this nether world that such tragic things take place: this is the cup that yieldeth bitter wine.[30]

*'Abdu'l-Bahá*

... no comfort can be secured by any soul in this world, from monarch down to the most humble commoner. If once this life should offer a man a sweet cup, a hundred bitter ones will follow; such is the condition of this world. The wise man, therefore, doth not attach himself to this mortal life and doth not depend upon it; at some moments, even, he eagerly wisheth for death that he may thereby be freed from these sorrows and afflictions.[31]

'Abdu'l-Bahá

# The Purpose of Tests:

## *To Teach Us to Depend upon God and Accept His Will*

# To Teach Us to Depend upon God and Accept His Will

O Son of Man! If adversity befall thee not in My path, how canst thou walk in the ways of them that are content with My pleasure? If trials afflict thee not in thy longing to meet Me, how wilt thou attain the light in thy love for My beauty?[32]

*Bahá'u'lláh*

## God bestows His favours on whom He wishes

Say: O people! Let not this life and its deceits deceive you, for the world and all that is therein is held firmly in the grasp of His Will. He bestoweth His favour on whom He willeth, and from whom He willeth He taketh it away. He doth whatsoever He chooseth.[33]

*Bahá'u'lláh*

## The tempests of trials should not hinder us

The winds of tests are powerless to hold back them that enjoy near access to Thee from setting their faces towards the horizon of Thy glory, and the tempests of trials must fail to draw away and hinder such as are wholly devoted to Thy will from approaching Thy court.

. . . Adversities are incapable of estranging them from Thy Cause, and the vicissitudes of fortune can never cause them to stray from Thy pleasure.[34]

*Bahá'u'lláh*

## God sends what will benefit us

. . . He will send down from the heaven of His mercy that which will benefit you, and whatever is graciously vouchsafed by Him shall enable you to dispense with all mankind.[35]

*The Báb*

. . . we must realize that everything which happens is due to some wisdom and that nothing happens without a reason.[36]

*'Abdu'l-Bahá*

## God is the real Protector

We are living in a day of reliance upon material conditions. Men imagine that the great size and strength of a ship, the perfection of machinery or the skill of a navigator will ensure safety, but these disasters [the sinking of the *Titanic*] sometimes take place that men may know that God is the real Protector. If it be the will of God to protect man, a little ship may escape destruction, whereas the greatest and most perfectly constructed vessel with the best and most skilful navigator may not survive a danger such as was present on the ocean. The purpose is that the people of the world may turn to God, the One Protector; that human souls may rely upon His preservation and know that He is the real safety . . .

Let no one imagine that these words imply that man should not be thorough and careful in his undertakings. God has endowed man with intelligence so that he may safeguard and protect himself. Therefore, he must provide and surround himself with all that scientific skill can produce. He must be deliberate, thoughtful and thorough in his purposes, build the best ship and provide the most experienced captain; yet, withal, let him rely upon God and consider God as the one Keeper. If God protects, nothing can imperil man's safety; and if it be not His will to safeguard, no amount of preparation and precaution will avail. [37]

*'Abdu'l-Bahá*

## To have more faith and confidence in God

While he [Shoghi Effendi] would urge you to courageously meet and overcome the many obstacles that stand in your way, he would at the same time advise you that in case of failure and no matter what befalls you, you should remain radiantly content at, and entirely submissive to, the Divine will. Our afflictions, tests and trials are sometimes blessings in disguise, as they teach us to have more faith and confidence in God, and bring us nearer to Him.[38]

*Written on behalf of Shoghi Effendi*

## Everything happens for a reason; there is a wisdom in suffering

Suffering is both a reminder and a guide. It stimulates us better to adapt ourselves to our environmental conditions, and thus leads the way to self improvement. In every suffering one can find a meaning and a wisdom. But it is not always easy to find the secret of that wisdom. It is sometimes only when all our suffering has passed that we become aware of its usefulness. What man considers to be evil turns often to be a cause of infinite blessings. And this is due to his desire to know more than he can. God's wisdom is, indeed, inscrutable to us all, and it is no use pushing too far trying to discover that which shall always remain a mystery to our mind.[39]

*Written on behalf of Shoghi Effendi*

It is strange how much suffering man has to put up with while on this earth. Our consolation should be however that it is part of a divine plan whose worth we cannot yet fathom . . .[40]

*Written on behalf of Shoghi Effendi*

## Suffering and free will

In his letter of 19 August 1994 . . . raises a number of questions on the subjects of suffering and free will. He asks if all tests are sent by God, 'aside from the tests we cause ourselves or each other', for the individual or collective purification of humanity, or if some are 'purely coincidental', such as an earthquake or a terminal illness. He also wants to know if 'man's free will is ever utilized to bring about God's Will'. To exemplify this question, he points to the murder of the Covenant-breaker Siyyid Muḥammad-i-Isfahání by three of the Bahá'ís living with Bahá'u'lláh in 'Akká at that time. He notes that Bahá'u'lláh forbade such an action, and was dismayed when it happened, and yet, in the Kitáb-i-Aqdas, He points to the death of Siyyid Muḥammad as a warning to Mírzá Yaḥyá and declares, 'Behold! God hath laid hold on him [Siyyid Muḥammad] who led thee astray.' That is, it could appear in this instance that God used innocent and faithful people to commit a repugnant deed in order to accomplish His own purpose . . .

As . . . has noted from the materials he has already studied, the questions of suffering and free will are both profound and hard to understand. In some pilgrims' notes, 'Abdu'l-Bahá indicates that the suffering of innocent creatures and human free will are two of God's three great mysteries, the third being the mystery of good and evil. Nevertheless, a number of Bahá'í texts shed light on these subjects . . . We especially note the following points . . .:

- There are two kinds of suffering, one for testing, one for punishment

- Humanity as a whole is experiencing divine punishment, retributory calamity, including 'upheavals, war, famine, and pestilence'

- Some tests are a result of man's choices, his free will

- God's foreknowledge of events does not cause them

- Everything that happens is good for God's loved ones

- God uses everything that happens for His own purposes

THE PURPOSE OF TESTS

This last point is, perhaps, especially pertinent to a consideration of the murder of Siyyid Muḥammad-i-Isfahání by faithful followers of Bahá'u'lláh. It cannot be said that committing the murder accorded with the Will of God, as it was a clear breach of the Law of God as directed by Bahá'u'lláh Himself. However, the statement that 'God rendereth His Cause victorious at one time through the aid of His enemies, and at another by virtue of the assistance of His chosen ones' seems to imply that everyone, including those who out of their free will choose to oppose the Cause of God or to disobey His laws, in the last analysis remains an instrument of God. This accords with the assumption that everything that happens is an expression or instrument of Divine Will, that 'all are His servants and all abide by His bidding', although everything that happens is not necessarily *caused* by God. The difference between those who consciously choose to turn to God and those who oppose or disobey Him, it would seem, is that the former consciously choose 'the complete surrender of one's will to the Will of God'. (This argument is taken from a commentary by Arash Abizadeh, published in *The Journal off Bahá'í Studies*, vol. 3, no. 1, pp. 67-73.)

. . . may also wish to refer to the presentation of J. E. Esslemont, made in *Bahá'u'lláh and the New Era* . . . on the subject of universal suffering . . .[41]

*Memorandum of the Research Department*

*The Purpose of Tests:*

*To Prove Our Sincerity*

# To Prove Our Sincerity

But for the tribulations which are sustained in Thy path, how could Thy true lovers be recognized; and were it not for the trials which are borne for love of Thee, how could the station of such as yearn for Thee be revealed? Thy might beareth me witness! The companions of all who adore Thee are the tears they shed, and the comforters of such as seek Thee are the groans they utter, and the food of them who haste to meet Thee is the fragments of their broken hearts.[42]

*Bahá'u'lláh*

. . . the Almighty hath tried, and will continue to try, His servants, so that light may be distinguished from darkness, truth from falsehood, right from wrong, guidance from error, happiness from misery, and roses from thorns. Even as He hath revealed: 'Do men think when they say "We believe" they shall be let alone and not be put to proof?'[43]

*Bahá'u'lláh*

But for tribulations, how could the assured be distinguished from the doubters among Thy servants? They who have been inebriated with the wine of Thy knowledge, these, verily, hasten to meet every manner of adversity in their longing to pass into Thy presence.[44]

*Bahá'u'lláh*

He Who is the Day Spring of Truth is, no doubt, fully capable of rescuing from such remoteness wayward souls and of causing them to draw nigh unto His court and attain His Presence. 'If God had pleased He had surely made all men one people.'

His purpose, however, is to enable the pure in spirit and the detached in heart to ascend, by virtue of their own innate powers, unto the shores of the Most Great Ocean, that thereby they who seek the Beauty of the All-Glorious may be distinguished and separated from the wayward and perverse. Thus hath it been ordained by the all-glorious and resplendent Pen . . . [45]

*Bahá'u'lláh*

. . . inasmuch as the divine Purpose hath decreed that the true should be known from the false, and the sun from the shadow, He hath, therefore, in every season sent down upon mankind the showers of tests from His realm of glory. [46]

*Bahá'u'lláh*

## Tribulations are the lot of His chosen ones

Know ye that trials and tribulations have, from time immemorial, been the lot of the chosen Ones of God and His beloved, and such of His servants as are detached from all else but Him, they whom neither merchandise nor traffic beguile from the remembrance of the Almighty, they that speak not till He hath spoken, and act according to His commandment. Such is God's method carried into effect of old, and such will it remain in the future. [47]

*Bahá'u'lláh*

Tests and trials only cause agitation to weak hearts. But to the pure souls, a hundred thousand tests are but to them like mirage, imagination and shadow. The shadow cannot withstand the rays of the sun and pure fragrances of holiness will not be concealed through the doubts of the beetle. The headache of wavering (or hesitancy) will not affect those exhilarated with the wine of the love of God. [48]

*'Abdu'l-Bahá*

## *To distinguish gems from pebbles, gold from dross*

Were it not for tests, pure gold could not be distinguished from the impure. Were it not for tests, the courageous could not be separated from the cowardly. Were it not for tests, the people of faithfulness could not be known from the disloyal. Were it not for tests, the intellectuals and the faculties of the scholars in great colleges would not develop. Were it not for tests, sparking gems could not be known from worthless pebbles. Were it not for tests, nothing would progress in this contingent world.[49]

*'Abdu'l-Bahá*

Not until man is tried doth the pure gold distinctly separate from the dross. Torment is the fire of test wherein the pure gold shineth resplendently and the impurity is burned and blackened.[50]

*'Abdu'l-Bahá*

Thou didst write of afflictive tests that have assailed thee. To the loyal soul, a test is but God's grace and favour; for the valiant doth joyously press forward to furious battle on the field of anguish, when the coward, whimpering with fright, will tremble and shake. So too, the proficient student, who hath with great competence mastered his subjects and committed them to memory, will happily exhibit his skills before his examiners on the day of his tests. So too will solid gold wondrously gleam and shine out in the assayer's fire.

It is clear, then, that tests and trials are, for sanctified souls, but God's bounty and grace, while to the weak, they are a calamity, unexpected and sudden.[51]

*'Abdu'l-Bahá*

Thy detailed letter was received. Its perusal produced the utmost happiness, for it evidences the fact that thou has attained to the knowledge of the reality of tests; that tests endured in the path of God are conducive to confirmation; nay, rather, they are heavenly powers and the bounties of the Realm of Might. But to weak believers tests are trials and examination, for, on account of the weakness of their faith and assurance they fall into difficulties and vicissitudes.

However, to those souls who are firm and steadfast, tests are the greatest favours. Consider thou that at the time of an examination in sciences and arts, the dull and lazy pupil finds himself in calamity. But to the intelligent and sagacious student examination in learning produces honour and infinite happiness. Alloyed gold, subjected to the fire, portrays its baseness, while the intensity of the flame enhances the beauty of pure gold. Therefore, tests to the weak souls are calamity and to the veiled ones the cause of their disgrace and humiliation. The point is this, that in the path of Truth every difficulty is made plain and every trial is the matchless bounty. Therefore, the believers of God and maid-servants of the Merciful must not relax during trial and no disaster must deter their service in the Cause of God.[52]

*'Abdu'l-Bahá*

But regarding the tests: Undoubtedly they must be violent so that those souls who are weak may fall back, while the souls who are firm and sincere may shine forth from the horizon of the Most Great Guidance like unto the sparkling stars.[53]

*'Abdu'l-Bahá*

## Sincerity can only be proved through deeds

Those who declare a wish to suffer much for Christ's sake must prove their sincerity; those who proclaim their longing to make great sacrifices can only prove their truth by their deeds. Job proved the fidelity of his love for God by being faithful through his great adversity, as well as during the prosperity of his life. The apostles of Christ who steadfastly bore all their trials and sufferings – did they not prove their faithfulness? Was not their endurance the best proof?

These griefs are now ended. Caiaphas lived a comfortable and happy life while Peter's life was full of sorrow and trial; which of these two is the more enviable? Assuredly we should choose the present state of Peter, for he possesses immortal life whilst Caiaphas has won eternal shame. The trials of Peter tested his fidelity.[54]

*'Abdu'l-Bahá*

## To increase our firmness and sincerity in the Cause

It is easy to approach the Kingdom of Heaven, but hard to stand firm and staunch within it, for the tests are rigorous, and heavy to bear.[55]

*'Abdu'l-Bahá*

Thy letter was received and its contents noted. In truth, thou hast been thrown amid dire ordeals, enduring agonizing afflictions. These trials were according to the consummate wisdom, therefore they were for the best. It is good for man to endure (in such moments).

Reflect upon his holiness Job: What trials, calamities and perplexities did he not endure! But these tests were like unto the fire and his holiness Job was like unto pure gold. Assuredly gold is purified by being submitted to the fire and if it contain any alloy or imperfection, it will disappear. That is the reason why violent tests become the cause of the everlasting glory of the righteous and are conducive to the destruction and disappearance of the unrighteous.

The wisdom of all these tribulations that poured successively upon thee was this, that thou shouldst be prepared and made ready for this Cause, that thou mightest expect the attainment to the greatest guidance, for all these trials were but a preparation for thine entrance into the Most Exalted Paradise and the beginning of obtaining this most great benefit.

Unless the season of winter appear, thunder roll, lightning flash, snow and rain fall, hail and frost descend and the intensity of cold execute its command, the season of the soul-refreshing spring would not come, the fragrant breeze would not waft, the moderation of temperature would not be realized, the roses and hyacinths would not grow, the surface of the earth would not become a delectable paradise, the trees would not bloom, neither would they bring forth fruits and leaves. That fierce inclemency of cold, snow, frost and tempest was the beginning of the manifestation of these roses, hyacinths, buds, blossoms and fruits.

Therefore, be not distressed on account of those adversities which fell upon thee; nay, rather, arise and render thanks that the ultimate goal is the attainment to this eminent bounty and the enjoyment of this highest gift of the almighty God. Consequently gird up the loins of thine endeavour, that thereby some results might be produced, some fruits gathered, the lamp of everlasting life ignited and the gifts of the Lord of the Kingdom be manifest, so that thou mayest accomplish again, with great yearning and exaltation, the worship of the Lord of Hosts.[56]

*'Abdu'l-Bahá*

O ye friends and maidservants of the Merciful! From the Spiritual Assembly of Los Angeles a letter hath been received. It was indicative of the fact that the blessed souls in California, like unto an immovable mountain, are withstanding the gale of violation, have, like unto blessed trees, been planted in the soil of the Covenant and are most firm and steadfast. The hope is entertained, therefore, that through the blessings of the Sun of Truth they may daily increase in their firmness and steadfastness. The tests of every dispensation are in direct proportion to the greatness of the Cause, and as heretofore such a manifest Covenant, written by the Supreme Pen, hath not been entered upon, the tests are proportionately more severe. These trials cause the feeble souls to waver while those who are firm are not affected.[57]

*'Abdu'l-Bahá*

The tests of God are surrounding you from all directions and many afflictions have occurred; but thanks be to God that you and your honourable husband are patient, thankful and constant. The necessity and the particularity of the assured and believing ones is to be firm in the Cause of God and withstand the hidden and evident tests. Thanks be to God that you are distinguished and made eminent by this blessing. In circumstances of ease and comfort, health and well-being, gratification and felicity, anyone can live contentedly; but to remain happy and contented in the face of difficulty, hardship and the onslaught of disease and sickness – this is an indication of nobility. Praise be to God that His dear handmaiden evinceth endless patience in the face of affliction, and gives thanks where others might repine.

Verily I am pleased with both you and [your husband], and I ask God that you may find pleasure and ease in another world – for this earthly world is narrow, dark and frightful, rest cannot be imagined and happiness really is non-existent, everyone is captured in the net of sorrow, and is day and night enslaved by the chain of calamity; there is no one who is at all free or at rest from grief and affliction. Still, as the believers of God are turning to the limitless world, they do not become very depressed and sad by disastrous calamities – there is something to console them; but the others in no way have anything to comfort them at the time of calamity. Whenever a calamity and a hardship occurs, they become sad and disappointed, and hopeless of the bounty and the mercy of the Glorious Lord.[58]

'Abdu'l-Bahá

*To distinguish sincere believers from the mass of humanity*

It is precisely by reason of the patent evils which, notwithstanding its [America's] other admittedly great characteristics and achievements, an excessive and binding materialism has unfortunately engendered within it that the Author of their

Faith and the Centre of His Covenant have singled it out to become the standard-bearer of the New World Order envisaged in their writings. It is by such means as this that Bahá'u'lláh can best demonstrate to a heedless generation His almighty power to raise up from the very midst of a people immersed in a sea of materialism, a prey to one of the most virulent and long-standing forms of racial prejudice, and notorious for its political corruption, lawlessness and laxity in moral standards, men and women who, as time goes by, will increasingly exemplify those essential virtues of self-renunciation, of moral rectitude, of chastity, of indiscriminating fellowship, of holy discipline, and of spiritual insight that will fit them for the preponderating share they will have in calling into being that World Order and that World Civilization of which their country, no less than the entire human race, stands in desperate need.[59]

*Shoghi Effendi*

## The future of the Faith depends on tested believers

There is always an important difference between friends and tested friends. No matter how precious the first type may be, the future of the Cause rests upon the latter.[60]

*Written on behalf of Shoghi Effendi*

*The Purpose of Tests:*

## To Correct Our Actions

# To Correct Our Actions

O people of God! That which traineth the world is Justice, for it is upheld by two pillars, reward and punishment. These two pillars are the sources of life to the world.[61]

*Bahá'u'lláh*

The structure of world stability and order hath been reared upon, and will continue to be sustained by, the twin pillars of reward and punishment . . . Justice hath a mighty force at its command. It is none other than reward and punishment for the deeds of men. By the power of this force the tabernacle of order is established throughout the world, causing the wicked to restrain their natures for fear of punishment.[62]

*Bahá'u'lláh*

## We are kept back from God by our deeds

I know not, O my God, what the Fire is which Thou didst kindle in Thy land. Earth can never cloud its splendour, nor water quench its flame . . . Some, O my God, Thou didst, through Thy strengthening grace, enable to approach it, while others Thou didst keep back by reason of what their hands have wrought in Thy days.[63]

*Bahá'u'lláh*

The trials of man are of two kinds. (a) The consequences of his own actions. If a man eats too much, he ruins his digestion; if he takes poison he becomes ill or dies. If a person gambles he will lose his money; if he drinks too much he will lose his equilibrium. All these sufferings are caused by the man him-

45

self, it is quite clear therefore that certain sorrows are the result of our own deeds.

(b) Other sufferings there are, which come upon the Faithful of God. Consider the great sorrows endured by Christ and by His apostles![64]

*'Abdu'l-Bahá*

War and rapine with their attendant cruelties are an abomination to God, and bring their own punishment, for the God of love is also a God of justice and each man must inevitably reap what he sows.[65]

*'Abdu'l-Bahá*

## Punishment is truly God's kindness to man

Thou hast asked about ordeal, adversities and tribulations, whether they are of God or the result of man's evil deeds.

Know thou that ordeals are of two kinds. One is for tests, and the other for punishment of misdeeds. That which is for testing is for one's education and development, and that which is for punishment of deeds is severe retribution.

The father and the teacher sometimes show tenderness towards the children and at other times deal harshly with them. Such severity is for educational purposes; it is true tenderness and absolute bounty and grace. Although in appearance it is wrath, in reality it is kindness. Although outwardly it is an ordeal, inwardly it is a cooling draught.

In both cases prayers and supplications should be offered at the sacred Threshold, so that thou mayest remain firm in tests, and patient in ordeals.[66]

*'Abdu'l-Bahá*

## Two kinds of torment

Know that there are two kinds of torment: subtile and gross. For example, ignorance itself is a torment, but it is a subtile torment; indifference to God is itself a torment; so also are falsehood, cruelty and treachery. All the imperfections are torments, but they are subtile torments. Certainly for an intelligent man death is better than sin, and a cut tongue is better than lying or calumny. The other kind of torment is gross – such as penalties, imprisonment, beating, expulsion and banishment. But for the people of God separation from God is the greatest torment of all.[67]

'Abdu'l-Bahá

## Sin can cause physical ailments

It is certainly the case that sins are a potent cause of physical ailments. If humankind were free from the defilements of sin and waywardness, and lived according to a natural, inborn equilibrium, without following wherever their passions led, it is undeniable that diseases would no longer take the ascendant, nor diversify with such intensity.

But man hath perversely continued to serve his lustful appetites, and he would not content himself with simple foods. Rather, he prepared for himself food that was compounded of many ingredients, of substances differing one from the other. With this, and with the perpetrating of vile and ignoble acts, his attention was engrossed, and he abandoned the temperance and moderation of a natural way of life. The result was the engendering of diseases both violent and diverse.[68]

'Abdu'l-Bahá

## For humankind's failure to accept God

There are two factors, God's Will and our free will: we are not puppets, if we make mistakes we have to pay for them. Bahá'u'lláh sought to prevent and avert wars of the last 50 years or so. No one listened. We are being chastised for our good now, by all this suffering, but there was an easier way, to accept the Message sent by God. We would not take that way; therefore He sends us this one . . .

... there are calamities for testing and for punishment –
there are also accidents, plain cause and effect![69]
*Written on behalf of Shoghi Effendi*

## Violating spiritual laws causes us injury

In considering the effect of obedience to the laws on individual
lives, one must remember that the purpose of this life is to
prepare the soul for the next. Here one must learn to control
and direct one's animal impulses, not to be a slave to them.
Life in this world is a succession of tests and achievements,
of falling short and of making new spiritual advances. Sometimes the course may seem very hard, but one can witness,
again and again, that the soul who steadfastly obeys the Law
of Bahá'u'lláh, however hard it may seem, grows spiritually,
while the one who compromises with the law for the sake of
his own apparent happiness is seen to have been following a
chimera: he does not attain the happiness he sought, he
retards his spiritual advance and often brings new problems
upon himself.[70]
*Written on behalf of the Universal House of Justice*

Just as there are laws governing our physical lives, requiring
that we must supply our bodies with certain foods, maintain
them within a certain range of temperatures, and so forth, if
we wish to avoid physical disabilities, so also there are laws
governing our spiritual lives. These laws are revealed to mankind in each age by the Manifestation of God, and obedience
to them is of vital importance if each human being, and mankind in general, is to develop properly and harmoniously.
Moreover, these various aspects are interdependent. If an
individual violates the spiritual laws for his own development
he will cause injury not only to himself but to the society in
which he lives. Similarly, the condition of society has a direct
effect on the individuals who must live within it.[71]
*The Universal House of Justice*

## Turning stumbling blocks into stepping stones

We Bahá'ís firmly believe that it is possible, if we have the right spirit, to make our stumbling blocks stepping-stones to progress. You have already, through at last facing yourself and acknowledging that you have both failed and erred in managing your life so far, set your feet on the right path. But now this new and spiritual condition in you is going to be proved – and the proving, the testing, will surely consist of the way you determine to take your punishment. Life is based on laws: physical, man-made, and spiritual. As you have broken the laws of the society in which you live, you will have to stand up like a man and take your punishment. The spirit in which you do this is the most important thing, and constitutes a great opportunity for you . . . at present, until your sentence is up, you must live within yourself in a way not to spoil the new future awaiting you. You must not become bitter – for after all you are only reaping what you planted. Bahá'u'lláh and 'Abdu'l-Bahá, through no crime of their own, spent the better part of their lives in exile and imprisoned, but they never became embittered although they were the victims of injustice. You, on the other hand, are the victim of injustice which you have inflicted on yourself – therefore you certainly have no right to be bitter towards the world.

He urges you to grasp firmly the teachings of our Faith, the love of your family and many Bahá'í friends, to put the past behind entirely, realizing that it can do you no more harm; on the contrary, through changing you and making you spiritually aware, this very past can be a means of enriching your life in the future![72]

*Written on behalf of Shoghi Effendi*

## Punishment can free us from past weaknesses

He (Shoghi Effendi) encouraged him to face manfully the future, accept the legitimate sanction of society as punishment for his admittedly anti-social conduct, and realise that his very suffering, humiliation and punishment can – if he will let it – be the means of freeing him from many of his past weaknesses and mistakes, and making him a worthy member of society. He should look to the future, for there is in his power, with Bahá'u'lláh's help, to shape into a worthy and constructive way of life . . . [73]

*Written on behalf of Shoghi Effendi*

# The Purpose of Tests:

## For the Growth of the Cause

# For the Growth of the Cause

Behold how in this Dispensation the worthless and foolish have fondly imagined that by such instruments as massacre, plunder and banishment they can extinguish the Lamp which the Hand of Divine power hath lit, or eclipse the Day Star of everlasting splendour. How utterly unaware they seem to be of the truth that such adversity is the oil that feedeth the flame of this Lamp! Such is God's transforming power. He changeth whatsoever He willeth; He verily hath power over all things. . .[74]

*Bahá'u'lláh*

## Persecution leads people to investigate the truth

This is the result of the slanderer's work: to be the cause of guiding men to a discovery of the truth.

We know that all the falsehoods spread about Christ and His apostles and all the books written against Him, only led the people to inquire into His doctrine; then, having seen the beauty and inhaled the fragrance, they walked evermore amidst the roses and the fruits of that celestial garden.[75]

*'Abdu'l-Bahá*

. . . the attacks and the obstructiveness of the ignorant but cause the Word of God to be exalted, and spread His signs and tokens far and wide. Were it not for this opposition by the disdainful, this obduracy of the slanderers, this shouting from the pulpits, this crying and wailing of great and small alike, these accusations of unbelief levelled by the ignorant, this uproar from the foolish – how could news of the advent of the Primal Point and the bright dawning of the Day-Star of Bahá ever have reached to east and west? How else could the planet have been rocked from pole to pole? . . . All these blessings and bestowals, the very means of proclaiming the Faith, have come about through the scorn of the ignorant, the opposition of the foolish, the stubbornness of the dull-witted, the violence of the aggressor. Had it not been for these things, the news of the Báb's advent would not, to this day, have reached even into lands hard by. Wherefore we should never grieve over the blindness of the unwitting, the attacks of the foolish, the hostility of the low and base, the heedlessness of the divines, the charges of infidelity brought against us by the empty of mind.[76]

*'Abdu'l-Bahá*

## Persecutions strengthen our faith

For the history of the Cause, particularly in Persia, is a clear illustration of the truth that such persecutions invariably serve to strengthen the believers in their faith, by stimulating the spiritual powers latent in their hearts, and by awakening in them a new and deeper consciousness of their duties and responsibilities towards the Faith.[77]

*Written on behalf of Shoghi Effendi*

. . . the Cause is bound sooner or later to suffer from all kinds of attacks and persecutions, that these in fact constitute the life-blood of its institutions, and as such constitute an inseparable and intrinsic part of its development and growth. Trials and tribulations, as Bahá'u'lláh says, are the oil that feed the lamp of the Cause, and are indeed blessings in disguise. The friends should therefore be confident that all these attacks to which the Cause is now subjected in . . . are a necessary part of the development of the Cause, and that their outcome would be beneficial to its best interests.[78]

*Written on behalf of Shoghi Effendi*

## Opposition will proclaim the Cause

But after I leave, some people may arise in opposition, heaping persecutions upon you in their bitterness, and in the newspapers there may be articles published against the Cause. Rest ye in the assurance of firmness. Be well poised and serene, remembering that this is only as the harmless twittering of sparrows and that it will soon pass away. . . Therefore, my purpose is to warn and strengthen you against accusations, criticisms, revilings and derision in newspaper articles or other publications. Be not disturbed by them. They are the very confirmation of the Cause, the very source of upbuilding to the Movement.[79]

*'Abdu'l-Bahá*

May God confirm the day when a score of ministers of the churches may arise and with bared heads cry at the top of their voices that the Bahá'ís are misguided. I would like to see that day, for that is the time when the Cause of God will spread. Bahá'u'lláh has pronounced such as these the couriers of the Cause. They will proclaim from pulpits that the Bahá'ís are fools, that they are a wicked and unrighteous people, but be ye steadfast and unwavering in the Cause of God. They will spread the message of Bahá'u'lláh.[80]

*'Abdu'l-Bahá*

## Severe trials have strengthened the heavenly tree

The amazing history of this glorious century will conclusively demonstrate to every opponent of the Cause throughout the World that violent upheavals have strengthened the root of this heavenly Tree, severe trials and hardships have reinforced the foundation of the divine Edifice. Dire abasement became a vesture of glory, while adversity and tribulation were the oil which fed the flame of the lamp of God's Revelation. Fierce attacks and violence produced steadfastness and constancy, and persecution and privation created interest, and led to conversion and proclamation.[81]

*Shoghi Effendi*

As opposition to the Faith, from whatever source it may spring, whatever form it may assume, however violent its outbursts, is admittedly the motive-power that galvanizes, on the one hand, the souls of its valiant defenders, and taps for them, on the other, fresh springs of that Divine and inexhaustible Energy, we who are called upon to represent, defend, and promote its interests, should, far from regarding any manifestation of hostility as an evidence of the weakening of the pillars of the Faith, acclaim it as both a God-sent gift and a God-sent opportunity which, if we remain undaunted, we can utilize for the furtherance of His Faith and routing and complete elimination of its adversaries.

. . . Fierce and relentless will be the opposition which this crystallization and emergence must provoke. The alarm it must and will awaken, the envy it will certainly arouse, the misrepresentations to which it will remorselessly be subjected, the setbacks it must, sooner or later sustain, the commotions to which it must eventually give rise, the fruits it must in the end garner, the blessings it must inevitably bestow and the glorious, the Golden Age it must irresistibly usher in, are just beginning to be faintly perceived, and will, as the old Order crumbles beneath the weight of so stupendous a Revelation, become increasingly apparent and arresting.[82]

*Shoghi Effendi*

Meanwhile the Faith that had been the object of such monstrous betrayals, and the target for such woeful assaults, was going from strength to strength, was forging ahead, undaunted and undivided by the injuries it had received. In the midst of trials it had inspired its loyal followers with a resolution that no obstacle, however formidable, could undermine. It had lighted in their hearts a faith that no misfortune, however black, could quench. It had infused into their hearts a hope that no force, however determined, could shatter.[83]

*Shoghi Effendi*

## The recent persecutions in Iran

The current persecution has resulted in bringing the name and character of our beloved Faith to the attention of the world as never before in its history. As a direct result of the protests sent by the world-wide community of the Most Great Name to the rulers in Iran, of the representations made to the media when those protests were ignored, of direct approach by Bahá'í institutions at national and international level to governments, communities of nations, international agencies and the United Nations itself, the Faith of Bahá'u'lláh has not only been given sympathetic attention in the world's councils, but also its merits and violated rights have been discussed and resolutions of protest sent to the Iranian authorities by sovereign governments, singly and in unison. The world's leading newspapers, followed by the local press, have presented sympathetic accounts of the Faith to millions of readers, while television and radio stations are increasingly making the persecutions in Iran the subject of their programmes . . . Indeed, this new wave of persecution sweeping the Cradle of the Faith may well be seen as a blessing in disguise, a 'providence' whose 'calamity' is, as always, borne heroically by the beloved Persian community. It may be regarded as the latest move in God's Major Plan, another trumpet blast to awaken the heedless from their slumber . . .[84]

*The Universal House of Justice*

Shoghi Effendi perceived in the organic life of the Cause a dialectic of victory and crisis. The unprecedented triumphs, generated by the adamantine steadfastness of the Iranian friends, will inevitably provoke opposition to test and increase our strength. Let every Bahá'í in the world be assured that whatever may befall this growing Faith of God is but incontrovertible evidence of the loving care with which the King of Glory and His martyred Herald, through the incomparable Centre of His Covenant and our beloved Guardian, are preparing His humble followers for ultimate and magnificent triumph.[85]

*The Universal House of Justice*

## The Cause is protected by ordeals and hardships

. . . the most effective means whereby this light of truth is safeguarded and protected is the onslaught of the enemies, grievous ordeals and manifold hardships. The globe of this lamp is the tempestuous winds and the safety of this ship lieth in the violence of tumultuous waves.

Therefore one must show forth gratitude in the face of Job-like afflictions and must evince joy and pleasure at the unyielding cruelty of evil-doers, inasmuch as such tribulations lead to immortality, and serve as the supreme factor to attract His consummate blessings and infinite bestowals.[86]

*'Abdu'l-Bahá*

## God's Cause proceeds despite every obstacle

If men had a sense of justice, when they observe that even during such periods of awful turmoil and with so many obstacles raised against it, still the Cause of God continues on its steady forward course – they would acknowledge its truth . . . It is obvious that, were this Cause not the truth, such turmoil, such hindrances, would already have put out its light. Since, however, this is God's Cause, it goes forward in spite of every obstacle, and torrents of hatred only feed its flame.[87]

*Attributed to 'Abdu'l-Bahá*

. . . were one to observe with a discerning eye, it would become clear and evident that commotion in itself, the very succession of calamities, upheavals and hardships, and the recurrence of trials, adversities and sufferings have lent an impetus to the power latent in the Cause and reinforced its compelling force and pervasive influence.

Indeed as a result of the onrushing tempests of tribulation and the raging hurricanes of tests and trials, the Faith's scope of operation has been enlarged, its pillars have been raised to loftier heights, its foundation has become more secure, its glory more resplendent, the spread of its influence more rapid, its ascendancy and dominion more conspicuous and evident.

Every blow that the hands of the wrongdoer have inflicted upon the community of the followers of the Cause of God from without, has proved to be the means of a fresh victory and triumph for the Faith, and every agitation provoked from within through the intrigues and plottings of perfidious traitors has led to a remarkable success for the Cause and to the revelation of its wondrous glory . . . [88]

*Shoghi Effendi*

. . . viewed in their proper perspective, each of them [the crises the Faith has sustained] can be confidently pronounced a blessing in disguise, affording a providential means for the release of a fresh outpouring of celestial strength, a miraculous escape from imminent and still more dreadful calamities, an instrument for the fulfilment of age-old prophecies, an agency for the purification and revitalization of the life of the community, an impetus for the enlargement of its limits and the propagation of its influence, and a compelling evidence of the indestructibility of its cohesive strength. Sometimes at the height of the crisis itself, more often when the crisis was past, the significance of these trials has manifested itself to men's eyes, and the necessity of such experiences has been demonstrated, far and wide and beyond the shadow of a doubt, to both friend and foe. Seldom, if indeed at any time, has the mystery underlying these portentous, God-sent upheavals remained undisclosed, or the profound purpose and meaning of their occurrence been left hidden from the minds of men.[89]

*Shoghi Effendi*

## Each trial has a cause, purpose and result

In such an afflicted time, when mankind is bewildered and the wisest of men are perplexed as to the remedy, the people of Bahá, who have confidence in His unfailing grace and divine guidance, are assured that each of these tormenting trials has a cause, a purpose, and a definite result, and all are essential instruments for the establishment of the immutable Will of God on earth. In other words, on the one hand humanity is struck by the scourge of His chastisement which will inevitably bring together the scattered and vanquished tribes of the earth; and on the other, the weak few whom He has nurtured under the protection of His loving guidance are, in this Formative Age and period of transition, continuing to build amidst these tumultuous waves an impregnable stronghold which will be the sole remaining refuge for those lost multitudes. Therefore, the dear friends of God who have such a broad and clear vision before them are not perturbed by such events, nor are they panic-stricken by such thundering sounds, nor will they face such convulsions with fear and trepidation, nor will they be deterred, even for a moment, from fulfilling their sacred responsibilities.[90]

*The Universal House of Justice*

## Every trial is fraught with infinite wisdom

I am however assured and sustained by the conviction, never dimmed in my mind, that whatsoever comes to pass in the Cause of God, however disquieting in its immediate effects, is fraught with infinite Wisdom and tends ultimately to promote its interests in the world. Indeed, our experiences of the distant past, as well as of recent events, are too numerous and varied to permit of any misgiving or doubt as to the truth of this basic principle – a principle which throughout the vicissitudes of our sacred mission in this world we must never disregard or forget.[91]

*Shoghi Effendi*

## Tests prepare hearts to accept the Cause

These perils, sufferings and commotions are blessings in disguise, which pave the way and prepare the hearts of those who face and sustain them for a deeper realization and an earlier and fuller acceptance of the Divine Message of Bahá'u'lláh.[92]

*Shoghi Effendi*

Adversity prepares the hearts of men, and paves the way for a wholehearted and general acceptance of the tenets and claims of our beloved Faith.[93]

*Shoghi Effendi*

The friends must not feel too crushed by the sufferings that are so piteously afflicting humanity. They must realize that the hotter the fire the more malleable the metal becomes, and take hope that out of the agony of the present the future will be born – the glorious future of peace and unity amongst the sons of men. Evidently only intense misery will prove sufficiently strong to purge the hearts of men.[94]

*Written on behalf of Shoghi Effendi*

## We shall win under all conditions

Whatsoever occurreth in the world of being is light for His loved ones and fire for the people of sedition and strife. Even if all the losses of the world were to be sustained by one of the friends of God, he would still profit thereby, whereas true loss would be borne by such as are wayward, ignorant and contemptuous. Although the author of the following saying had intended it otherwise, yet We find it pertinent to the operation of God's immutable Will: 'Even or odd, thou shalt win the wager.' The friends of God shall win and profit under all conditions, and shall attain true wealth. In fire they remain cold, and from water they emerge dry. Their affairs are at variance with the affairs of men. Gain is their lot, whatever the deal. To this testifieth every wise one with a discerning eye, and every fair-minded one with a hearing ear.[95]

*Bahá'u'lláh*

## Enemies have utterly failed

Numerous and powerful have been the forces that have schemed, both from within and from without, in lands both far and near, to quench its light and abolish its holy name. Some have apostatized from its principles, and betrayed ignominiously its cause. Others have hurled against it the fiercest anathemas which the embittered leaders of any ecclesiastical institution are able to pronounce. Still others have heaped upon it the afflictions and humiliations which sovereign authority can alone, in the plenitude of its power, inflict.

The utmost its avowed and secret enemies could hope to achieve was to retard its growth and obscure momentarily its purpose. What they actually accomplished was to purge and purify its life, to stir it to still greater depths, to galvanize its soul, to prune its institutions, and cement its unity. A schism, a permanent cleavage in the vast body of its adherents, they could never create.[96]

*Shoghi Effendi*

## Be confident of final victory

As the Faith grows stronger and attracts the serious attention and consideration of the world outside, the friends must expect a similar, if not a greater, increase in the forces of opposition which from every direction, both secular and religious, will be massed to undermine the very basis of its existence. The final outcome of such a struggle, which will be surely gigantic, is clear to us believers. A Faith born of God and guided by His Divine and all-pervasive spirit cannot but finally triumph and firmly establish itself, no matter how persistent and insidious the forces with which it has to contend. The friends should be confident, and act with the utmost wisdom and moderation, and should particularly abstain from any provocative act. The future is surely theirs.[97]

*Written on behalf of Shoghi Effendi*

## Whatever may befall the Faith, the future is bright

Whatever may befall this infant Faith of God in future decades or in succeeding centuries, whatever the sorrows, dangers and tribulations which the next stage in its world-wide development may engender, from whatever quarter the assaults to be launched by its present or future adversaries may be unleashed against it, however great the reverses and setbacks it may suffer, we, who have been privileged to apprehend, to the degree our finite minds can fathom, the significance of these marvellous phenomena associated with its rise and establishment, can harbour no doubt that what it has already achieved in the first hundred years of its life provides sufficient guarantee that it will continue to forge ahead, capturing loftier heights, tearing down every obstacle, opening up new horizons and winning still mightier victories until its glorious mission, stretching into the dim ranges of time that lie ahead, is totally fulfilled.[98]

*Shoghi Effendi*

# The Purpose of Tests:

## Gifts of God

# Gifts of God

O Son of Man! My calamity is My providence, outwardly it is fire and vengeance, but inwardly it is light and mercy. Hasten thereunto that thou mayest become an eternal light and an immortal spirit. This is My command unto thee, do thou observe it.[99]

*Bahá'u'lláh*

## God sends only what will profit us

Thou lookest upon them that are dear to Thee with the eyes of Thy loving-kindness, and sendest down for them only that which will profit them through Thy grace and Thy gifts.[100]

*Bahá'u'lláh*

## Tests are a healing medicine

O Thou Whose tests are a healing medicine to such as are nigh unto Thee, Whose sword is the ardent desire of all them that love Thee, Whose dart is the dearest wish of those hearts that yearn after Thee, Whose decree is the sole hope of them that have recognized Thy truth![101]

*Bahá'u'lláh*

O Thou . . . Whose trial is the healer of the sicknesses of them who have embraced Thy Cause, Whose calamity is the highest aspiration of such as are rid of all attachment to any one but Thyself![102]

*Bahá'u'lláh*

The trials Thou sendest are a salve to the sores of all them who are devoted to Thy will . . .[103]

*Bahá'u'lláh*

## Gifts bestowed on Thy chosen ones

Every vexation borne for love of Thee is a token of Thy mercy unto Thy creatures, and every ordeal suffered in Thy path is but a gift from Thee bestowed on Thy chosen ones.[104]

*Bahá'u'lláh*

Whatever befalleth in the path of God is the beloved of the soul and the desire of the heart. Deadly poison in His path is pure honey, and every tribulation a draught of crystal water.[105]

*Bahá'u'lláh*

Verily God hath made adversity as a morning dew upon His green pasture, and a wick for His lamp which lighteth earth and heaven.[106]

*Bahá'u'lláh*

How sweet is the thought of Thee in times of adversity and trial, and how delightful to glorify Thee when compassed about with the fierce winds of Thy decree![107]

*Bahá'u'lláh*

## Adversity blessed by divine favour

Prosperity, contentment, and freedom, however much desired and conducive to the gladness of the human heart, can in no wise compare with the trials of homelessness and adversity in the pathway of God; for such exile and banishment are blessed by the divine favour, and are surely followed by the mercy of Providence.[108]

*'Abdu'l-Bahá*

## A garden of delight

I hear thou art grieved and distressed at the happenings of the world and the vicissitudes of fortune. Wherefore this fear and sorrow? The true lovers of the Abhá Beauty, and they that have quaffed the Cup of the Covenant fear no calamity, nor feel depressed in the hour of trial. They regard the fire of adversity as their garden of delight, and the depth of the sea the expanse of heaven.[109]

*'Abdu'l-Bahá*

## Affliction is the essence of bounty

Whatsoever may happen is for the best, because affliction is but the essence of bounty, and sorrow and toil are mercy unalloyed, and anguish is peace of mind, and to make a sacrifice is to receive a gift, and whatsoever may come to pass hath issued from God's grace.[110]

*'Abdu'l-Bahá*

# The Sources of Tests

# The Sources of Tests:

# The Self

# The Self

Arise, O people, and, by the power of God's might, resolve to gain the victory over your own selves, that haply the whole earth may be freed and sanctified from its servitude to the gods of its idle fancies – gods that have inflicted such loss upon, and are responsible for the misery of, their wretched worshippers. These idols form the obstacle that impedeth man in his efforts to advance in the path of perfection. We cherish the hope that the Hand of Divine power may lend its assistance to mankind, and deliver it from its state of grievous abasement.[111]

*Bahá'u'lláh*

Sharp must be thy sight, O Dhabíh, and adamant thy soul, and brass-like thy feet, if thou wishest to be unshaken by the assaults of the selfish desires that whisper in men's breasts.[112]

*Bahá'u'lláh*

## The darkness of the self

Watch over yourselves, for the Evil One is lying in wait, ready to entrap you. Gird yourselves against his wicked devices, and, led by the light of the name of the All-Seeing God, make your escape from the darkness that surroundeth you. Let your vision be world-embracing, rather than confined to your own self. The Evil One is he that hindereth the rise and obstructeth the spiritual progress of the children of men.[113]

*Bahá'u'lláh*

## Pride abases us

Humility exalteth man to the heaven of glory and power, whilst pride abaseth him to the depths of wretchedness and degradation.[114]

*Bahá'u'lláh*

## Our powers are obscured by worldly desires

Upon the reality of man. . . He hath focused the radiance of all of His names and attributes, and made it a mirror of His own Self. Alone of all created things man hath been singled out for so great a favour, so enduring a bounty. These energies with which the Day Star of Divine bounty and Source of heavenly guidance hath endowed the reality of man lie, however, latent within him, even as the flame is hidden within the candle and the rays of light are potentially present in the lamp. The radiance of these energies may be obscured by worldly desires even as the light of the sun can be concealed beneath the dust and dross which cover the mirror. Neither the candle nor the lamp can be lighted through their own unaided efforts, nor can it ever be possible for the mirror to free itself from its dross. It is clear and evident that until a fire is kindled the lamp will never be ignited, and unless the dross is blotted out from the face of the mirror it can never represent the image of the sun nor reflect its light and glory.[115]

*Bahá'u'lláh*

## The dangers of jealousy and anger

O Son of Earth! Know, verily, the heart wherein the least remnant of envy yet lingers, shall never attain My everlasting dominion, nor inhale the sweet savours of holiness breathing from My kingdom of sanctity.[116]

*Bahá'u'lláh*

Jealousy consumeth the body and anger doth burn the liver: avoid these two as you would a lion.[117]

*'Abdu'l-Bahá*

How many a soul hath turned itself unto the Lord and entered into the protective shadow of His Word, and become famed throughout the world – for example, Judas Iscariot. And then, when the tests grew harsh and the violence thereof intensified, their feet slipped on the pathway and they turned backward from the Faith after having acknowledged its truth, and they denied it, and fell away from harmony and love into mischief and hate. Thus became visible the power of tests, which maketh mighty pillars to tremble and shake.

Judas Iscariot was the greatest of the disciples, and he summoned the people to Christ. Then it seemed to him that Jesus was showing increasing regard to the Apostle Peter, and when Jesus said, 'Thou art Peter, and upon this rock I will build My church,' these words addressed to Peter, and this singling out of Peter for special honour, had a marked effect on the Apostle, and kindled envy within the heart of Judas. For this reason he who had once drawn nigh did turn aside, and he who had believed in the Faith denied it, and his love changed to hate, until he became a cause of the crucifixion of that glorious Lord, that manifest Splendour. Such is the outcome of envy, the chief reason why men turn aside from the Straight Path. So hath it occurred, and will occur, in this great Cause. But it doth not matter, for it engendereth loyalty in the rest, and maketh souls to arise who waver not, who are fixed and unshakable as the mountains in their love for the Manifest Light.[118]

*'Abdu'l-Bahá*

. . . desire is a flame that has reduced to ashes uncounted lifetime harvests of the learned, a devouring fire that even the vast sea of their accumulated knowledge could never quench. How often has it happened that an individual who was graced with every attribute of humanity and wore the jewel of true understanding, nevertheless followed after his passions until his excellent qualities passed beyond moderation and he was forced into excess. His pure intentions changed to evil ones, his attributes were no longer put to uses worthy of them, and the power of his desires turned him aside from righteousness and its rewards into ways that were dangerous and dark. A good character is in the sight of God and His chosen ones and the possessors of insight, the most excellent and praiseworthy of all things, but always on condition that its centre of emanation should be reason and knowledge and its base should be true moderation.[119]

*'Abdu'l-Bahá*

## Tests can be caused by our weaknesses and failings

To what extent do they form a part of those mental tests and trials destined at various times by the Almighty to stir and reinvigorate the body of His Cause, and how far are they traceable to our imperfect state of understanding, to our weaknesses and failings?[120]

*Shoghi Effendi*

And yet, if it is the lot of the chosen ones of God, the people of Bahá, to face adversity and suffer tribulation before achieving ultimate victory, are we to believe that whatever befalls us is divinely ordained, and in no wise the result of our faint-heartedness and negligence?[121]

*Shoghi Effendi*

Life is a constant struggle, not only against forces around us, but above all against our own 'ego'. We can never afford to rest on our oars, for if we do, we soon see ourselves carried downstream again. Many of those who drift away from the Cause do so for the reason that they had ceased to go on developing. They became complacent, or indifferent, and consequently ceased to draw the spiritual strength and vitality from the Cause which they should have.[122]

*Written on behalf of Shoghi Effendi*

... the complete and entire elimination of the ego would imply perfection – which man can never completely attain – but the ego can and should be ever-increasingly subordinated to the enlightened soul of man. This is what spiritual progress implies.[123]

*Written on behalf of Shoghi Effendi*

... self has really two meanings, or is used in two senses, in the Bahá'í writings; one is self, the identity of the individual created by God. This is the self mentioned in such passages as 'he hath known God who hath known himself', etc. The other self is the ego, the dark, animalistic heritage each one of us has, the lower nature that can develop into a monster of selfishness, brutality, lust and so on. It is this self we must struggle against, or this side of our natures, in order to strengthen and free the spirit within us and help it to attain perfection.[124]

*Written on behalf of Shoghi Effendi*

## Beware of intellectual pride

The House of Justice feels that Bahá'í scholars must beware of the temptations of intellectual pride. 'Abdu'l-Bahá has warned the friends in the West that they would be subjected to intellectual tests, and the Guardian reminded them of this warning. There are many aspects of western thinking which have been exalted to a status of unassailable principle in the general mind, that time may well show to have been erroneous or, at least, only partially true. Any Bahá'í who rises to eminence in academic circles will be exposed to the powerful influence of such thinking.[125]

*Written on behalf of the Universal House of Justice*

*The Sources of Tests:*

*Each Other*

# Each Other

O My Son! The company of the ungodly increaseth sorrow, whilst fellowship with the righteous cleanseth the rust from off the heart. He that seeketh to commune with God, let him betake himself to the companionship of His loved ones; and he that desireth to hearken unto the word of God, let him give ear to the words of His chosen ones.[126]

*Bahá'u'lláh*

Time and again have We admonished Our beloved ones to avoid, nay to flee from, anything whatsoever from which the odour of mischief can be detected. The world is in great turmoil, and the minds of its people are in a state of utter confusion.[127]

*Bahá'u'lláh*

O Son of Dust! Beware! Walk not with the ungodly and seek not fellowship with him, for such companionship turneth the radiance of the heart into infernal fire.[128]

*Bahá'u'lláh*

## Dissension and strife bring great harm upon the Cause

He, Who is the Eternal Truth, beareth Me witness! Nothing whatever can, in this Day, inflict a greater harm upon this Cause than dissension and strife, contention, estrangement and apathy, among the loved ones of God. Flee them, through the power of God and His sovereign aid, and strive ye to knit together the hearts of men, in His Name, the Unifier, the All-Knowing, the All-Wise.[129]

*Bahá'u'lláh*

## No one has power over our spirits

Let not the deeds of those who reject the Truth shut you out
as by a veil. Such people have warrant over your bodies only,
and God hath not reposed in them power over your spirits,
your souls and your hearts.[130]

*The Báb*

## Be on your guard and ever wakeful

No day goeth by but someone raiseth the standard of revolt
and spurreth his charger into the arena of discord. No hour
passeth but the vile adder bareth its fangs and scattereth its
deadly venom.

The beloved of the Lord are wrapped in utter sincerity and
devotion, unmindful of this rancour and malice. Smooth and
insidious are these snakes, these whisperers of evil, artful in
their craft and guile. Be ye on your guard and ever wakeful!
Quick-witted and keen of intellect are the faithful, and firm
and steadfast are the assured. Act ye with all circumspection!

'Fear ye the sagacity of the faithful, for he seeth with the
divine light!'

Beware lest any soul privily cause disruption or stir up strife.
In the Impregnable Stronghold be ye brave warriors, and for
the Mighty Mansion a valiant host. Exercise the utmost care,
and day and night be on your guard, that thereby the tyrant
may inflict no harm.

Study the Tablet of the Holy Mariner that ye may know the
truth and consider that the Blessed Beauty hath fully foretold
future events. Let them who perceive take warning. Verily in
this is a bounty for the sincere![131]

*'Abdu'l-Bahá*

## Others can raise our spirits or depress us

There are persons with whom we associate and converse whose
utterances are life-imparting, joy-giving. The withered and

faded are refreshed, the joyless become happy, the extinct become enkindled and the lifeless are quickened with the breaths of the Holy Spirit. The one drowned in the sea of hesitation and doubt is saved by the life-boat of certainty and assurance; the one attached to this material world becomes severed and the one steeped in blameworthy deeds is adorned with praiseworthy attributes. On the other hand there are some persons whose very respiration extinguishes the light of faith; whose conversation weakens firmness and steadfastness in the Cause of God; whose company diverts one's attention from the kingdom of Abhá.[132]

*Attributed to 'Abdu'l-Bahá*

## *No one can remove a soul from its intended place*

To be approved of God alone should be one's aim.

When God calls a soul to a high station, it is because that soul has capacity for that station as a gift of God, and because that soul has supplicated to be taken into His service. No envies, jealousies, calumnies, slanders, plots nor schemes will ever move God to remove a soul from its intended place, for by the grace of God, such actions on the part of the people are the test of the servant, testing his strength, forbearance, endurance and sincerity under adversity. At the same time those who show forth envies, jealousies, etc., toward a servant, are depriving themselves of their own stations, and not another of his, for they prove by their own acts that they are not only unworthy of being called to any station awaiting them, but also prove that they cannot withstand the very first test – that of rejoicing over the success of their neighbour, at which God rejoices. Only by such a sincere joy can the gift of God descend into a pure heart.

Envy closes the door of Bounty, and jealousy prevents one from ever attaining to the Kingdom of Abhá.

No! Before God! No one can deprive another of his rightful station, that can only be lost by one's unwillingness or failure to do the will of God, or by seeking to use the Cause of God for one's own gratification or ambition.

No one save a severed soul or a sincere heart finds response from God. By assisting in the success of another servant in the Cause does one in reality lay the foundation for one's own success and aspirations. Ambitions are an abomination before the Lord. How regrettable! Some even use the affairs of the Cause and its activities as a means of revenge on account of some personal spite, or fancied injury, interfering with the work of another, or seeking its failure. Such only destroy their own success, did they know the truth.[133]

*Attributed to 'Abdu'l-Bahá*

## The corrosion of racial prejudice

As to racial prejudice, the corrosion of which, for well nigh a century, has bitten into the fibre, and attacked the whole social structure of American society, it should be regarded as constituting the most vital and challenging issue confronting the Bahá'í community at the present stage of its evolution. The ceaseless exertions which this issue of paramount importance calls for, the sacrifices it must impose, the care and vigilance it demands, the moral courage and fortitude it requires, the tact and sympathy it necessitates, invest this problem, which the American believers are still far from having satisfactorily resolved, with an urgency and importance that cannot be overestimated.[134]

*Shoghi Effendi*

## We can be each other's greatest test

Perhaps the greatest test Bahá'ís are ever subjected to is from each other; but for the sake of the Master they should be ever ready to overlook each other's mistakes, apologize for harsh words they have uttered, forgive and forget. He strongly recommends to you this course of action.[135]

*Written on behalf of Shoghi Effendi*

You should not allow the remarks made by the Bahá'ís to hurt or depress you, but should forget the personalities, and arise to do all you can, yourself, to teach the Faith. Bahá'u'lláh enjoins work on all. No one need ever be ashamed of his job.[136]

*Written on behalf of Shoghi Effendi*

We are Bahá'ís because we believe it is the Truth for this day, and not because of any hopes we may have for an easier passage through this troubled world! Our tests often come from each other; but for the sake of Bahá'u'lláh we must endure them patiently and rise above them.[137]

*Written on behalf of Shoghi Effendi*

... the believers need to be deepened in their knowledge and appreciation of the Covenants of both Bahá'u'lláh and 'Abdu'l-Bahá. This is the stronghold of the Faith of every Bahá'í, and that which enables him to withstand every test and the attacks of the enemies outside the Faith, and the far more dangerous, insidious, lukewarm people inside the Faith who have no real attachment to the Covenant, and consequently uphold the intellectual aspect of the teachings while at the same time undermining the spiritual foundation upon which the whole Cause of God rests.[138]

*Written on behalf of Shoghi Effendi*

## Do not look on the believers as the standard

You should, under no circumstances, feel discouraged, and allow such difficulties [community problems], even though they may have resulted from the misconduct, or the lack of capacity and vision of certain members of the Community, to make you waver in your faith and basic loyalty to the Cause. Surely, the believers, no matter how qualified they may be, whether as teachers or administrators, and however high their intellectual and spiritual merits, should never be looked upon as a standard whereby to evaluate and measure the divine authority and mission of the Faith. It is to the Teachings, themselves, and to the lives of the Founders of the Cause that the believers should look for their guidance and inspiration, and only by keeping strictly to such true attitude can they hope to establish their loyalty to Bahá'u'lláh upon an enduring and unassailable basis.[139]

*Written on behalf of Shoghi Effendi*

## The suffering of innocents

Your letter . . . in which you express great anguish at the plight of babies and children who suffer at the hands of exploitative and disturbed individuals, was received by the Universal House of Justice. We are instructed to convey this reply to you.

On this plane of existence, there are many injustices that the human mind cannot fathom. Among these are the heart-rending trials of the innocent. Indeed, even the Prophets of God Themselves have borne Their share of grievous afflictions in every age. Yet in spite of the evidence of all this suffering, God's Manifestations, Whose lives and wisdom show Them to have been far above human beings in understanding, unitedly bear testimony to the justice, love and mercy of God.

With regard to the spiritual significance of the suffering of children 'who are afflicted at the hands of the oppressor', 'Abdu'l-Bahá not only states that for those souls 'the afflictions that they bear in life become a cause for them of . . . an outpouring of divine mercy and bestowal', He also explains that to be a recipient of God's mercy is 'preferable to a hundred thousand earthly comforts', and He promises that 'in the world to come a mighty recompense awaiteth such souls'. Thus:

> As regards the questions of young children and of weak, defenceless souls who are afflicted at the hand of the oppressor, in this a great wisdom is concealed. The question is one of cardinal importance, but briefly it may be stated that in the world to come a mighty recompense

awaiteth such souls. Much, indeed, might be said upon this theme, and upon how the afflictions that they bear in life become cause for them of such an outpouring of Divine mercy and bestowal as is preferable to a hundred thousand comforts and to a world of growth and development in this transitory abode . . . (from a Tablet, translated from the Persian)

You enquire why some souls, notably those born to loving parents, are seemingly favoured by God, while those born to abusing and rejecting parents are destined to endure a lifetime of suffering, since children growing up in such a destructive atmosphere are more likely as adults to perpetuate abuse on their own children, thus repeating the cycle of violence and thereby further placing in jeopardy their relationship to God. Clearly, only God is able to know the true state of any soul. It is therefore important to appreciate that God in His bounty has endowed every created thing, however humble, 'with the capacity to exercise a particular influence, and been made to possess a distinct virtue'. And, reminiscent of the parable of the talents (Matthew 25:14-30), Bahá'u'lláh, in the *Gleanings* (p. 149), draws attention to the need to make efforts to develop and demonstrate in action our God-given potential:

> All that which ye potentially possess can, however, be manifested only as a result of your own volition. Your own acts testify to this truth.

Is it not an evidence of the justice of God that each of us, irrespective of family background, is assessed in terms of the efforts we have made to seize whatever opportunities existed in our lives, to develop and use our allotted talent, be it large or small. 'Each shall receive his share from thy Lord,' is Bahá'u'lláh's assurance.

Sufferings and trials, sent by God to test and perfect His creatures, are an integral part of life. They contain the potential for man's progress or retrogression, depending on the individual's response. As 'Abdu'l-Bahá explains:

The souls who bear the tests of God become the manifestations of great bounties; for the divine trials cause some souls to become entirely lifeless, while they cause the holy souls to ascend to the highest degree of love and solidity.

In addition, we know from the Bahá'í writings that man's soul 'is independent of all infirmities of body or mind', and not only continues to exist 'after departing from this mortal world', but progresses 'through the bounty and grace of the Lord'. Therefore, an evaluation of man's material existence and achievements cannot ignore the potential spiritual development stimulated by the individual's desire to manifest the attributes of God and his response to the exigencies of his life, nor can it exclude the possibility of the operation of God's mercy in terms of compensation for earthly suffering in the next life.[140]

*Written on behalf of the Universal House of Justice*

*The Sources of Tests:*

*The World and Its Qualities*

# The World and Its Qualities

O Son of Being! Busy not thyself with this world, for with fire We test the gold, and with gold We test Our servants.[141]

*Bahá'u'lláh*

O Son of Man! Should prosperity befall thee, rejoice not, and should abasement come upon thee, grieve not, for both shall pass away and be no more.[142]

*Bahá'u'lláh*

## The test of gold

O Son of Man! Thou dost wish for gold and I desire thy freedom from it. Thou thinkest thyself rich in its possession, and I recognize thy wealth in thy sanctity therefrom. By My life! This is My knowledge, and that is thy fancy; how can My way accord with thine?[143]

*Bahá'u'lláh*

O Ye that Pride Yourselves on Mortal Riches! Know ye in truth that wealth is a mighty barrier between the seeker and his desire, the lover and his beloved. The rich, but for a few, shall in no wise attain the court of His presence nor enter the city of content and resignation. Well is it then with him, who, being rich, is not hindered by his riches from the eternal kingdom, nor deprived by them of imperishable dominion.[144]

*Bahá'u'lláh*

93

Be not troubled in poverty nor confident in riches, for poverty is followed by riches, and riches are followed by poverty.[145]

*Bahá'u'lláh*

Cleanse thyself from the defilement of riches and in perfect peace advance into the realm of poverty; that from the well-spring of detachment thou mayest quaff the wine of immortal life.[146]

*Bahá'u'lláh*

By God! In earthly riches fear is hidden and peril is concealed . . . Fleeting are the riches of the world; all that perisheth and changeth is not, and hath never been, worthy of attention, except to a recognized measure.[147]

*Bahá'u'lláh*

## Let not this life deceive you

Say: O people! Let not this life and its deceits deceive you, for the world and all that is therein is held firmly in the grasp of His Will. He bestoweth His favour on whom He willeth, and from whom He willeth He taketh it away. He doth whatsoever He chooseth. Had the world been of any worth in His sight, He surely would never have allowed His enemies to possess it, even to the extent of a grain of mustard seed. He hath, however, caused you to be entangled with its affairs, in return for what your hands have wrought in His Cause. This, indeed, is a chastisement which ye, of your own will, have inflicted upon yourselves, could ye but perceive it. Are ye rejoicing in the things which, according to the estimate of God, are contemptible and worthless, things wherewith He proveth the hearts of the doubtful?[148]

*Bahá'u'lláh*

Indeed shouldst Thou desire to confer blessing upon a servant Thou wouldst blot out from the realm of his heart every mention or disposition except Thine Own mention; and shouldst Thou ordain evil for a servant by reason of that which his hands have unjustly wrought before Thy face, Thou wouldst test him with the benefits of this world and of the next that he might become preoccupied therewith and forget Thy remembrance.[149]

*The Báb*

## The earth supplies only disappointment

Every soul seeketh an object and cherisheth a desire, and day and night striveth to attain his aim. One craveth riches, another thirsteth for glory and still another yearneth for fame, for art, for prosperity and the like. Yet finally all are doomed to loss and disappointment. One and all they leave behind them all that is theirs and empty-handed hasten to the realm beyond, and all their labours shall be in vain. To dust they shall all return, denuded, depressed, disheartened and in utter despair.[150]

*'Abdu'l-Bahá*

. . . woe and misery to the soul that seeketh after comforts, riches, and earthly delights while neglecting to call God to mind![151]

*'Abdu'l-Bahá*

## Suffering is the outcome of material things

Wealth has a tempting and drawing quality. It bewilders the sight of its charmed victims with showy appearances and draws them on and on to the edge of yawning chasms. It makes a person self-centred, self-occupied, forgetful of God and of holy things.[152]

*Attributed to 'Abdu'l-Bahá*

95

## The destructive power of materialism

... an evil which the nation [America], and indeed all those within the capitalist system ... share ... is the crass materialism, which lays excessive and ever-increasing emphasis on material well-being, forgetful of those things of the spirit on which alone a sure and stable foundation can be laid for human society. It is this same cancerous materialism, born originally in Europe, carried to excess in the North American continent, contaminating the Asiatic peoples and nations, spreading its ominous tentacles to the borders of Africa, and now invading its very heart, which Bahá'u'lláh in unequivocal and emphatic language denounced in His Writings, comparing it to a devouring flame and regarding it as the chief factor in precipitating the dire ordeals and world-shaking crises that must necessarily involve the burning of cities and the spread of terror and consternation in the hearts of men. Indeed a foretaste of the devastation which this consuming fire will wreak upon the world, and with which it will lay waste the cities of the nations participating in this tragic world-engulfing contest, has been afforded by the last World War [II], marking the second stage in the global havoc which humanity, forgetful of its God and heedless of the clear warnings uttered by His appointed Messenger for this day, must, alas, inevitably experience.[153]

*Shoghi Effendi*

## Formidable obstacles we must overcome

The gross materialism that engulfs the entire nation at the present hour; the attachment to worldly things that enshrouds the souls of men; the fears and anxieties that distract their minds; the pleasure and dissipation that fill their time, the prejudices and animosities that darken their outlook, the apathy and lethargy that paralyze their spiritual faculties – these are among the formidable obstacles that stand in the path of every would-be warrior in the service of Bahá'u'lláh, obstacles which he must battle against and surmount in his crusade for the redemption of his own countrymen.[154]

*Shoghi Effendi*

The steady and alarming deterioration in the standard of morality as exemplified by the appalling increase of crime, by political corruption in ever widening and ever higher circles, by the loosening of the sacred ties of marriage, by the inordinate craving for pleasure and diversion, and by the marked and progressive slackening of parental control, is no doubt the most arresting and distressing aspect of the decline that has set in, and can be clearly perceived, in the fortunes of the entire nation.[155]

*Shoghi Effendi*

The Bahá'ís should realize that today's intensely materialistic civilization, alas, most perfectly exemplified by the United States, has far exceeded the bounds of moderation, and, as Bahá'u'lláh has pointed out in His Writings, civilization itself, when carried to extremes, leads to destruction. The Canadian friends should be on their guard against this deadly influence to which they are so constantly exposed, and which we can see is undermining the moral strength of not only America, but indeed of Europe and other parts of the world to which it is rapidly spreading.[156]

*Written on behalf of Shoghi Effendi*

The people of Bahá should, then, lead their lives and conduct their affairs with the highest degree of sanctity and godliness, and uncompromisingly repudiate and dissociate themselves from the disreputable practices, the deplorable modes and customs prevalent among the people of the West. Piety and devotion should be the object of all who would be accounted lovers of this Cause, and the adornment of every righteous soul; otherwise, slowly but surely, the illumination conferred on the innermost reality of men's hearts by the virtues of the human world will flicker and fade and die away, to be overwhelmed by the engulfing darkness of vice and depravity. Courtesy and dignity are what bring nobility and standing to a man; whereas frivolity and facetiousness, ribaldry and effrontery will lead to his abasement, degradation and humiliation. The Bahá'ís should, indeed must, seek to distinguish themselves in all things, for what difference else would there be between them and others? Any action, therefore, that is calculated to detract from the dignity of man's station must be steadfastly avoided and shunned.[157]

*Written on behalf of Shoghi Effendi*

## Our materialistic civilization

... the chief reason for the evils now rampant in society is the lack of spirituality. The materialistic civilization of our age has so much absorbed the energy and interest of mankind that people in general do no longer feel the necessity of raising themselves above the forces and conditions of their daily material existence. There is not sufficient demand for things that we should call spiritual to differentiate them from the needs and requirements of our physical existence.

The universal crisis affecting mankind is, therefore, essentially spiritual in its causes. The spirit of the age, taken on the whole, is irreligious. Man's outlook on life is too crude and materialistic to enable him to elevate himself into the higher realms of the spirit.

It is this condition, so sadly morbid, into which society has fallen, that religion seeks to improve and transform. . .[158]

*Written on behalf of Shoghi Effendi*

It would be perhaps impossible to find a nation or people not in a state of crisis today. The materialism, the lack of true religion and the consequent baser forces in human nature which are being released, have brought the whole world to the brink of probably the greatest crisis it has ever faced or will have to face. The Bahá'ís are a part of the world. They too feel the great pressures which are brought to bear upon all people today, whoever and wherever they may be.[159]

*Written on behalf of Shoghi Effendi*

## America's suffering

Many and divers are the setbacks and reverses which this nation [America], extolled so highly by 'Abdu'l-Bahá, and occupying at present so unique a position among its fellow nations, must, alas, suffer. The road leading to its destiny is long, thorny and tortuous. The impact of various forces upon the structure and polity of that nation will be tremendous. Tribulations, on a scale unprecedented in its history, and calculated to purge its institutions, to purify the hearts of its people, to fuse its constituent elements, and to weld it into one entity with its sister nations in both hemispheres, are inevitable.[160]

*Shoghi Effendi*

The American nation . . . stands, indeed, from whichever angle one observes its immediate fortunes, in grave peril. The woes and tribulations which threaten it are partly avoidable but mostly inevitable and God-sent, for by reason of them a government and people clinging tenaciously to the obsolescent doctrine of absolute sovereignty and upholding a political system, manifestly at variance with the needs of a world already contracted into a neighbourhood and crying out for unity, will find itself purged of its anachronistic conceptions, and prepared to play a preponderating role, as foretold by 'Abdu'l-Bahá, in the hoisting of the standard of the Lesser Peace, in the unification of mankind, and in the establishment of a world federal government on this planet. These same fiery tribulations will not only firmly weld the American nation to its sister nations in both hemispheres, but will through their cleansing effect, purge it thoroughly of the accumulated dross which ingrained racial prejudice, rampant materialism, widespread ungodliness and moral laxity have combined, in the course of successive generations, to produce, and which have prevented her thus far from assuming the role of world spiritual leadership forecast by 'Abdu'l-Bahá's unerring pen – a role which she is bound to fulfil through travail and sorrow.[161]

*Shoghi Effendi*

## Beware that you are not affected by the world

People are so markedly lacking in spirituality these days that the Bahá'ís should consciously guard themselves against being caught in what one might call the undertow of materialism and atheism, sweeping the world these days. Scepticism, cynicism, disbelief, immorality and hard-heartedness are rife, and as the friends are those who stand for the antithesis of all these things they should beware lest the atmosphere of the present world affects them without their being conscious of it.[162]

*Written on behalf of Shoghi Effendi*

He [Shoghi Effendi] quite understands how the friends can sometimes feel, as you put it, 'spiritually depleted', for the condition of the world is such today that it is like a great negative undertow trying to pull down all but the strongest and most firmly rooted. The friends should realize this and draw closer to each other, knowing that they form one spiritual family, closer to each other, in the sight of God, than those united by ties of blood.

He will pray for you, and that you may be able to draw the believers into a more conscious effort at unity, and to inspire them to see in each that which the Master would wish them to, and not what their own intolerant personalities are so prone to seeing: namely faults![163]

*Written on behalf of Shoghi Effendi*

## Do not feel depressed about not finding the right job

You should never be too depressed about your dissatisfaction concerning not finding a job you like, a place in the world that fits you. If you analyse it this general sense of mis-fit is one of the curses of your generation, one of the products of the world's disequilibrium and chaos. It is not confined to your life, it is pretty general.[164]

*Written on behalf of Shoghi Effendi*

## The darkness of society

In other lands, such as those of Western Europe, the faithful believers have to struggle to convey the message in the face of widespread indifference, materialistic self-satisfaction, cynicism and moral degradation.[165]

*The Universal House of Justice*

. . . we cannot forget that the dark passage of the Age of Transition has not been fully traversed; it is as yet long, slippery and tortuous. For godlessness is rife, materialism rampant. Nationalism and racism still work their treachery in men's hearts, and humanity remains blind to the spiritual foundations of the solution to its economic woes. For the Bahá'í community the situation is a particular challenge, because time is running out and we have serious commitments to keep.[166]

*The Universal House of Justice*

One of the signs of a decadent society, a sign which is very evident in the world today, is an almost frenetic devotion to pleasure and diversion, an insatiable thirst for amusement, a fanatical devotion to games and sport, a reluctance to treat any matter seriously, and a scornful, derisory attitude towards virtue and solid worth. Abandonment of 'a frivolous conduct' does not imply that a Bahá'í must be sour-faced or perpetually solemn. Humour, happiness, joy are characteristics of a true Bahá'í life. Frivolity palls and eventually leads to boredom and emptiness, but true happiness and joy and humour that are parts of a balanced life that includes serious thought, compassion and humble servitude to God, are characteristics that enrich life and add to its radiance. Shoghi Effendi's choice of words was always significant, and each one is important in understanding his guidance. In this particular passage [from *The Advent of Divine Justice*, p. 30], he does not forbid 'trivial' pleasures, but he does warn against 'excessive attachment' to them and indicates that they can often be 'misdirected'. One is reminded of 'Abdu'l-Bahá's caution that we should not let a pastime become a waste of time.[167]

*Written on behalf of the Universal House of Justice*

# The Sources of Tests:

# Persecutions of the Believers

# Persecutions of the Believers

Know ye that trials and tribulations have, from time immemorial, been the lot of the chosen Ones of God and His beloved, and such of His servants as are detached from all else but Him, they whom neither merchandise nor traffic beguile from the remembrance of the Almighty, they that speak not till He hath spoken, and act according to His commandment. Such is God's method carried into effect of old, and such will it remain in the future.[168]

*Bahá'u'lláh*


Thy glory is my witness! At each daybreak they who love Thee wake to find the cup of woe set before their faces, because they have believed in Thee and acknowledged Thy signs. Though I firmly believe that Thou hast a greater compassion on them than they have on their own selves, though I recognize that Thou hast afflicted them for no other purpose except to proclaim Thy Cause, and to enable them to ascend into the heaven of Thine eternity and the precincts of Thy court, yet Thou knowest full well the frailty of some of them, and art aware of their impatience in their sufferings.

Help them through Thy strengthening grace, I beseech Thee, O my God, to suffer patiently in their love for Thee, and unveil to their eyes what Thou hast decreed for them behind the Tabernacle of Thine unfailing protection, so that they may rush forward to meet what is preordained for them in Thy path, and may vie in hasting after tribulation in their love towards Thee.[169]

*Bahá'u'lláh*

## Throughout the ages the righteous have suffered

. . . throughout all ages and centuries the righteous have been made a target to the darts of adversity and have fallen victim to the swords of oppression. At one time they quaffed the cup of dire ordeal, at another they tasted the venom of bitter woe. Not for a moment did they enjoy rest and comfort, nor did they repose for a fleeting breath upon the couch of tranquillity. Rather did they endure agonizing torment and patiently carry the burden of hardship that every oppressor was wont to impose on them. Having been consigned to dungeons and prisons, they severed themselves from the world and all its peoples.

. . . In brief, there is not a spike whose tip is not tinged with the blood of the martyrs, nor is there a place not dyed crimson with the blood of His ardent lovers. The purpose is to enable you to know that one of the tenets of those that thirst after Him and the highest aspiration of such as long to behold His face is to endure hardship, to submit to trials and martyrdom in the path of the Lord of grace. Therefore it behoveth you to render thanks unto God for the bounty of having drunk your fill from this draught and for having tasted deadly poison in the path of the Best-Beloved. Indeed far from being a poison this is pure honey and sugar, far from being bitter in taste, this is the essence of sweetness.[170]

*'Abdu'l-Bahá*

## A multitude will arise against us

. . . a large multitude of people will arise against you, showing oppression, expressing contumely and derision, shunning your society, and heaping upon you ridicule. However, the Heavenly Father will illumine you to such an extent that, like unto the rays of the sun, you shall scatter the dark clouds of superstition, shine gloriously in the midst of Heaven and illumine the face of the earth. You must make firm the feet at the time when these trials transpire, and demonstrate forbearance and patience. You must withstand them with the utmost love and kindness; consider their oppression and persecution as the caprice of children, and do not give any importance to whatever they do.[171]

*'Abdu'l-Bahá*

How great, how very great is the Cause! How very fierce the onslaught of all the peoples and kindreds of the earth. Ere long shall the clamour of the multitude throughout Africa, throughout America, the cry of the European and of the Turk, the groaning of India and China, be heard from far and near. One and all, they shall arise with all their power to resist His Cause. Then shall the knights of the Lord, assisted by His grace from on high, strengthened by faith, aided by the power of understanding, and reinforced by the legions of the Covenant, arise and make manifest the truth of the verse: 'Behold the confusion that hath befallen the tribes of the defeated!'[172]

*'Abdu'l-Bahá*

## The friends in the West will have their share of tests

... the friends in the West will unquestionably have their share of the calamities befalling the friends in the East. It is inevitable that, walking the pathway of Bahá'u'lláh, they too will become targets for persecution by the oppressors ...

Now ye, as well, must certainly become my partners to some slight degree, and accept your share of tests and sorrows. But these episodes shall pass away, while that abiding glory and eternal life shall remain unchanged forever. Moreover, these afflictions shall be the cause of great advancement.[173]

*'Abdu'l-Bahá*

## There are many obstacles

Look thou around the world of existence: A little worldly transaction cannot be brought about except through surmounting many an obstacle. How much more important are the objects of the Supreme World! Certainly there existeth troubles, trials, afflictions, persecution, censure and contempt. When thou didst occupy thy time in the past to give out religious exhortations and advices, thou experienced some persecutions and trouble. But thou canst not realize in this present moment what great ordeals are in store and what unbearable calamities, affliction and adversity exist, and that to give up life is the easiest of all those calamities. But the end of all these is bliss, overflowing joy, everlasting exultation, happiness and supreme contentment. It is eternal life, never ending glory, a lordly gift and divine sovereignty![174]

*'Abdu'l-Bahá*

The intent of what I wrote to thee in my previous letter was this, that when exalting the Word of God, there are trials to be met with, and calamities; and that in loving Him, at every moment there are hardships, torments, afflictions.

It behoveth the individual first to value these ordeals, willingly accept them, and eagerly welcome them; only then should he proceed with teaching the Faith and exalting the Word of God.[175]

*'Abdu'l-Bahá*

O spiritual friends and loved ones of the All-Merciful! In every Age believers are many but the tested are few. Render ye praise unto God that ye are tested believers, that ye have been subjected to every kind of trial and ordeal in the path of the supreme Lord. In the fire of ordeals your faces have flushed aglow like unto pure gold, and amidst the flames of cruelty and oppression which the wicked had kindled, ye suffered yourselves to be consumed while remaining all the time patient. Thus ye have initiated every believer into the ways of steadfastness and fortitude. You showed them the meaning of forbearance, of constancy, and of sacrifice, and what leadeth to dismay and distress. This indeed is a token of the gracious providence

of God and a sign of the infinite favours vouchsafed by the
Abhá Beauty Who hath singled out the friends of that region
to bear grievous sufferings in the path of His love. Outwardly
they are fire, but inwardly light and an evidence of His glory.
Ye have been examples of the verse: 'Let them that are men
of action follow in their footsteps.' 'And to this let those aspire
who aspire unto bliss.'[176]

*'Abdu'l-Bahá*

## The Cause will be affected by world crises

How can the beginnings of a world upheaval, unleashing forces
that are so gravely deranging the social, the religious, the
political, and the economic equilibrium of organized society,
throwing into chaos and confusion political systems, racial
doctrines, social conceptions, cultural standards, religious
associations, and trade relationships – how can such agitations,
on a scale so vast, so unprecedented, fail to produce any
repercussions on the institutions of a Faith of such tender age
whose teachings have a direct and vital bearing on each of
these spheres of human life and conduct?

Little wonder, therefore, if they who are holding aloft the
banner of so pervasive a Faith, so challenging a Cause, find
themselves affected by the impact of these world-shaking
forces. Little wonder if they find that in the midst of this
whirlpool of contending passions their freedom has been
curtailed, their tenets contemned, their institutions assaulted,
their motives maligned, their authority jeopardized, their
claim rejected.[177]

*Shoghi Effendi*

## The Cause will face many adversaries

For let every earnest upholder of the Cause of Bahá'u'lláh
realize that the storms which this struggling Faith of God must
needs encounter, as the process of the disintegration of society
advances, shall be fiercer than any which it has already experi-

enced. Let him be aware that so soon as the full measure of the stupendous claim of the Faith of Bahá'u'lláh comes to be recognized by those time-honoured and powerful strongholds of orthodoxy, whose deliberate aim is to maintain their stranglehold over the thoughts and consciences of men, this infant Faith will have to contend with enemies more powerful and more insidious than the cruellest torture-mongers and the most fanatical clerics who have afflicted it in the past.[178]

*Shoghi Effendi*

## Storms of abuse and ridicule

In the conduct of this twofold crusade the valiant warriors struggling in the name and for the Cause of Bahá'u'lláh must, of necessity, encounter stiff resistance, and suffer many a setback. Their own instincts, no less than the fury of conservative forces, the opposition of vested interests, and the objections of a corrupt and pleasure-seeking generation, must be reckoned with, resolutely resisted, and completely overcome. As their defensive measures for the impending struggle, are organized and extended, storms of abuse and ridicule, and campaigns of condemnation and misrepresentation, may be unloosed against them. Their Faith, they may soon find, has been assaulted, their motives misconstrued, their aims defamed, their aspirations derided, their institutions scorned, their influence belittled, their authority undermined, and their Cause, at times, deserted by a few who will either be incapable of appreciating the nature of their ideals, or unwilling to bear the brunt of the mounting criticisms which such a contest is sure to involve. 'Because of 'Abdu'l-Bahá', the beloved Master has prophesied, 'many a test will be visited upon you. Troubles will befall you, and suffering afflict you.'[179]

*Shoghi Effendi*

It was not mere physical torture that the friends in Persia had to endure but also moral persecution for they were cursed and vilified by all the people, especially when they ceased to defend themselves . . . the Master used to say sometimes that the western friends will be severely persecuted but theirs will be primarily moral . . .[180]

*Written on behalf of Shoghi Effendi*

## Maintain unity in the face of opposition

Undoubtedly, as the influence of God's Faith becomes more pervasive, the number of those who wish to obstruct its progress will also grow; new and increasingly formidable adversaries will come to the fore; and mischief-makers, appearing under various extraordinary guises, will seek surreptitiously to goad to action all those who harbour resentment or bear ill will towards this Cause, and will raise aloft the standards of sedition. Under these circumstances it is essential for the friends on the one hand to be alert and watchful, and on the other to arouse the vigilance and strengthen the allegiance of their fellow-believers, to guard the integrity of the Word of God, and to maintain harmony and unity amongst His loved ones. Herein lies the supreme duty of the friends of God, and the highest means by which they can render service to His Cause.[181]

*Written on behalf of Shoghi Effendi*

## Critical contests lie ahead

We feel strongly that . . . the time has come for them [the friends] to clearly grasp the inevitability of the critical contests which lie ahead, give you their full support in repelling with confidence and determination 'the darts' which will be levelled against them by 'their present enemies, as well as those whom Providence will, through His mysterious dispensations raise up from within or from without,' and aid and enable the Faith of God to scale loftier heights, win more signal triumphs, and traverse more vital stages in its predestined course to complete victory and world-wide ascendancy.[182]

*The Universal House of Justice*

As the Bahá'í community continues to emerge inexorably from obscurity, it will be confronted by enemies, from both within and without, whose aim will be to malign and misrepresent its principles, so that its admirers might be disillusioned and the faith of its adherents might be shaken.[183]

*Written on behalf of the Universal House of Justice*

*The Sources of Tests:*

## Calamities in the World

# Calamities in the World

So blind hath become the human heart that neither the disruption of the city, nor the reduction of the mountain in dust, nor even the cleaving of the earth, can shake off its torpor. The allusions made in the Scriptures have been unfolded, and the signs recorded therein have been revealed, and the prophetic cry is continually being raised. And yet all, except such as God was pleased to guide, are bewildered in the drunkenness of their heedlessness!

Witness how the world is being afflicted with a fresh calamity every day. Its tribulation is continually deepening. From the moment the Súriy-i-Ra'ís (Tablet to Ra'ís) was revealed until the present day, neither hath the world been tranquillized, nor have the hearts of its peoples been at rest. At one time it hath been agitated by contentions and disputes, at another it hath been convulsed by wars, and fallen a victim to inveterate diseases. Its sickness is approaching the stage of utter hopelessness, inasmuch as the true Physician is debarred from administering the remedy, whilst unskilled practitioners are regarded with favour, and are accorded full freedom to act. [184]

*Bahá'u'lláh*

## Darkness hath fallen on every land

O God, my God! Thou seest how black darkness is enshrouding all regions, how all countries are burning with the flame of dissension, and the fire of war and carnage is blazing throughout the East and the West. Blood is flowing, corpses bestrew the ground, and severed heads are fallen on the dust of the battlefield.

. . . O Lord! Wars have persisted. Distress and anxiety have waxed great and every flourishing region is laid waste. O Lord! Hearts are heavy and souls are in anguish. Have mercy on these poor souls and do not leave them to the excesses of their own desires.

. . . O Lord! The ocean of rebellion is surging, and these tempests will not be stilled save through Thy boundless grace which hath embraced all regions.

O Lord! Verily, the people are in the abyss of passion, and naught can save them but Thine infinite bounties.

O Lord! Dispel the darkness of these corrupt desires, and illumine the hearts with the lamp of Thy love through which all countries will erelong be enlightened.[185]

*'Abdu'l-Bahá*

## Until the people are forced to turn to God

Know thou that hardship and privation shall increase day by day, and the people shall thereby be afflicted. The doors of joy and happiness shall be closed on all sides, and terrible wars shall occur. Frustration and despair shall encompass the people until they are forced to turn to the One True God. Then will the light of most joyful tidings so illumine the horizons that the cry of 'Yá Bahá'u'l-Abhá' will be raised from every direction. This shall come to pass.[186]

*'Abdu'l-Bahá*

## A tempest is sweeping the face of the earth

A tempest, unprecedented in its violence, unpredictable in its course, catastrophic in its immediate effects, unimaginably glorious in its ultimate consequences, is at present sweeping the face of the earth. Its driving power is remorselessly gaining in range and momentum. Its cleansing force, however much undetected, is increasing with every passing day. Humanity, gripped in the clutches of its devastating power, is smitten by the evidences of its resistless fury. It can neither perceive its origin, nor probe its significance, nor discern its outcome. Bewildered, agonized and helpless, it watches this great and mighty wind of God invading the remotest and fairest regions of the earth, rocking its foundations, deranging its equilibrium, sundering its nations, disrupting the homes of its peoples, wasting its cities, driving into exile its kings, pulling down its bulwarks, uprooting its institutions, dimming its light, and harrowing up the souls of its inhabitants.[187]

*Shoghi Effendi*

## The purpose of the tempest

This judgement of God, as viewed by those who have recognized Bahá'u'lláh as His Mouthpiece and His greatest Messenger on earth, is both a retributory calamity and an act of holy and supreme discipline. It is at once a visitation from God and a cleansing process for all mankind. Its fires punish the perversity of the human race, and weld its component parts into one organic, indivisible, world-embracing community. Mankind, in these fateful years, which at once signalize the passing of the first century of the Bahá'í Era and proclaim the opening of a new one, is, as ordained by Him Who is both the Judge and the Redeemer of the human race, being simultaneously called upon to give account of its past actions, and is being purged and prepared for its future mission. It can neither escape the responsibilities of the past, nor shirk those of the future. God, the Vigilant, the Just, the Loving, the All-Wise Ordainer, can, in this supreme Dispensation, neither allow the sins of an unregenerate humanity, whether of omission or of commission, to go unpunished, nor will He be willing to abandon His children to their fate, and refuse them that culminating and blissful stage in their long, their slow and painful evolution throughout the ages, which is at once their inalienable right and their true destiny.

. . . 'The whole earth', Bahá'u'lláh, on the other hand, forecasting the bright future in store for a world now wrapt in darkness, emphatically asserts, 'is now in a state of pregnancy.

The day is approaching when it will have yielded its noblest fruits, when from it will have sprung forth the loftiest trees, the most enchanting blossoms, the most heavenly blessings.' 'The time is approaching when every created thing will have cast its burden. Glorified be God Who hath vouchsafed this grace that encompasseth all things, whether seen or unseen!' 'These great oppressions', He, moreover, foreshadowing humanity's golden age, has written, 'are preparing it for the advent of the Most Great Justice.' This Most Great Justice is indeed the Justice upon which the structure of the Most Great Peace can alone, and must eventually, rest, while the Most Great Peace will, in turn, usher in that Most Great, that World Civilization which shall remain forever associated with Him Who beareth the Most Great Name.[188]

*Shoghi Effendi*

## Difficult times must precede the promised dawn

. . . as the horizons of the world grow darker, as its agitation becomes more severe and the prevailing chaos and confusion more widespread, the dawn of the Promised Day will correspondingly draw nearer, and the means for the splendours of His light to be shed abroad will be more readily provided.

However, the fulfilment of glad-tidings, so glorious and heart-uplifting, must needs be heralded by awesome and distressing events, inasmuch as the realization of these irrevocable and divinely-ordained promises depends on the awakening and the stirring of the conscience of the entire human race, while this cannot be achieved save through the occurrence of unnumbered afflictions, manifold convulsions and growing adversities.[189]

*Shoghi Effendi*

## The stage of purgation is indispensable

You seem to complain about the calamities that have befallen humanity. In the spiritual development of man a stage of purgation is indispensable, for it is while passing through it that the over-rated material needs are made to appear in their proper light. Unless society learns to attribute more importance to spiritual matters, it would never be fit to enter the golden era foretold by Bahá'u'lláh. The present calamities are parts of this process of purgation, through them alone will man learn his lesson. They are to teach the nations that they have to view things internationally, they are to make the individual attribute more importance to his moral, than his material welfare.[190]

*Written on behalf of Shoghi Effendi*

## Bahá'ís should not hope to remain unaffected by calamities

In such a process of purgation, when all humanity is in the throes of dire suffering, the Bahá'ís should not hope to remain unaffected. Should we consider the beam that is in our own eye, we would immediately find that these sufferings are also meant for ourselves, who claimed to have attained. Such world crisis is necessary to awaken us to the importance of our duty and the carrying on of our task. Suffering will increase our energy in setting before humanity the road to salvation, it will move us from our repose for we are far from doing our best in teaching the Cause and conveying the Message with which we have been entrusted . . .[191]

*Written on behalf of Shoghi Effendi*

When such a crisis sweeps over the world no person should hope to remain intact. We belong to an organic unit and when one part of the organism suffers all the rest of the body will feel its consequence. This is in fact the reason why Bahá'u'lláh calls our attention to the unity of mankind. But as Bahá'ís we should not let such hardship weaken our hope in the future . . .[192]

*Written on behalf of Shoghi Effendi*

## Only Bahá'u'lláh's message can heal the world

We have no indication of exactly what nature the apocalyptic upheaval will be; it might be another war . . . but as students of our Bahá'í Writings, it is clear that the longer the 'Divine Physician' (i.e. Bahá'u'lláh) is withheld from healing the ills of the world, the more severe will be the crisis, and the more terrible the sufferings of the patient.[193]

*Written on behalf of Shoghi Effendi*

No doubt to the degree we Bahá'ís the world over strive to spread the Cause and live up to its teachings, there will be some mitigation of the suffering of the peoples of the world. But it seems apparent that the great failure to respond to Bahá'u'lláh's instructions, appeals and warnings issued in the 19th century, has now sent the world along a path, or released forces, which must culminate in a still more violent upheaval and agony. The thing is out of hand, so to speak, and it is too late to avert catastrophic trials.[194]

*Written on behalf of Shoghi Effendi*

## We know the future is serene and bright

It is quite natural for anyone, observing the present state of the world, to feel very depressed and apprehensive of the future. Any intelligent person must be wondering what you are wondering. It is indeed hard to see what lies ahead of us in the near future – but we, as Bahá'ís, unlike most people, have absolute assurance that the distant future is serene and bright. We do not know if there will be another Great War; what we do know is this: that unless people become spiritually awakened in time, great suffering, maybe in the form of war, will come upon them, for humanity must be unified, must be redeemed. If men refuse absolutely to take the easier road of faith, of seeking out God's Manifestation for this age and accepting Him, then they will bring upon themselves a fresh crisis in human affairs and very great affliction. What we, as Bahá'ís, must do is our duty; we cannot do other people's duty for them, alas, but we can fulfil our own sacred responsibilities by serving our fellow-men, living a Bahá'í life, teaching the Faith, and strengthening its budding world order. [195]

*Written on behalf of Shoghi Effendi*

## Do not dwell on the dark side of things

He [Shoghi Effendi] has been told that some of the friends are disturbed over reports brought back by the pilgrims concerning the dangers facing America in the future whenever another world conflagration breaks out.

He does not feel that the Bahá'ís should waste time dwelling on the dark side of things. Any intelligent person can understand from the experiences of the last world war, and keeping abreast of what modern science has developed in the way of weapons for any future war, that big cities all over the world are going to be in tremendous danger. This is what the Guardian has said to the pilgrims.

Entirely aside from this, he has urged the Bahá'ís, for the sake of serving the Faith, to go out from these centres of intense materialism, where life nowadays is so hurried and grinding and, dispersing to towns and villages, carry the Message far and wide throughout the cities of the American Union. He strongly believes that the field outside the big cities is more fertile, that the Bahá'ís in the end will be happier for having made this move, and that, in case of an outbreak of war, it stands to reason they will be safer, just the way any other person living in the country, or away from the big industrial areas is safer.

It is remarks such as these that the pilgrims have carried back in their notes. He sees no cause for alarm, but he certainly believes that the Bahá'ís should weigh these thoughts, and take action for the sake of spreading the Faith of Bahá'u'lláh, and for their own ultimate happiness as well. Indeed the two things go together. [196]

*Written on behalf of Shoghi Effendi*

121

## Current dangers and opportunities facing the world

With the fresh tide of political freedom resulting from the collapse of the strongholds of communism has come an explosion of nationalism. The concomitant rise of racism in many regions has become a matter of serious global concern. These are compounded by an upsurge in religious fundamentalism which is poisoning the wells of tolerance. Terrorism is rife, Widespread uncertainty about the condition of the economy indicates a deep disorder in the management of the material affairs of the planet, a condition which can only exacerbate the sense of frustration and futility affecting the political realm. The worsening state of the environment and of the health of huge populations is a source of alarm. And yet an element of this change is the amazing advances in communications technology making possible the rapid transmission of information and ideas from one part of the world to the other. It is against such 'simultaneous processes of rise and fall, of integration and of disintegration, of order and chaos, with their continuous and reciprocal reactions on each other', that a myriad new opportunities for the next stage in the unfoldment of the beloved Master's Divine Plan present themselves.[197]

*The Universal House of Justice*

. . . the believers should understand that a catastrophic breakdown of human society as a result of mankind's ignoring His Message has been clearly foretold by Bahá'u'lláh, and that we are, indeed, in the midst of such a breakdown. The main concern of the Bahá'ís should be, not how to preserve themselves physically, but how to seize the opportunities that these conditions present to convey the healing teachings of the Faith to their fellow-citizens. The rising level of concern at this time may well be one of the keys that will assist the friends to open the eyes of the peoples of Europe to the true nature of their predicament and to win their allegiance to the Cause of God.[198]

*The Universal House of Justice*

The House of Justice is deeply concerned at the plight of so many of the indigenous and aboriginal peoples in various parts of the world who have been denied their rights as a consequence of actions by oppressive majorities. Such inequities and injustices are to be found in many countries. The purpose of the coming of Bahá'u'lláh is to lift the yoke of oppression from his loved ones, to liberate all the people of the world, and to provide the means for their abiding happiness.

The Bahá'í approach to resolution of the manifold problems affecting human society rests upon the assertion by Bahá'u'lláh that these ills are but various symptoms and side effects of the basic disease, which the Divine Physician has diagnosed to be disunity. Bahá'u'lláh has made it abundantly clear that the first step essential for the health and harmony of the whole of mankind is its unification. He says, 'The well-being of mankind, its peace and security are unattainable unless and until its unity is firmly established' (*The World Order of Bahá'u'lláh*, p. 203). By contrast, the approach of most people is the exact opposite: their concentration is on attempts to remedy the multitude of ills besetting mankind, with the expectation that the resolution of these problems will lead ultimately to unity.[199]

*Written on behalf of the Universal House of Justice*

Let us consider the First World War, which Shoghi Effendi has described in his writings as 'the first stage in the titanic convulsion long predicted by Bahá'u'lláh'. Although it ended outwardly in a Treaty of Peace, 'Abdu'l-Bahá remarked: 'Peace, Peace, the lips of potentates and peoples unceasingly proclaim, whereas the fire of unquenched hatred still smoulders in their hearts.' And then in 1920, He wrote: 'The ills from which the world now suffers will multiply; the gloom which envelops it will deepen.' And again: 'Another war, fiercer than the last, will assuredly break out.' After the Second World War broke out in 1939, Shoghi Effendi called it a 'tempest, unprecedented in its violence', and the 'great and mighty wind of God invading the remotest and fairest regions of the earth'. After the termination of this War and the creation of the United Nations, the Guardian wrote in 1948, anticipating 'still more violent convulsions' and referred to the 'winds' of yet another 'conflict', destined to 'darken the international horizon'.[200]

*Written on behalf of the Universal House of Justice*

. . . the Pen of the Centre of the Covenant has repeatedly prophesied the intolerable calamities which must best beset this wayward humanity ere it heeds the life-giving Teachings of Bahá'u'lláh. 'Chaos and confusion are daily increasing in the world. They will attain such intensity as to render the frame of mankind unable to bear them. Then will men be awakened and become aware that religion is the impregnable stronghold and the manifest light of the world, and its laws, exhortations and teachings the source of life on earth.' Every discerning eye clearly sees that the early stages of this chaos have daily manifestations affecting the structure of human society; its destructive forces are uprooting time-honoured institutions which were a haven and refuge for the inhabitants of the earth in bygone days and centuries, and around which revolved all human affairs. The same destructive forces are also deranging the political, economic, scientific, literary, and moral equilibrium of the world and are destroying the fairest fruits of the present civilization. Political machinations of those in authority have placed the seal of obsolescence upon the root principles of the world's order. Greed and passion, deceit, hypocrisy, tyranny, and pride are dominating features afflicting human relations. Discoveries and inventions, which are the fruit of scientific and technological advancements, have become the means and tools of mass extermination and destruction and are in the hands of the ungodly. Even music, art, and literature, which are to represent and inspire the noblest sentiments and highest aspirations and should be a source of comfort and tranquillity for troubled souls, have strayed from the straight path and are now the mirrors of the soiled hearts of this confused, unprincipled and disordered age. Perversions such as these shall result in the ordeals which have been prophesied by the Blessed Beauty in the following words: '. . . the earth will be tormented by a fresh calamity every day and unprecedented commotions will break out.' 'The day is approaching when its (civilization's) flame will devour the cities.' In such an afflicted time, when mankind is bewildered and the wisest of men are perplexed as to the remedy, the people of Bahá, who have confidence in His unfailing grace and divine guidance, are assured that each of these tormenting trials has a cause, a purpose, and a definite result, and all are essential instruments for the establishment of the immutable Will of God on earth. In other words, on the one hand humanity is struck by the scourge of His chastisement which will inevitably bring together the scattered and vanquished tribes of the earth; and on the other, the weak few whom He has nurtured under the protection of his loving guidance are, in this Formative Age and period of transition, continuing to build amidst these tumultuous waves an impregnable stronghold which will be the sole remaining refuge for those lost multitudes. Therefore, the dear friends of God who have such a broad and clear vision before them are not perturbed by such events, nor are they panic-stricken by such thundering sounds, nor will they face such convulsions with fear and trepidation, nor will they be deterred, even for a moment, from fulfilling their sacred responsibilities.

One of their sacred responsibilities is to exemplify in their lives those attributes which are acceptable at His Sacred Threshold.[201]

*Written on behalf of the Universal House of Justice*

# Solutions to Tests

*Solutions to Tests:*

# *Faith and Confidence*

# Faith and Confidence

Place not thy reliance on thy treasures. Put thy whole confidence in the grace of God, thy Lord. Let Him be thy trust in whatever thou doest, and be of them that have submitted themselves to His Will.[202]

*Bahá'u'lláh*

Put your whole trust and confidence in God, Who hath created you, and seek ye His help in all your affairs. Succor cometh from Him alone. He succoreth whom He will with the hosts of the heavens and of the earth.[203]

*Bahá'u'lláh*

Be confident that a confirmation will be granted unto you and a success on His part is given unto you.[204]

*Bahá'u'lláh*

My army is My reliance on God; My people, the force of My confidence in Him.[205]

*Bahá'u'lláh*

. . . and he that placeth his complete trust in God, God shall, verily, protect him from whatsoever may harm him, and shield him from the wickedness of every evil plotter.[206]

*Bahá'u'lláh*

Be not afraid of anyone, place thy whole trust in God, the Almighty, the All-Knowing.[207]

*Bahá'u'lláh*

Whatever hath befallen you, hath been for the sake of God. This is the truth, and in this there is no doubt. You should, therefore, leave all your affairs in His Hands, place your trust in Him, and rely upon Him. He will assuredly not forsake you. In this, likewise, there is no doubt. No father will surrender his sons to devouring beasts; no shepherd will leave his flock to ravening wolves. He will most certainly do his utmost to protect his own. If, however, for a few days, in compliance with God's all-encompassing wisdom, outward affairs should run their course contrary to one's cherished desire, this is of no consequence and should not matter. Our intent is that all the friends should fix their gaze on the Supreme Horizon, and cling to that which hath been revealed in the Tablets.[208]

*Bahá'u'lláh*

In God, Who is the Lord of all created things, have I placed My whole trust. There is no God but Him, the Peerless, the Most Exalted. Unto Him have I resigned Myself and into His hands have I committed all My affairs.[209]

*The Báb*

## The light of trust and detachment

Well is it with him who hath been illumined with the light of trust and detachment. The tribulations of that Day will not hinder or alarm him.[210]

*Bahá'u'lláh*

## God sufficeth all things

Rid thou thyself of all attachments to aught except God, enrich thyself in God by dispensing with all else besides Him, and recite this prayer:

> Say: God sufficeth all things above all things, and nothing in the heavens or in the earth or in whatever lieth between them but God, thy Lord, sufficeth. Verily, He is in Himself the Knower, the Sustainer, the Omnipotent.

Regard not the all-sufficing power of God as an idle fancy. It is that genuine faith which thou cherishest for the Manifestation of God in every Dispensation. It is such faith which sufficeth above all the things that exist on the earth, whereas no created thing on earth besides faith would suffice thee. If thou art not a believer, the Tree of divine Truth would condemn thee to extinction. If thou art a believer, thy faith shall be sufficient for thee above all things that exist on earth, even though thou possess nothing.[211]

*The Báb*

## With a look He granteth a hundred thousand hopes

O thou who art turning thy face towards God! Close thine eyes to all things else, and open them to the realm of the All-Glorious. Ask whatsoever thou wishest of Him alone; seek whatsoever thou seekest from Him alone. With a look He granteth a hundred thousand hopes, with a glance He healeth a hundred thousand incurable ills, with a nod He layeth balm on every wound, with a glimpse He freeth the hearts from the shackles of grief. He doeth as He doeth, and what recourse have we? He carrieth out His Will, He ordaineth what He pleaseth. Then better for thee to bow down thy head in submission, and put thy trust in the All-Merciful Lord.[212]

*'Abdu'l-Bahá*

The friends of God are supported by the Kingdom on high and they win their victories through the massed armies of the most great guidance. Thus for them every difficulty will be made smooth, every problem will most easily be solved.[213]

*'Abdu'l-Bahá*

Rest assured in the protection of God. He will preserve his own children under all circumstances. Be ye not afraid nor be ye agitated. He holds the scepter of power in his hand, and like unto a hen he gathereth his chickens under his wings. 'To everything there is a season, and a time for every purpose under the sun. A time to be born, and a time to die, a time to weep and a time to laugh; a time to keep silent and a time to speak.' Now, friends, this is the time of assurance and faith and not fear and dread.[214]

*Attributed to 'Abdu'l-Bahá*

## God's bounties never cease flowing

Never lose thy trust in God. Be thou ever hopeful, for the bounties of God never cease to flow upon man. If viewed from one perspective they seem to decrease, but from another they are full and complete. Man is under all conditions immersed in a sea of God's blessings. Therefore, be thou not hopeless under any circumstances, but rather be firm in thy hope.[215]

*'Abdu'l-Bahá*

## Thanking God increases His bounties to us

Be thou happy and well pleased and arise to offer thanks to God, in order that thanksgiving may conduce to the increase of bounty.[216]

*'Abdu'l-Bahá*

## True happiness

Happiness consists of two kinds; physical and spiritual. The physical happiness is limited; its utmost duration is one day, one month, one year. It hath no result. Spiritual happiness is eternal and unfathomable. This kind of happiness appeareth in one's soul with the love of God and suffereth one to attain to the virtues and perfections of the world of humanity. Therefore, endeavour as much as thou art able in order to illumine the lamp of thy heart by the light of love.[217]

*'Abdu'l-Bahá*

SOLUTIONS TO TESTS

## Have perfect confidence in the grace of God

O army of God! When calamity striketh, be ye patient and composed. However afflictive your sufferings may be, stay ye undisturbed, and with perfect confidence in the abounding grace of God, brave ye the tempest of tribulations and fiery ordeals.[218]

'Abdu'l-Bahá

Depend thou upon God. Forsake thine own will and cling to His, set aside thine own desires and lay hold of His, that thou mayest become an example, holy, spiritual, and of the Kingdom, unto His handmaids.[219]

'Abdu'l-Bahá

Let them cling to the hem of Almighty God, and put their faith in the Beauty of the Most High; let them lean on the unfailing help that cometh from the Ancient Kingdom, and depend on the care and protection of the generous Lord.[220]

'Abdu'l-Bahá

## The magnet of faith

Faith is the magnet which draws the confirmation of the Merciful One.[221]

'Abdu'l-Bahá

## When we have faith

When a man has faith, all the mountains of the world cannot turn him back. No, he will endure any trial, any disaster, and nothing will weaken him. But one who is not a true believer, one who lacks real faith, will lament over the least disappointment, and cry out against the slightest thing which mars his peace and pleasure.[222]

Attributed to 'Abdu'l-Bahá

A man of faith bears every trial, every hardship, with self-control and patience. One without faith is always wailing, lamenting, carrying on. He cannot endure hardship, he never thinks of better times coming that will take the place of present ills.[223]

*Attributed to 'Abdu'l-Bahá*

... I say unto you that anyone who will rise up in the Cause of God at this time shall be filled with the spirit of God, and that He will send His hosts from heaven to help you, and that nothing shall be impossible to you if you have faith. And now I give you a commandment that shall be for a covenant between you and me – that ye have faith; that your faith be steadfast as a rock that no storms can move, that nothing can disturb, and that it endure through all things even to the end ... As ye have faith so shall your powers and blessings be. This is the balance – this is the balance – this is the balance.[224]

*Attributed to 'Abdu'l-Bahá*

When one is released from the prison of self, that is, indeed, freedom! For self is the greatest prison.

When this release takes place, one can never be imprisoned. Unless one accepts dire vicissitudes, not with dull resignation, but with radiant acquiescence, one cannot attain this freedom.[225]

*'Abdu'l-Bahá*

The darkness of this gloomy night shall pass away. Again the Sun of Reality will dawn from the horizon of the hearts. Have patience – wait, but do not sit idle; work while you are waiting; smile while you are wearied with monotony; be firm while everything around you is being shaken; be joyous while the ugly face of despair grins at you; speak aloud while the malevolent forces of the nether world try to crush your mind; be

valiant and courageous while men all around you are cringing
with fear and cowardice.[226]

*'Abdu'l-Bahá*

## Our greatest exploits will coincide with the darkest days

The champion builders of Bahá'u'lláh's rising World Order
must scale nobler heights of heroism as humanity plunges into
greater depths of despair, degradation, dissension and distress.
Let them forge ahead into the future serenely confident that
the hour of their mightiest exertions and the supreme opportunity for their greatest exploits must coincide with the apocalyptic upheaval marking the lowest ebb in mankind's fast-
declining fortunes.[227]

*Shoghi Effendi*

## Repose our confidence in Bahá'u'lláh

The greatest divine bounty is a confident heart. When the
heart is confident, all the trials of the world will be as child's
play. Should they throw him into a prison, should they cast
him into a black well, should they heap upon him all manner
of afflictions, still his heart is content, peaceful and assured.[228]

*'Abdu'l-Bahá*

The Bahá'ís all over the world are subject sometimes to suffering, along with their fellow-men. Whatever vicissitudes befall
their country, they will be protected though, and watched over
by Bahá'u'lláh, and should not fear the future but rather fear
any failure on their part to carry out the work of His Cause.[229]

*Written on behalf of Shoghi Effendi*

Be . . . confident in Bahá'u'lláh's help. His Spirit will lead
you, and will feed your soul with that spiritual sustenance
whereby you will be able to overcome the obstacles which seem
to so hopelessly beset your path.[230]

*Written on behalf of Shoghi Effendi*

Bahá'u'lláh has given us [a] promise that should we persevere in our efforts and repose all our confidence in Him the doors of success will be widely open before us . . .[231]

*Written on behalf of Shoghi Effendi*

Reliance on God is indeed the strongest and safest weapon which the Bahá'í teacher can carry. For by its means no earthly power can remain unconquered, and no obstacle become insuperable.[232]

*Written on behalf of Shoghi Effendi*

The Bahá'í teacher must be all confidence. Therein lies his strength and the secret of his success.[233]

*Written on behalf of Shoghi Effendi*

. . . when we put our trust in Him, Bahá'u'lláh solves our problems and opens the way.[234]

*Written on behalf of Shoghi Effendi*

## Turn firmly to the divine Manifestation

Naturally there will be periods of distress and difficulty, and even severe tests, but if that person turns firmly toward the divine Manifestation, studies carefully His spiritual teachings and receives the blessings of the Holy Spirit, he will find that in reality these tests and difficulties have been the gifts of God to enable him to grow and develop.[235]

*Written on behalf of Shoghi Effendi*

## God will give us strength to meet our tests

There is no need to fear opposition from without if the life within be sound and vigorous. Our Heavenly Father will always give us the strength to meet and overcome tests if we turn with all our hearts to Him, and difficulties if they are met in the

SOLUTIONS TO TESTS

right spirit only make us rely on God more firmly and completely.[236]

*Written on behalf of Shoghi Effendi*

All humanity is disturbed and suffering and confused; we cannot expect to not be disturbed and not to suffer – but we don't have to be confused. On the contrary, confidence and assurance, hope and optimism are our prerogative.[237]

*Written on behalf of Shoghi Effendi*

## The light of faith eliminates dark thoughts and feelings

Through the light of faith the darkness which envelops our thoughts and feelings gives way to a radiance and a splendour before which every gloom vanishes.[238]

*Written on behalf of Shoghi Effendi*

There are dark forces in the world today of despair and hatred and suspicion; the believers must, as the Master said, turn their backs on these and their faces to Him, confident of His help and protection.[239]

*Written on behalf of Shoghi Effendi*

He fully understands indeed the rather difficult situation in which you have been placed through the sheer development of circumstances, but nevertheless feels you have no reason to get so discouraged, and wishes you therefore to rest assured, confident that through such difficulties you will be enabled to further deepen in your love and devotion to the Cause, and receive fresh opportunities of serving and promoting its truth.[240]

*Written on behalf of Shoghi Effendi*

## Feelings of failure are self-fulfilling

We feel that an over-anxiousness on your part about a breakthrough [in teaching] and an undue worry over the state of society can be counter-productive. While there are opportunities for greater growth than is occurring, neither your Assembly nor the friends must burden themselves with feelings of failure at every disappointment, for such feelings are self-fulfilling and can easily cause stagnation in the expansion of the Cause. The tendency toward frustration, sometimes induced by a desire for instant gratification, must be resisted by an effort to gain a deeper appreciation of the divine process.[241]

*The Universal House of Justice*

## To develop confidence, learn greater dependence on Bahá'u'lláh

As [the believers] discharge their spiritual responsibilities and learn greater dependence on the confirmations of Bahá'u'lláh, they find that their faith gains new vitality, and their hearts fresh confidence. These are all areas where the action of the individual need not wait for either urging or help. Alone, and aided solely by the power of the Almighty, each believer is challenged to develop these spiritual strengths which will contribute beyond measure to the evolution of the community.[242]

*The Universal House of Justice*

*Solutions to Tests:*

# Strength and Resolution

# Strength and Resolution

Arise, O people, and, by the power of God's might, resolve to gain the victory over your own selves, that haply the whole earth may be freed and sanctified from its servitude to the gods of its idle fancies – gods that have inflicted such loss upon, and are responsible for the misery of, their wretched worshippers. These idols form the obstacle that impedeth man in his efforts to advance in the path of perfection. We cherish the hope that the Hand of Divine power may lend its assistance to mankind, and deliver it from its state of grievous abasement.[243]

*Bahá'u'lláh*

## Nothing should keep us back

I implore Thee . . . to send down upon Thy loved ones what will enable them to dispense with all else except Thee. Endue them, then, with such constancy that they will arise to proclaim Thy Cause, and will call on Thy name, before all that are in Thy heaven and on Thy earth, in such wise that the Pharaonic cruelties inflicted by the oppressors among Thy servants will not succeed in keeping them back from Thee.[244]

*Bahá'u'lláh*

## We have the power to overcome all tests

He will never deal unjustly with any one, neither will He task a soul beyond its power. He, verily, is the Compassionate, the All-Merciful.[245]

*Bahá'u'lláh*

## Fixed resolve

Sharp must be thy sight, O <u>Dh</u>abíh, and adamant thy soul, and brass-like thy feet, if thou wishest to be unshaken by the assaults of the selfish desires that whisper in men's breasts.[246]

*Bahá'u'lláh*

Blessed is the believer who hath in this Day embraced the Truth and the man of fixed resolve whom the hosts of tyranny have been powerless to affright.[247]

*Bahá'u'lláh*

I implore Thee to assist me and them that love me to magnify Thy Word, and to endow us with such strength that the ills of this world and its tribulations will be powerless to hinder us from remembering Thee and from extolling Thy virtues.[248]

*Bahá'u'lláh*

Fully alive to the unfailing efficacy of the power of Bahá'u'lláh, and armed with the essential weapons of wise restraint and inflexible resolve, let him wage a constant fight against the inherited tendencies, the corruptive instincts, the fluctuating fashions, the false pretences of the society in which he lives and moves.[249]

*Shoghi Effendi*

Who knows but that these few remaining, fast-fleeting years, may not be pregnant with events of unimaginable magnitude, with ordeals more severe than any that humanity has as yet experienced, with conflicts more devastating than any which have preceded them. Dangers, however sinister, must, at no time, dim the radiance of their new-born faith. Strife and confusion, however bewildering, must never befog their vision. Tribulations, however afflictive, must never shatter their resolve. Denunciations, however clamorous, must never sap their loyalty. Upheavals, however cataclysmic, must never deflect their course.[250]

*Shoghi Effendi*

## Stand unmoved

As for you, O ye lovers of God, make firm your steps in His Cause, with such resolve that ye shall not be shaken though the direst of calamities assail the world. By nothing, under no conditions, be ye perturbed.[251]

*'Abdu'l-Bahá*

Be thou strong and firm. Be thou resolute and steadfast. When the tree is firmly rooted, it will bear fruit. Therefore, it is not permitted to be agitated by any test. Be thou not disheartened. Be thou not discouraged. The trials of God are many, but if man remains firm and steadfast, test itself is a stepping stone for the progress of humanity.[252]

*'Abdu'l-Bahá*

Convey thou unto the handmaids of the Merciful the message that when a test turneth violent they must stand unmoved, and faithful to their love for Bahá. In winter come the storms, and the great winds blow, but then will follow spring in all its beauty, adorning hill and plain with perfumed plants and red anemones, fair to see. Then will the birds trill out upon the branches their songs of joy, and sermonize in lilting tones from the pulpits of the trees. Ere long shall ye bear witness that the lights are streaming forth, the banners of the realm above are waving, the sweet scents of the All-Merciful are wafted abroad, the hosts of the Kingdom are marching down, the angels of heaven are rushing forward, and the Holy Spirit is breathing upon all those regions. On that day thou shalt behold the waverers, men and women alike, frustrated of their hopes and in manifest loss. This is decreed by the Lord, the Revealer of Verses.[253]

*'Abdu'l-Bahá*

O ye loved ones of God! Be ye firm of foot, and fixed of heart, and through the power of the Blessed Beauty's help, stand ye committed to your purpose. Serve ye the Cause of God. Face ye all nations of the world with the constancy and the endurance of the people of Bahá, that all men may be astounded and ask how this could be, that your hearts are as well-springs of confidence and faith, and as mines so rich in the love of God. Be ye so, that ye shall neither fail nor falter on account of these tragedies in the Holy Land; let not these dread events make you despondent. And if all the believers be put to the sword, and only one be left, let that one cry out in the name of the Lord and tell the joyous tidings; let that one rise up and confront all the peoples of the earth.[254]

*'Abdu'l-Bahá*

## The importance of high resolve

. . . the happiness and greatness, the rank and station, the pleasure and peace, of an individual have never consisted in his personal wealth, but rather in his excellent character, his high resolve, the breadth of his learning, and his ability to solve difficult problems.[255]

*'Abdu'l-Bahá*

The children must be carefully trained to be most courteous and well-behaved. They must be constantly encouraged and made eager to gain all the summits of human accomplishment, so that from their earliest years they will be taught to have high aims, to conduct themselves well, to be chaste, pure, and undefiled, and will learn to be of powerful resolve and firm of purpose in all things. Let them not jest and trifle, but earnestly advance unto their goals, so that in every situation they will be found resolute and firm.[256]

*'Abdu'l-Bahá*

It is sure you will have to endure many difficulties in this Cause and that great obstacles will come before you. You will have many hindrances. But you must confront all and you must endure all these difficulties.[257]

*Attributed to 'Abdu'l-Bahá*

## Work is the source of happiness

Perfection of work is man's greatest reward. When a man sees his work perfected and this perfection is the result of incessant labour and application he is the happiest man in the world. Work is the source of human happiness.[258]

*Attributed to 'Abdu'l-Bahá*

Devotion to and love for one's vocation accomplishes miracles.[259]

*Attributed to 'Abdu'l-Bahá*

There are certain forms of work which are beyond human endurance and others which are within it; and these differ according to the early environment and training of each individual . . . The struggling, winning, successful man is he who accustoms himself to the accomplishment of those things which are considered to be beyond human endurance. Only a soul thus great can stand the tests of life and come out of the crucible pure and unspotted. (But) if one cannot rise to this height he can at least school himself to perform the tasks which are within the range of his endurance. If a man cannot qualify in one of these two classes he becomes a social burden.[260]

*Attributed to 'Abdu'l-Bahá*

Man must be tireless in his effort. Once his effort is directed in the proper channel if he does not succeed today, he will succeed tomorrow. Effort in itself is one of the noblest traits of human character. Devotion to one's calling, effort in its speedy execution, simplicity of spirit and steadfastness through all the ups and downs, these are the hallmarks of success. A person characterized with these attributes will gather the fruits of his labours and will win the happiness of the kingdom.[261]

*Attributed to 'Abdu'l-Bahá*

## The power is available to us if we make the effort

However severe the challenge, however multiple the tasks, however short the time, however sombre the world outlook, however limited the material resources of a hard-pressed adolescent community, the untapped sources of celestial strength from which it can draw are measureless in their potencies, and will unhesitatingly pour forth their energizing influences if the necessary daily effort be made and the required sacrifices be willingly accepted.[262]

*Shoghi Effendi*

. . . in the reverses they may temporarily suffer, in the opposition they will meet with, in the tests and trials they will undergo, His unfailing guidance will be vouchsafed to them in direct proportion to the degree of their consecration to their task, and the perseverance, the courage and fidelity they will display as they discharge their duties.[263]

*Shoghi Effendi*

## Exert greater effort as world darkens

The champion builders of Bahá'u'lláh's rising World Order must scale nobler heights of heroism as humanity plunges into greater depths of despair, degradation, dissension and distress. Let them forge ahead into the future serenely confident that the hour of their mightiest exertions and the supreme opportunity for their greatest exploits must coincide with the apocalyptic upheaval marking the lowest ebb in mankind's fast-declining fortunes.[264]

*Shoghi Effendi*

# The power of prayer and determined effort

Such hindrances [i.e. illness and outer difficulties], no matter how severe and insuperable they may at first seem, can and should be effectively overcome through the combined and sustained power of prayer and of determined and continued effort. For have not Bahá'u'lláh and 'Abdu'l-Bahá both repeatedly assured us that the Divine and unseen hosts of victory will ever reinforce and strengthen those who valiantly and confidently labour in their name? . . . Whatever the particular field of service you may choose, whether teaching or administrative, the essential is for you to persevere, and not allow any consciousness of your limitations to dampen your zeal, much less to deter you from serving joyously and actively.[265]
*Written on behalf of Shoghi Effendi*

. . . when the determination is strong and the faith firm, the friends can work wonders and surprise even themselves![266]
*Written on behalf of Shoghi Effendi*

## Make every stumbling-block a stepping-stone

He is very happy to see that you have put into practice one of the most encouraging precepts of 'Abdu'l-Bahá in which He said that we should try and make every stumbling-block a stepping-stone to progress. In the course of your past life you have all stumbled very gravely; but, far from being embittered or defeated by this experience, you are determined to make it a means of purifying your natures, improving your characters, and enabling you to become better citizens in the future. This is truly pleasing in the eyes of God.[267]
*Written on behalf of Shoghi Effendi*

## Like soldiers under attack

The friends must, at all times, bear in mind that they are, in a way, like soldiers under attack. The world is at present in an exceedingly dark condition spiritually; hatred and prejudice, of every sort, are literally tearing it to pieces. We, on the other hand, are the custodians of the opposite forces, the forces of love, of unity, of peace and integration, and we must constantly be on our guard, whether as individuals or as an Assembly or Community, lest through us these destructive, negative forces enter into our midst. In other words we must beware lest the darkness of society become reflected in our acts and attitudes, perhaps all unconsciously. Love for each other, the deep sense that we are a new organism, the dawn-breakers of a New World Order, must constantly animate our Bahá'í lives, and we must pray to be protected from the contamination of society which is so diseased with prejudice.[268]

*Written on behalf of Shoghi Effendi*

He is very sorry that such undesirable things are every now and then cropping up in . . . and discouraging you in your work, keeping you from devoting all your spare time in teaching the Cause and spreading its principles. He does not wish you, however, to lose heart from such things. As the Cause grows its difficulties will increase and its problems will become more numerous. The friends, especially the older ones, should therefore try and stand unmoved by them. In fact the more their difficulties will increase the more they have to take courage and try to solve them. The Master has often said that sorrows are like furrows, the deeper they go the more productive the land becomes. If this problem . . . should be settled other problems will arise. Are the friends to become discouraged or are they to follow the footsteps of the Master and consider them more as chances to show their tenacity of belief and spirit of sacrifice?[269]

*Written on behalf of Shoghi Effendi*

He urges you to make up your minds to do great, great deeds for the Faith; the condition of the world is steadily growing worse, and your generation must provide the saints, heroes, martyrs and administrators of future years. With dedication and will power you can rise to great heights![270]

*Written on behalf of Shoghi Effendi*

## Prove our capacity to endure living sacrifice

Undoubtedly, the highly esteemed American believers who bear the designation 'spiritual descendants of the Dawn-breakers', know quite well that they must now seize their chance at this critical time to prove their capacity to endure that living sacrifice which, as Shoghi Effendi said, in contrast to dying, is required of them in the scriptures of our Faith. May they be granted the celestial strength to pass, over and over again, the mental tests which 'Abdu'l-Bahá promised He would send them to purify them, thus enabling them to achieve their divinely conferred potential as a force for change in the world.[271]

*The Universal House of Justice*

## Resolve not to be seduced by the world

In the midst of a civilization torn by strife and enfeebled by materialism, the people of Bahá are building a new world. We face at this time opportunities and responsibilities of vast magnitude and great urgency. Let each believer in his inmost heart resolve not to be seduced by the ephemeral allurements of the society around him nor to be drawn into its feuds and short-lived enthusiasms, but instead to transfer all he can from the old world to that new one which is the vision of his longing and will be the fruit of his labours.[272]

*The Universal House of Justice*

*Solutions to Tests:*

# Prayer and Deepening

# Prayer and Deepening

Who is there that hath cried after Thee, and whose prayer hath remained unanswered? Where is he to be found who hath reached forth towards Thee, and whom Thou hast failed to approach?[273]

*Bahá'u'lláh*

Peruse ye every day the verses revealed by God. Blessed is the man who reciteth them and reflecteth upon them. He truly is of them with whom it shall be well.[274]

*Bahá'u'lláh*

Whoso reciteth, in the privacy of his chamber, the verses revealed by God, the scattering angels of the Almighty shall scatter abroad the fragrance of the words uttered by his mouth, and shall cause the heart of every righteous man to throb. Though he may, at first, remain unaware of its effect, yet the virtue of the grace vouchsafed unto him must needs sooner or later exercise its influence upon his soul.[275]

*Bahá'u'lláh*

Peruse My verses with joy and radiance. Verily they will attract you unto God and will enable you to detach yourselves from aught else save Him. Thus have ye been admonished in God's Holy Writ and in this resplendent Tablet.[276]

*Bahá'u'lláh*

Gather ye together with the utmost joy and fellowship and recite the verses revealed by the merciful Lord. By so doing the doors to true knowledge will be opened to your inner beings, and ye will then feel your souls endowed with steadfastness and your hearts filled with radiant joy.[277]

*Bahá'u'lláh*

## Removing difficulties

Bid them recite: 'Is there any Remover of difficulties save God? Say: Praised be God! He is God! All are His servants, and all abide by His bidding!' Tell them to repeat it five hundred times, nay, a thousand times, by day and by night, sleeping and waking, that haply the Countenance of Glory may be unveiled to their eyes, and tiers of light descend upon them.[278]

*Bahá'u'lláh*

If sorrow and adversity visit us, let us turn our faces to the Kingdom and heavenly consolation will be outpoured.

If we are sick and in distress let us implore God's healing, and He will answer our prayer.

When our thoughts are filled with the bitterness of this world, let us turn our eyes to the sweetness of God's compassion and He will send us heavenly calm![279]

*'Abdu'l-Bahá*

Pray for strength. It will be given to you, no matter how difficult the conditions.[280]

*'Abdu'l-Bahá*

I supplicate God to alleviate thy trials and look upon thee with the eye of His mercy under all aspects. Turn thou to the Kingdom of thy great Lord with a truthful heart and with all devotion, sincerity and great spirituality and ask to be healed from pain and passions and be confident in the great bounty of thy Lord.[281]

*'Abdu'l-Bahá*

## The greatest power to recreate us is prayer

It is not sufficient for a believer to merely accept and observe the teachings. He should, in addition, cultivate the sense of spirituality, which he can acquire chiefly by the means of prayer. The Bahá'í Faith, like all other Divine religions, is thus fundamentally mystic in character. Its chief goal is the development of the individual and society, through the acquisition of spiritual virtues and powers. It is the soul of man that has first to be fed. And this spiritual nourishment prayer can best provide. Laws and institutions, as viewed by Bahá'u'lláh, can become really effective only when our inner spiritual life has been perfected and transformed. Otherwise religion will degenerate into a mere organization, and become a dead thing.

The believers, particularly the young ones, should therefore fully realize the necessity of praying. For prayer is absolutely indispensable to their inner spiritual development, and this, as already stated, is the very foundation and purpose of the Religion of God.[282]

*Written on behalf of Shoghi Effendi*

. . . not everyone achieves easily and rapidly the victory over self. What every believer, new or old, should realize is that the Cause has the spiritual power to re-create us if we make the effort to let that power influence us, and the greatest help in this respect is prayer. We must supplicate Bahá'u'lláh to assist us to overcome the failings in our own characters, and also exert our own will-power in mastering ourselves.[283]

*Written on behalf of Shoghi Effendi*

## Prayer and effort

Such hindrances (i.e. illness and outer difficulties) no matter how severe and insuperable they may at first seem, can and should be effectively overcome through the combined and sustained power of prayer and of determined and continued effort.[284]

*Written on behalf of Shoghi Effendi*

## God answers all prayers

God will answer the prayer of every servant if that prayer is urgent. His mercy is vast, illimitable. He answers the prayers of all His servants . . .

But we ask for things which the divine wisdom does not desire for us, and there is no answer to our prayer. His wisdom does not sanction what we wish. We pray, 'O God! Make me wealthy!' If this prayer were universally answered, human affairs would be at a standstill. There would be none left to work in the streets, none to till the soil, none to build, none to run the trains. Therefore, it is evident that it would not be well for us if all prayers were answered. The affairs of the world would be interfered with, energies crippled and progress hindered. But whatever we ask for which is in accord with divine wisdom, God will answer. Assuredly!

For instance, a very feeble patient may ask the doctor to give him food which would be positively dangerous to his life and condition. He may beg for roast meat. The doctor is kind and wise. He knows it would be dangerous to his patient so he refuses to allow it. The doctor is merciful; the patient, ignorant. Through the doctor's kindness the patient recovers; his life is saved. Yet the patient may cry out that the doctor is unkind, not good, because he refuses to answer his pleading.

God is merciful. In His mercy He answers the prayers of all His servants when according to His supreme wisdom it is necessary.[285]

*'Abdu'l-Bahá*

Although you seem to feel that your prayers have not so far been answered, and do no longer have any hope that your material conditions will ameliorate, the Guardian wishes you nevertheless not to allow such disappointments to undermine your faith in the power of prayer, but rather to continue entreating the Almighty to enable you to discover the great wisdom which may be hidden behind all these sufferings. For are not our sufferings often blessings in disguise, through which God wishes to test the sincerity and depth of our faith, and thereby make us firmer in His Cause?[286]

*Written on behalf of Shoghi Effendi*

## Ask God to conform our will to His

The true worshipper, while praying, should endeavour not so much to ask God to fulfil his wishes and desires, but rather to adjust these and make them conform to the Divine Will. Only through such an attitude can one derive that feeling of inner peace and contentment which the power of prayer alone can confer.[287]

*Written on behalf of Shoghi Effendi*

## Prayer and fasting protect us from tests

. . . prayer and fasting is the cause of awakening and mindfulness and conducive to protection and preservation from tests.[288]

*'Abdu'l-Bahá*

## To solve problems: fives steps of prayer

Regarding the five steps of prayer outlined by the Guardian, and recorded by Mrs Moffett in her booklet the 'Call to Prayer': these, he wishes me to explain, are merely personal suggestions and need not, therefore, be adopted strictly and universally by the believers.[289]

*Written on behalf of Shoghi Effendi*

159

*After encouraging me to stress the need of more prayer and meditation among the friends, he [Shoghi Effendi] said to use these five steps if we have a problem of any kind for which we desire a solution or wish help:*

**First step.** *Pray and meditate about it.* Use the prayers of the Manifestations as they have the greatest power. Then remain in the silence of contemplation for a few minutes.

**Second step.** *Arrive at a decision and hold to this.* This decision is usually born during the contemplation. It may seem almost impossible of accomplishment but if it seems to be an answer to a prayer or a way of solving the problem, then immediately take the next step.

**Third step.** *Have determination to carry the decision through.* Many fail here. The decision, budding into determination, is blighted and instead becomes a wish or a vague longing. When determination is born, immediately take the next step.

**Fourth step.** *Have faith and confidence* that the power will flow through you, the right way will appear, the door will open, the right book will be given to you. Have confidence, and the right thing will come to your need. Then, as you rise from prayer, take at once the fifth step.

**Fifth step.** *Act as though it had all been answered.* Act with tireless, ceaseless energy, And as you act, you, yourself, will become a magnet, which will attract more power to your being, until you become an unobstructed channel for the Divine Power to flow through you. Many pray but do not remain for the last half of the first step. Some who meditate arrive at a decision, but fail to hold it. Few have the determination of carry the decision through, and still fewer have the confidence that the right thing will come to their need. But how many remember to act as though it had all been answered? How true are those words – 'Greater than the prayer is the spirit in which it is uttered, but greater than the way it is uttered is the spirit in which it is carried out.'[290]

*Attributed to Shoghi Effendi*

## We are informed and strengthened during meditation

Through the faculty of meditation man attains to eternal life; through it he receives the breath of the Holy Spirit – the bestowal of the Spirit is given in reflection and meditation.

The spirit of man is itself informed and strengthened during meditation; through it affairs of which man knew nothing are unfolded before his view. Through it he receives Divine inspiration, through it he receives heavenly food.

. . . This faculty of meditation frees man from the animal nature, discerns the reality of things, puts man in touch with God.[291]

*'Abdu'l-Bahá*

## Obtaining answers in dreams

Meditate thou, perform the ablution and pray to God before sleeping; and whatever the Merciful One may inspire unto thee at the time of revelation in a dream, that will be consistent with obtaining thy wishes.[292]

*'Abdu'l-Bahá*

## The Greatest Name

That the Most Great Name exerciseth influence over both physical and spiritual matters is sure and certain.[293]

*'Abdu'l-Bahá*

The Greatest Name should be found upon the lips in the first awaking moment of early dawn. It should be fed upon by constant use in daily invocation, in trouble, under opposition, and should be the last word breathed when the head rests upon the pillow at night. It is the name of comfort, protection, happiness, illumination, love and unity.

. . . The use of the Greatest Name and dependence upon it, cause the soul to strip itself of the husks of mortality and to step forth freed, reborn, a new creature . . .[294]

*'Abdu'l-Bahá*

# *Reading* Nabíl's Narrative *can allay distress*

FEEL IMPELLED APPEAL ENTIRE BODY AMERICAN BELIEVERS
HENCEFORTH REGARD NABÍL'S SOUL STIRRING NARRATIVE AS
ESSENTIAL ADJUNCT TO RECONSTRUCTED TEACHING PROGRAM,
AS UNCHALLENGEABLE TEXTBOOK IN THEIR SUMMER SCHOOLS,
AS SOURCE OF INSPIRATION IN ALL LITERARY ARTISTIC PUR-
SUITS, AS AN INVALUABLE COMPANION IN TIMES OF LEISURE, AS
INDISPENSABLE PRELIMINARY TO FUTURE PILGRIMAGE TO
BAHÁ'U'LLÁH'S NATIVE LAND AND AS UNFAILING INSTRUMENT
TO ALLAY DISTRESS AND RESIST ATTACKS OF CRITICAL DISILLU-
SIONED HUMANITY.[295]

*Shoghi Effendi*

Shoghi Effendi found great pleasure and spiritual upliftment
while working on the translation of *Nabíl's Narrative*. The life
of those who figure in it is so stirring that everyone who reads
those accounts is bound to be affected and impelled to follow
their footsteps of sacrifice in the path of the Faith. The Guardian believes, therefore, that it should be studied by the friends,
especially the youth who need some inspiration to carry them
through these troubled days.[296]

*Written on behalf of Shoghi Effendi*

## *Immersion in the teachings brings safety*

Indeed if an avowed follower of Bahá'u'lláh were to immerse
himself in, and fathom the depths of, the ocean of these
heavenly teachings, and with utmost care and attention deduce
from each of them the subtle mysteries and consummate
wisdom that lie enshrined therein, such a person's life, materi-
ally, intellectually and spiritually, will be safe from toil and
trouble, and unaffected by setbacks and perils, or any sadness
or despondency.[297]

*Shoghi Effendi*

## To lay a foundation that no amount of trials can destroy

He [Shoghi Effendi] is very happy to have this opportunity of welcoming you into the service of our glorious Faith, and he urges you to quietly and steadily read the Teachings, as in this way you will fit yourself to teach others, and also deepen your own understanding and lay a foundation in your own soul and character which no amount of tests and trials can change or destroy.[298]

*Written on behalf of Shoghi Effendi*

Bahá'í scholarship is needed really more than worldly scholarship, for one is spiritual, the other more or less transient. There is a real lack in the Cause of people who know the Teachings *thoroughly*, especially their deeper truths, and who can consequently teach the souls properly and lay a permanent foundation, one that tests and trials will not shake down.[299]

*Written on behalf of Shoghi Effendi*

## To withstand every test, study the Covenant

He feels that in your contact with the believers and in teaching new souls, you should help them to obtain a full knowledge and understanding of the Covenant and the Will and Testament. This will strengthen them to meet every test, and to understand the nature of the spiritual disease which afflicts those who turn against the Institutions of the Faith. These are, indeed, times of testing and of trial, for the whole world and for the believers too.[300]

*Written on behalf of Shoghi Effendi*

*Solutions to Tests:*

*Accept the Will of God*

# Accept the Will of God

Blessed is the man that hath acknowledged his belief in God and in His signs, and recognized that 'He shall not be asked of His doings'. Such a recognition hath been made by God the ornament of every belief, and its very foundation. Upon it must depend the acceptance of every goodly deed. Fasten your eyes upon it, that haply the whisperings of the rebellious may not cause you to slip.

. . . Whoso hath not recognized this sublime and fundamental verity, and hath failed to attain this most exalted station, the winds of doubt will agitate him, and the sayings of the infidels will distract his soul. He that hath acknowledged this principle will be endowed with the most perfect constancy.[301]

*Bahá'u'lláh*

The second Tajallí [Effulgence] is to remain steadfast in the Cause of God – exalted be His glory – and to be unswerving in His love. And this can in no wise be attained except through full recognition of Him; and full recognition cannot be obtained save by faith in the blessed words: 'He doeth whatsoever He willeth.' Whoso tenaciously cleaveth unto this sublime word and drinketh deep from the living waters of utterance which are inherent therein, will be imbued with such a constancy that all the books of the world will be powerless to deter him from the Mother Book.[302]

*Bahá'u'lláh*

## God's Will is reflected in His Tablets

It behoveth thee to consecrate thyself to the Will of God.

Whatsoever hath been revealed in His Tablets is but a reflection of His Will. So complete must be thy consecration, that every trace of worldly desire will be washed from thine heart. This is the meaning of true unity.[303]

*Bahá'u'lláh*

## Merge our will in the Will of God

O Son of Earth! Wouldst thou have Me, seek none other than Me; and wouldst thou gaze upon My beauty, close thine eyes to the world and all that is therein; for My will and the will of another than Me, even as fire and water, cannot dwell together in one heart.[304]

*Bahá'u'lláh*

By self-surrender and perpetual union with God is meant that men should merge their will wholly in the Will of God, and regard their desires as utter nothingness beside His Purpose. Whatsoever the Creator commandeth His creatures to observe, the same must they diligently, and with the utmost joy and eagerness, arise and fulfil. They should in no wise allow their fancy to obscure their judgement, neither should they regard their own imaginings as the voice of the Eternal . . . In this consisteth the complete surrender of one's will to the Will of God.[305]

*Bahá'u'lláh*

If it be Thy pleasure, make me to grow as a tender herb in the meadows of Thy grace, that the gentle winds of Thy will may stir me up and bend me into conformity with Thy pleasure, in such wise that my movement and my stillness may be wholly directed by Thee.[306]

*Bahá'u'lláh*

The source of all good is trust in God, submission unto His

command, and contentment with His holy will and pleasure.
. . . The source of all glory is acceptance of whatsoever the
Lord hath bestowed, and contentment with that which God
hath ordained.[307]

*Bahá'u'lláh*


We hear thy cry and supplication at thy remoteness from the
Dawning-Place of Lights. Be patient and do not bewail thy
plight. Be content with that which God hath ordained for thee.
He, verily, payeth the due recompense of those who are patient. Hast thou not seen My incarceration, My affliction, My
injury, My suffering? Follow then the ways of thy Lord, and
among His methods is the suffering of His well-favoured
servants. Let nothing grieve thee. Put thy trust in thy Lord. He
shall verily confirm thee, draw thee nigh unto Him and grant
thee victory. Should affliction overtake thee in My path and
abasement in My name, rejoice and be of the thankful. Thus
have We imparted unto thee the word of truth so that when
calamities descend upon thee, thy feet may not slip and thou
shalt be as firm and steadfast as a mountain in the Cause of thy
Lord . . .[308]

*Bahá'u'lláh*


Know thou, O fruit of My Tree, that the decrees of the Sovereign Ordainer, as related to fate and predestination, are of two
kinds. Both are to be obeyed and accepted. The one is irrevocable, the other is, as termed by men, impending. To the
former all must unreservedly submit, inasmuch as it is fixed
and settled. God, however, is able to alter or repeal it. As the
harm that must result from such a change will be greater than
if the decree had remained unaltered, all, therefore, should
willingly acquiesce in what God hath willed and confidently
abide by the same.

The decree that is impending, however, is such that prayer
and entreaty can succeed in averting it.

God grant that thou who art the fruit of My Tree, and they

that are associated with thee, may be shielded from its evil consequences.[309]

*Bahá'u'lláh*

Fate is of two kinds: one is decreed, and the other is conditional or impending. The decreed fate is that which cannot change or be altered, and conditional fate is that which may occur. So, for this lamp, the decreed fate is that the oil burns and will be consumed; therefore, its eventual extinction is a decree which it is impossible to alter or to change because it is a decreed fate. In the same way, in the body of man a power of life has been created, and as soon as it is destroyed and ended, the body will certainly be decomposed, so when the oil in this lamp is burnt and finished, the lamp will undoubtedly become extinguished.[310]

*'Abdu'l-Bahá*

## Contentment with our circumstances

This material world of ours is a world of contrasts. It has in itself abundance and destitution, joy and sorrow, youth and old age. It is all the time changing and one has to undergo these different stages. Hence it behooves every faithful person to be patient and to be grateful for that which he receives.

It is fitting for those in the Kingdom to be satisfied with their fate and look only toward the increase of the heavenly spark in their hearts for this, alone, will give them rest and consolation. And you, too, should endeavour to increase that spiritual flame, known as the love of God, for through its increase you will enter into a new world of love and contentment.

. . . Be comforted, and trust in the mercy of the Merciful One, for it is said, 'He who is not contented with what he receives, let him seek a God other than Me.'[311]

*'Abdu'l-Bahá*

Man must live in contentment with the conditions of his time. He must not make himself the slave of any habit. He must eat a piece of stale bread with the same relish and enjoyment as the most sumptuous dinner. Contentment is real wealth. If one develops within himself the quality of contentment he will become independent. Contentment is the creator of happiness. When one is contented he does not care either for riches or poverty. He lives above the influence of them and is indifferent to them.[312]

*Attributed to 'Abdu'l-Bahá*

## All abide by God's bidding

Is there any Remover of difficulties save God? Say: Praised be God! He is God! All are His servants and all abide by His bidding![313]

*The Báb*

## Commit all our affairs to God

It behooveth one like thee to endure every trial, to be pleased with the decree and to commit all thy affairs to God, so that thou mayest be a calm, approved and pleasing soul before God.[314]

*'Abdu'l-Bahá*

Verily thy Lord is gracious to His servants and He facilitates ere long every straight cause. But thou must submit to and rely upon God under all conditions and He will bestow upon thee that which is conducive to thy well-being. Verily He is merciful and compassionate! For how many an affair was involved in difficulty and then was straightened, and how many a problem was solved by the permission of God.[315]

*'Abdu'l-Bahá*

To attain the pleasure of God is the most important thing. Thank God thou art content with the will of God and art attached in heart to His divine wishes; and as thou art thus, all thy desires will be granted thee.[316]

*'Abdu'l-Bahá*

Your question raises a highly abstruse and philosophical issue which it is impossible for our finite minds to grasp and fully comprehend. Justice and mercy are both attributes of God and it is not for us to attempt to analyse why and how the Almighty in His infinite wisdom exercises and manifests these attributes to the righteous and sinner in the world to come. We must do our share in this world and place our trust in Him.[317]

*Shoghi Effendi*

## Remain radiantly content with the Will of God

While he [Shoghi Effendi] would urge you to courageously meet and overcome the many obstacles that stand in your way, he would at the same time advise you that in case of failure and no matter what befalls you, you should remain radiantly content at, and entirely submissive to, the Divine will. Our afflictions, tests and trials are sometimes blessings in disguise, as they teach us to have more faith and confidence in God, and bring us nearer to Him.[318]

*Written on behalf of Shoghi Effendi*

Self-sacrifice means to subordinate this lower nature and its desires to the more godly and noble side of our selves. Ultimately, in its highest sense, self-sacrifice means to give our will and our all to God to do with as He pleases. Then He purifies and glorifies our true self until it becomes a shining and wonderful reality.[319]

*Written on behalf of Shoghi Effendi*

*Solutions to Tests:*

*Steadfastness*

# Steadfastness

A twofold obligation resteth upon him who hath recognized the Day Spring of the Unity of God, and acknowledged the truth of Him Who is the Manifestation of His oneness. The first is steadfastness in His love, such steadfastness that neither the clamour of the enemy nor the claims of the idle pretender can deter him from cleaving unto Him Who is the Eternal Truth, a steadfastness that taketh no account of them whatever. The second is strict observance of the laws He hath prescribed – laws which He hath always ordained, and will continue to ordain, unto men, and through which the truth may be distinguished and separated from falsehood.[320]

*Bahá'u'lláh*

## Shelter of constancy

O My servants! Deprive not yourselves of the unfading and resplendent Light that shineth within the Lamp of Divine glory. Let the flame of the love of God burn brightly within your radiant hearts. Feed it with the oil of Divine guidance, and protect it within the shelter of your constancy. Guard it within the globe of trust and detachment from all else but God, so that the evil whisperings of the ungodly may not extinguish its light.[321]

*Bahá'u'lláh*

## Today is the day for steadfastness

O ye beloved of the Lord! Beware, beware lest ye hesitate and waver. Let not fear fall upon you, neither be troubled nor dismayed. Take ye good heed lest this calamitous day slacken the flames of your ardour, and quench your tender hopes.

Today is the day for steadfastness and constancy. Blessed are they that stand firm and immovable as the rock and brave the storm and stress of this tempestuous hour. They, verily, shall be the recipients of God's grace; they, verily, shall receive His divine assistance, and shall be truly victorious.[322]

*'Abdu'l-Bahá*

Now show thou forth firmness and steadfastness without wavering. If any test fall upon thee, it will be conducive to the strength of thy faith.[323]

*'Abdu'l-Bahá*

The beloved of the Lord must stand fixed as the mountains, firm as impregnable walls. Unmoved must they remain by even the direst adversities, ungrieved by the worst of disasters. Let them cling to the hem of Almighty God, and put their faith in the Beauty of the Most High; let them lean on the unfailing help that cometh from the Ancient Kingdom, and depend on the care and protection of the generous Lord. Let them at all times refresh and restore themselves with the dews of heavenly grace, and with the breaths of the Holy Spirit revive and renew themselves from moment to moment. Let them rise up to serve their Lord, and do all in their power to scatter His breathings of holiness far and wide. Let them be a mighty fortress to defend His Faith, an impregnable citadel for the hosts of the Ancient Beauty. Let them faithfully guard the edifice of the Cause of God from every side; let them become the bright stars of His luminous skies. For the hordes of darkness are assailing this Cause from every direction, and the peoples of the earth are intent on extinguishing this evident Light. And since all the kindreds of the world are mounting their attack, how can our attention be diverted, even for a moment? Assuredly be cognizant of these things, be watchful, and guard the Cause of God.[324]

*'Abdu'l-Bahá*

The souls who bear the tests of God become the manifestations of great bounties; for the divine trials cause some souls to become entirely lifeless, while they cause the holy souls to ascend to the highest degree of love and solidity. They cause progress and they also cause retrogression.[325]

*'Abdu'l-Bahá*

## The chosen ones must prove their worth

In this day every one must be tested, as the time of the 'chosen ones' to prove their worth is indeed very short. The day of attainment is drawing to a close for them. The 'first fruits' must be ripened in spirit, mellowed in love, and consumed by their self-sacrifice and severance. None other are acceptable as first fruits, and all who fail to attain to the standard through the tests, are relegated to the 'many who are called'.[326]

*Attributed to 'Abdu'l-Bahá*

## Follow in the footsteps of the martyrs

It behoveth you to ponder on all those well-beloved ones who hastened to the holy field of sacrifice, those precious souls who offered up their lives. Bear ye in mind what streams of sacred blood were poured away, how many a righteous heart was commingled with its gore, how many a breast was the target of tyranny's spear, how many a chaste body was ripped to shreds. How then could it be right for us even to think of saving ourselves! To curry favour with stranger or kin, and make a show of compromise! Should we not, rather, take the pathway of the righteous, and follow in the footsteps of those great ones gone before?[327]

*'Abdu'l-Bahá*

## Be stable, rock-solid and staunch

It is easy to approach the Kingdom of Heaven, but hard to stand firm and staunch within it, for the tests are rigorous, and heavy to bear. But the English remain steadfast under all conditions, neither at the first sign of trouble do their footsteps slip. They are not changeable, playing fast and loose with some project and soon giving it up. They do not, for some trivial reason, fail in enthusiasm and zeal, their interest gone. No, in all they do, they are stable, rock-solid and staunch.[328]

*'Abdu'l-Bahá*

The friends of God must arise with such steadfastness that if, at any moment, a hundred souls like 'Abdu'l-Bahá become the target for the arrows of affliction, they will not shift or waver in their resolve, their determination, their enkindlement, their devotion and service in the Cause of God.[329]

*'Abdu'l-Bahá*

There is no doubt that the tests are severe. The more a soul resists and shows firmness and steadfastness, the greater will be his progress, and he shall soar to the sublimest heights of the Kingdom.[330]

*'Abdu'l-Bahá*

Today no soul has any station or enjoys any title except the soul who is firm in the Covenant and steadfast in the Testament, who entirely forgets himself and is released from the world.[331]

*Attributed to 'Abdu'l-Bahá*

Firmness in the Covenant means obedience, so that no one may say this is my opinion, Nay, rather he must obey that which proceeds from the pen and tongue of the Covenant.[332]

*'Abdu'l-Bahá*

As thou hast realized thy own shortcomings, rest thou assured that thou art firm in the Covenant and Testament, and in the love of the True One art steadfast and growing.[333]

'Abdu'l-Bahá

## Stepping stones to progress

Be thou strong and firm. Be thou resolute and steadfast. When the tree is firmly rooted, it will bear fruit. Therefore, it is not permitted to be agitated by any test. Be thou not disheartened. Be thou not discouraged. The trials of God are many, but if man remains firm and steadfast, test itself is a stepping stone for the progress of humanity.[334]

'Abdu'l-Bahá

Thus he changes every stumbling block placed in his path to dishearten him from further progress into a stepping stone, advances with confident steps, ever rising higher, never looking backward but always forward, setting aside imperturbably all the seeming difficulties and finally planting his feet on the summit of the mountain of success, beatitude and undiminished glory. Such a man was Mirza Abul Fazl. On such an unshakable rock every person must lay the foundation of the palace of his life, so that the howling of the winds, the fury of the storms and the onslaught of the wild elements may not in the least shake it.[335]

Attributed to 'Abdu'l-Bahá

## Remain firm in times of trial

Without firmness there will be no result. Trees must be firm in the ground to give fruit. The foundation of a building must be very solid in order to support the building. If there be the slightest doubt in a believer, he will be without result. How often did Christ warn Peter to be steadfast! Therefore, consider how difficult it is to *remain* firm, especially in the time of trials. If man endure and overcome the trials, the more will be become firm and steadfast. When the tree is firmly rooted, the more the wind blows the more the tree will benefit; the more intense the wind the greater the benefit. But if weak, it will immediately fall.[336]

*Attributed to 'Abdu'l-Bahá*

Thou must be firm and unshakable in thy purpose, and never, never let any outward circumstances worry thee.[337]

*Attributed to 'Abdu'l-Bahá*

Who knows but that these few remaining, fast-fleeting years, may not be pregnant with events of unimaginable magnitude, with ordeals more severe than any that humanity has as yet experienced, with conflicts more devastating than any which have preceded them. Dangers, however sinister, must, at no time, dim the radiance of their new-born faith. Strife and confusion, however bewildering, must never befog their vision. Tribulations, however afflictive, must never shatter their resolve. Denunciations, however clamorous, must never sap their loyalty. Upheavals, however cataclysmic, must never deflect their course.[338]

*Shoghi Effendi*

*Solutions to Tests*

# Detachment

# Detachment

The world is but a show, vain and empty, a mere nothing, bearing the semblance of reality. Set not your affections upon it. Break not the bond that uniteth you with your Creator, and be not of those that have erred and strayed from His ways. Verily I say, the world is like the vapour in a desert, which the thirsty dreameth to be water and striveth after it with all his might, until when he cometh unto it, he findeth it to be mere illusion.[339]

*Bahá'u'lláh*

Know ye that by 'the world' is meant your unawareness of Him Who is your Maker, and your absorption in aught else but Him. The 'life to come', on the other hand, signifieth the things that give you a safe approach to God, the All-Glorious, the Incomparable. Whatsoever deterreth you, in this Day, from loving God is nothing but the world. Flee it, that ye may be numbered with the blest. Should a man wish to adorn himself with the ornaments of the earth, to wear its apparels, or partake of the benefits it can bestow, no harm can befall him, if he alloweth nothing whatever to intervene between him and God, for God hath ordained every good thing, whether created in the heavens or in the earth, for such of His servants as truly believe in Him. Eat ye, O people, of the good things which God hath allowed you, and deprive not yourselves from His wondrous bounties. Render thanks and praise unto Him, and be of them that are truly thankful.[340]

*Bahá'u'lláh*

Say: Doth it beseem a man while claiming to be a follower of his Lord, the All-Merciful, he should yet in his heart do the very deeds of the Evil One? Nay, it ill beseemeth him, and to this He Who is the Beauty of the All-Glorious will bear Me witness. Would that ye could comprehend it!

Cleanse from your hearts the love of worldly things, from your tongues every remembrance except His remembrance, from your entire being whatsoever may deter you from beholding His face, or may tempt you to follow the promptings of your evil and corrupt inclinations. Let God be your fear, O people, and be ye of them that tread the path of righteousness.

. . . Disencumber yourselves of all attachment to this world and the vanities thereof. Beware that ye approach them not, inasmuch as they prompt you to walk after your own lusts and covetous desires, and hinder you from entering the straight and glorious Path.[341]

*Bahá'u'lláh*

## No comfort can be secured by any soul in this world

Such is this mortal abode: a storehouse of afflictions and suffering. It is ignorance that binds man to it, for no comfort can be secured by any soul in this world, from monarch down to the most humble commoner. If once this life should offer a man a sweet cup, a hundred bitter ones will follow; such is the condition of this world. The wise man, therefore, doth not attach himself to this mortal life and doth not depend upon it; at some moments, even, he eagerly wisheth for death that he may thereby be freed from these sorrows and afflictions.[342]

*'Abdu'l-Bahá*

## This present life is but a mirage

O thou handmaid aflame with the fire of God's love! Grieve thou not over the troubles and hardships of this nether world, nor be thou glad in times of ease and comfort, for both shall pass away. This present life is even as a swelling wave, or a mirage, or drifting shadows. Could ever a distorted image on the desert serve as refreshing waters? No, by the Lord of

Lords! Never can reality and the mere semblance of reality be one, and wide is the difference between fancy and fact, between truth and the phantom thereof.

Know thou that the Kingdom is the real world, and this nether place is only its shadow stretching out. A shadow hath no life of its own; its existence is only a fantasy, and nothing more; it is but images reflected in water, and seeming as pictures to the eye.[343]

'Abdu'l-Bahá

Be thou not unhappy; the tempest of sorrow shall pass; regret will not last; disappointment will vanish; the fire of the love of God will become enkindled, and the thorns and briars of sadness and despondency will be consumed! Be thou happy; rest thou assured upon the favours of Bahá, so that uncertainty and hesitation may become non-existent and the invisible outpourings descend upon the arena of being!

If thou art seeking after spiritual tranquillity, turn thy face at all times toward the Kingdom of Abhá. If thou art desiring divine joy, free thyself from the bonds of attachment. If thou art wishing for the confirmation of the Holy Spirit, become thou engaged in teaching the Cause of God.

If the friends and relatives are keeping themselves at a distance from thee, be thou not sad, for God is near to thee. Associate thou, as much as thou canst, with the relatives and strangers; display thou loving kindness; show thou forth the utmost patience and resignation. The more they oppose thee, shower thou upon them the greater justice and equity; the more they show hatred and opposition toward thee, challenge thou them with great truthfulness, friendship and reconciliation.

Praise be to God, thou art near to the Kingdom of Abhá! Rest thou assured. With all my soul and spirit, I am thy companion at all moments. Know thou this of a certainty![344]

'Abdu'l-Bahá

These few brief days shall pass away, this present life shall vanish from our sight; the roses of this world shall be fresh and fair no more, the garden of this earth's triumphs and delights shall droop and fade. The spring season of life shall turn into the autumn of death, the bright joy of palace halls give way to moonless dark within the tomb. And therefore is none of this worth loving at all, and to this the wise will not anchor his heart.[345]

*'Abdu'l-Bahá*

## Put aside all thoughts of self

Let us not keep on forever with our fancies and illusions, with our analyzing and interpreting and circulating of complex dubieties. Let us put aside all thoughts of self; let us close our eyes to all on earth, let us neither make known our sufferings nor complain of our wrongs. Rather let us become oblivious of our own selves, and drinking down the wine of heavenly grace, let us cry out our joy, and lose ourselves in the beauty of the All-Glorious.[346]

*'Abdu'l-Bahá*

Life is a load which must be carried on while we are on earth, but the cares of the lower things of life should not be allowed to monopolize all the thoughts and aspirations of a human being.[347]

*'Abdu'l-Bahá*

## Be oblivious to the world below

Wherefore dwell thou ever in the Kingdom, and be thou oblivious of this world below. Be thou so wholly absorbed in the emanations of the spirit that nothing in the world of man will distract thee.[348]

*'Abdu'l-Bahá*

Stay ye entirely clear of this dark world's concerns, and become ye known by the attributes of those essences that make their home in the Kingdom. Then shall ye see how intense is the glory of the heavenly Day-Star, and how blinding bright are the tokens of bounty coming out of the invisible realm.[349]

*'Abdu'l-Bahá*

The mind and spirit of man advance when he is tried by suffering. The more the ground is ploughed the better the seed will grow, the better the harvest will be. Just as the plough furrows the earth deeply, purifying it of weeds and thistles, so suffering and tribulation free man from the petty affairs of this worldly life until he arrives at a state of complete detachment. His attitude in this world will be that of divine happiness. Man is, so to speak, unripe: the heat of the fire of suffering will mature him. Look back to the times past and you will find that the greatest men have suffered most.

. . . Through suffering he will attain to an eternal happiness which nothing can take from him. The apostles of Christ suffered: they attained eternal happiness.

. . . To attain eternal happiness one must suffer. He who has reached the state of self-sacrifice has true joy. Temporal joy will vanish.[350]

*'Abdu'l-Bahá*

## The impermanence of this world

Whenever you see tremendous personal problems in your private lives . . . you must remember that these afflictions are part of human life; and, according to our teachings one of their wisdoms is to teach us the impermanence of this world and the permanence of the spiritual bonds that we establish with God, His Prophet, and those who are alive in the faith of God. You must always remember that the Manifestations of God, Themselves, were not immune to suffering of the most human nature; and that from the hands of their relatives, they drank the bitterest potions, Bahá'u'lláh even being proffered poison by His half-brother, Mírzá Yaḥyá. Beside their afflictions, our afflictions, however terrible for us, must seem small in comparison.[351]

*Written on behalf of Shoghi Effendi*

## Detach ourselves from the turmoil affecting the world

Paradoxical as it may seem, the prospects toward the breakthrough you anticipate in the teaching field are conspicuous in the current, distressing state of society. You must realize that the worse conditions become, the more plentiful are the opportunities to teach the Cause, the greater the receptivity to the Divine Message. Bahá'u'lláh certainly gave ample foreknowledge about the radical, worldwide disturbance which His Revelation is creating as part of the transition toward the unity and peace that are the ultimate goal of His Faith. Your awareness of this inevitable transition should enable your members to detach themselves from the debilitating emotions aroused by the turmoil which characterizes this process . . .[352]

*The Universal House of Justice*

*Solutions to Tests:*

# Obey the Teachings

# Obey the Teachings

The beginning of all things is the knowledge of God, and the end of all things is strict observance of whatsoever hath been sent down from the empyrean of the Divine Will that pervadeth all that is in the heavens and all that is on the earth.[353]

*Bahá'u'lláh*

## Bahá'u'lláh's reaction to those who disobey His teachings

Every time My name 'the All-Merciful' was told that one of My lovers had breathed a word that runneth counter to My wish, it repaired, grief-stricken and disconsolate to its abode; and whenever My name 'the Concealer' discovered that one of My followers had inflicted any shame or humiliation on his neighbour, it, likewise, turned back chagrined and sorrowful to its retreats of glory, and there wept and mourned with a sore lamentation. And whenever My name 'the Ever-Forgiving' perceived that any one of My friends had committed any transgression, it cried out in its great distress, and, overcome with anguish, fell upon the dust, and was borne away by a company of the invisible angels to its habitation in the realms above.

. . . Every time the sin committed by any one amongst them was breathed in the Court of His Presence, the Ancient Beauty would be so filled with shame as to wish He could hide the glory of His countenance from the eyes of all men, for He hath, at all times, fixed His gaze on their fidelity, and observed its essential requisites.[354]

*Bahá'u'lláh*

## Our final victory depends on obedience

The ordinances of God have been sent down from the heaven of His most august Revelation. All must diligently observe them. Man's supreme distinction, his real advancement, his final victory, have always depended, and will continue to depend, upon them. Whoso keepeth the commandments of God shall attain everlasting felicity.[355]

*Bahá'u'lláh*

We can prove ourselves worthy of our Cause only if in our individual conduct and corporate life we sedulously imitate the example of our beloved Master, whom the terrors of tyranny, the storms of incessant abuse, the oppressiveness of humiliation, never caused to deviate a hair's breadth from the revealed Law of Bahá'u'lláh.

Such is the path of servitude, such is the way of holiness He chose to tread to the very end of His life. Nothing short of the strictest adherence to His glorious example can safely steer our course amid the pitfalls of this perilous age, and lead us on to fulfil our high destiny.[356]

*Shoghi Effendi*

The road is stony, and there are many tests; but as you say, if the friends will learn to live according to Bahá'u'lláh's teachings, they will discover that they work indeed in mysterious and forceful ways; and that there is always help at hand, that obstacles are overcome, and that success is assured in the end.[357]

*Written on behalf of Shoghi Effendi*

## The battle of life is within the individual

Ultimately all the battle of life is within the individual. No amount of organization can solve the inner problems or produce or prevent, as the case may be, victory or failure at a crucial moment. In such times as these particularly, individuals are torn by great forces at large in the world, and we see some weak ones suddenly become miraculously strong, and strong ones fail – we can only try, through loving advice . . . to bring about the act on the part of the believer which will be for the highest good of the Cause. Because obviously something bad for the Cause cannot be the highest good of the individual Bahá'í.[358]

*Written on behalf of Shoghi Effendi*

## The one power to overcome tests

You should rest assured that your strict adherence to the laws and observances enjoined by Bahá'u'lláh is the one power that can effectively guide and enable you to overcome the tests and trials of your life, and help you to continually grow and develop spiritually.[359]

*Written on behalf of Shoghi Effendi*

## Obedience to the institutions

. . . the Assembly may make a mistake, but, as the Master pointed out, if the Community does not abide by its decisions, or the individual Bahá'í, the result is worse, as it undermines the very institution which must be strengthened in order to uphold the principles and laws of the Faith. He tells us God will right the wrongs done. We must have confidence in this and obey our Assemblies.[360]

*Written on behalf of Shoghi Effendi*

Neither the administration, nor the general teaching work of the Cause . . . will progress, or be able to accomplish anything, unless the believers are truly firm, deep, spiritually convinced Bahá'ís. An intellectual grasp of the Teachings is purely superficial; with the first real test such believers are shaken from the bough! But once a Bahá'í has the profound conviction of the authority from God, vested in the Prophet, passed on to the

Master, and by Him, to the Guardians, and which flows out
through the Assemblies and creates order based on obedience
– once a Bahá'í has this, nothing can shake him . . .³⁶¹

*Written on behalf of Shoghi Effendi*

You must not make the great mistake of judging our Faith by
one community which obviously needs to study and obey the
Bahá'í teachings. Human frailties and peculiarities can be a
great test. But the only way, or perhaps I should say the first
and best way, to remedy such situations, is to oneself do what
is right. One soul can be the cause of the spiritual illumination
of a continent. Now that you have seen, and remedied, a great
fault in your own life, now that you see more clearly what is
lacking in your own community, there is nothing to prevent
you from arising and showing such an example, such a love
and spirit of service, as to enkindle the hearts of your fellow
Bahá'ís.³⁶²

*Written on behalf of Shoghi Effendi*

However, he [Shoghi Effendi] feels very strongly that if . . . is
in the state your letter would seem to indicate it is certainly
conducting its affairs in the wrong way. This does not mean
the Assembly, it means everyone. For where is Bahá'í love?
Where is putting unity and harmony first? Where is the willingness to sacrifice one's personal feelings and opinions to achieve
love and harmony? What makes the Bahá'ís think that when
they sacrifice the spiritual laws the administrative laws are
going to work?³⁶³

*Written on behalf of Shoghi Effendi*

## People will be attracted by our virtues

As humanity plunges deeper into the condition of which
Bahá'u'lláh wrote, 'to disclose it now would not be meet and
seemly', so must the believers increasingly stand out as assured,
oriented, and fundamentally happy beings, conforming to a

standard which, in direct contrast to the ignoble and amoral attitudes of modern society, is the source of their honour, strength, and maturity. It is this marked contrast between the vigour, unity, and discipline of the Bahá'í community on the one hand, and the increasing confusion, despair and feverish tempo of a doomed society on the other, which during the turbulent years ahead will draw the eyes of humanity to the sanctuary of Bahá'u'lláh's world-redeeming Faith.[364]

*The Universal House of Justice*

## Do not fear rejection

The world must see that, regardless of each passing whim or current fashion of the generality of mankind, the Bahá'í lives his life according to the tenets of his Faith. We must not allow the fear of rejection by our friends and neighbours to deter us from our goal to live the Bahá'í life.[365]

*The Universal House of Justice*

## Life is a succession of tests and achievements

Obedience to the Laws of Bahá'u'lláh will necessarily impose hardships in individual cases. No one should expect, upon becoming a Bahá'í, that his faith will not be tested, and to our finite understanding of such matters these tests may occasionally seem unbearable. But we are aware of the assurance which Bahá'u'lláh Himself has given the believers that they will never be called upon to meet a test greater than their capacity to endure.[366]

*The Universal House of Justice*

Man often lacks the understanding to fathom the wisdom of some of the ordinances which are not to his liking. It therefore becomes a matter of demonstration of the depth of his faith when he is faced with a divine command which he cannot at that time understand.[367]

*The Universal House of Justice*

In considering the effect of obedience to the laws on individual lives, one must remember that the purpose of this life is to prepare the soul for the next. Here one must learn to control and direct one's animal impulses, not to be a slave to them. Life in this world is a succession of tests and achievements, of falling short and of making new spiritual advances. Sometimes the course may seem very hard, but one can witness, again and again, that the soul who steadfastly obeys the Law of Bahá'u'lláh, however hard it may seem, grows spiritually, while the one who compromises with the law for the sake of his own apparent happiness is seen to have been following a chimera: he does not attain the happiness he sought, he retards his spiritual advance and often brings new problems upon himself.[368]

*The Universal House of Justice*

*Solutions to Tests:*

# *Have Patience and*
# *Look to the End of Things*

# Have Patience and Look to the End of Things

O Son of Man! Should prosperity befall thee, rejoice not, and should abasement come upon thee, grieve not, for both shall pass away and be no more.[369]

*Bahá'u'lláh*

## Be content under all circumstances

Verily the most necessary thing is contentment under all circumstances; by this one is preserved from morbid conditions and from lassitude.[370]

*Bahá'u'lláh*

Concerning thine own affairs, if thou wouldst content thyself with whatever might come to pass it would be praiseworthy. To engage in some profession is highly commendable, for when occupied with work one is less likely to dwell on the unpleasant aspects of life.[371]

*Bahá'u'lláh*

## Show patience in calamity

Say, O beloved of God! Fear none and let nothing grieve thee; be steadfast in the Cause. By God, those who have drunk of the love of God, the Glorious, the Effulgent, have no fear of anyone, and show patience in calamity, like unto the patience of the lover toward the good-pleasure of the beloved. With them affliction ranketh greater than that which the lovers perceive in the countenance of the beloved.[372]

*Bahá'u'lláh*

Blessed are the steadfastly enduring, they that are patient under ills and hardships, who lament not over anything that befalleth them, and who tread the path of resignation . . . [373]

*Bahá'u'lláh*


He, verily, shall increase the reward of them that endure with patience.[374]

*Bahá'u'lláh*


## Patience, nay, thankfulness in the midst of tribulation

The virtues and attributes pertaining unto God are all evident and manifest, and have been mentioned and described in all the heavenly Books. Among them are trustworthiness, truthfulness, purity of heart while communing with God, forbearance, resignation to whatever the Almighty hath decreed, contentment with the things His Will hath provided, patience, nay, thankfulness in the midst of tribulation, and complete reliance, in all circumstances, upon Him. These rank, according to the estimate of God, among the highest and most laudable of all acts.[375]

*Bahá'u'lláh*


Be generous in your days of plenty, and be patient in the hour of loss. Adversity is followed by success and rejoicings follow woe.[376]

*Bahá'u'lláh*


Merge thy will in His pleasure, for We have, at no time, desired anything whatsoever except His Will, and have welcomed each one of His irrevocable decrees. Let thine heart be patient, and be thou not dismayed. Follow not in the way of them that are sorely agitated.[377]

*Bahá'u'lláh*

## Accept patiently the Will of God

Life afflicts us with very severe trials sometimes, but we must always remember that when we accept patiently the Will of God He compensates us in other ways. With faith and love we must be patient, and He will surely reward us.[378]

*Written on behalf of Shoghi Effendi*

## Reflect over what may befall us in the future

Lament not in your hours of trial, neither rejoice therein; seek ye the Middle Way which is the remembrance of Me in your afflictions and reflection over that which may befall you in future.[379]

*Bahá'u'lláh*

## Look to the ends and results of tests

The essence of true safety is to observe silence, to look at the end of things and to renounce the world.[380]

*Bahá'u'lláh*

O My servants! Sorrow not if, in these days and on this earthly plane, things contrary to your wishes have been ordained and manifested by God, for days of blissful joy, of heavenly delight, are assuredly in store for you. Worlds, holy and spiritually glorious, will be unveiled to your eyes. You are destined by Him, in this world and hereafter, to partake of their benefits, to share in their joys, and to obtain a portion of their sustaining grace. To each and every one of them you will, no doubt, attain.[381]

*Bahá'u'lláh*

. . . this earthly life shall come to an end, and everyone shall expire and return unto my Lord God Who will reward with the choicest gifts the deeds of those who endure with patience.[382]

*The Báb*

Do ye not look upon the beginning of the affairs; attach your hearts to the ends and results. The present period is like unto the sowing time. Undoubtedly it is impregnated with perils and difficulties, but in the future many a harvest shall be gathered and benefits and results will become apparent. When one considers the issue and the end, exhaustless joy and happiness will dawn.[383]

*'Abdu'l-Bahá*

Be not sad nor sorrowful over what hath occurred. What hath transpired is for the best and in it is a sacred wisdom concealed which ere long will become manifest.[384]

*'Abdu'l-Bahá*

'Abdu'l-Bahá used often to say that the difference between a prophet and an ordinary person is that the latter looks only to the present. He does not try to imagine the future victories and thereby forget the present trivial obstructions. The prophet, however, having a deep insight in the future condition of things sees his ultimate victory and does not get disheartened even though he sees a whole-sale massacre of his followers.

As Bahá'ís we should follow the prophet's method. We know that the Cause will ultimately conquer and its ranks be fully united. We know that the Master's promises will ultimately be realized, therefore why be discouraged by trivial oppositions we see on our way. We should rather add to our zeal and persist in our prayers and endeavours . . . [385]

*Written on behalf of Shoghi Effendi*

## After the storm

O ye beloved of God! When the winds blow severely, rains fall fiercely, the lightning flashes, the thunder roars, the bolt descends and storms of trial become severe, grieve not; for after this storm, verily, the divine spring will arrive, the hills and fields will become verdant, the expanses of grain will joyfully wave, the earth will become covered with blossoms, the trees will be clothed with green garments and adorned with blossoms and fruits. Thus blessings become manifest in all countries. These favours are the results of those storms and hurricanes.

The discerning man rejoiceth at the day of trials, his breast becometh dilated at the time of severe storms, his eyes become brightened when seeing the showers of rain and gusts of wind, whereby trees are uprooted; because he foreseeth the result and the end, the leaves, blossoms and fruits; while the ignorant person becometh troubled when he seeth a storm, is saddened when it raineth severely, is terrified by the thunder and trembleth at the surging of the waves which storm the shores.

As ye have heard of the former times, when Christ – glory be to Him! – appeared, a storm of trials arose, afflictions appeared, the winds of tests blew, the thunder of temptation descended and hosts of people surrounded the houses of the friends; then the weak ones were shaken and were misled after once being guided; but the disciples withstood the hardships and endured the storms of ordeals, remaining firm in the Religion of God. Then observe that which occurred after the storm and what appeared subsequent to that severity, whereby the members trembled.

God changed the sorrow to joy, the destructive darkness of calamity into the shining light from the Supreme Concourse. The people at the beginning persecuted and reviled the believers in God and said of them: 'These are the people of aberration.' Then, when their light appeared, their stars shone and their lamps illuminated, the people returned into love and affinity; they prayed to them, offered words of glory night and day and remembered them in eulogy, reverence, honour and majesty.

Therefore, O ye beloved of God, be not grieved when people stand against you, persecute you, afflict and trouble you and say all manner of evil against you. The darkness will pass away and the light of the manifest signs will appear, the veil will be withdrawn and the Light of Reality will shine forth from the unseen Kingdom of El-Abhá. This we inform you before it occurs, so that when the hosts of people arise against you for my love, be not disturbed or troubled; nay, rather, be firm as a mountain, for this persecution and reviling of the people upon you is a pre-ordained matter. Blessed is the soul who is firm in the path![386]

*'Abdu'l-Bahá*

## Look toward the glorious future ahead

The immediate future, as clearly predicted by the Master, must necessarily be very dark for the Cause as well as for the whole world, but the promises He has repeatedly given us of a glorious future for the Faith and for mankind as a whole are of such character as should assuredly sustain and strengthen us amidst the trials and tribulations of the days ahead.[387]

*Written on behalf of Shoghi Effendi*

We Bahá'ís are indeed most blessed in that we know that, however dark the days immediately ahead of the human race, the future is blessed and glorious. It is for this future that the believers must labour day and night, heedless of the state of the world and the dangers threatening.[388]

*Written on behalf of Shoghi Effendi*

However gloomy the immediate future may seem to appear, the prospect which the distant future has in store for the community of German believers is of such immeasurable brightness as it cannot but afford the deepest comfort and encouragement to you in your moments of uttermost sorrow and distress.[389]

*Written on behalf of Shoghi Effendi*

## The Lord changeth grief into joy

Be not grieved if thy circumstances become exacting, and problems press upon thee from all sides. Verily, thy Lord changeth grief into joy, hardship into comfort, and affliction into absolute ease.[390]

*'Abdu'l-Bahá*

## Be patient, zealous and calm

Although this calamity hath been great and intense, thou shouldst, at the time of adversity and misfortune, be patient, zealous, calm, firm and long-suffering. These are the qualities that befit such as thee.[391]

*'Abdu'l-Bahá*

Grieve not at the divine trials. Be not troubled because of hardships and ordeals; turn unto God, bowing in humbleness and praying to Him, while bearing every ordeal, contented under all conditions and thankful in every difficulty. Verily thy Lord loveth His maid-servants who are patient, believing and firm. He draws them nigh unto Him through these ordeals and trials.[392]

*'Abdu'l-Bahá*

Great is the multitude who will rise up to oppose you, who will oppress you, heap blame upon you, rejoice at your misfortunes, account you people to be shunned, and visit injury upon you; yet shall your heavenly Father confer upon you such spiritual illumination that ye shall become even as the rays of the sun which, as they chase away the sombre clouds, break forth to flood the surface of the earth with light. It is incumbent upon you, whensoever these tests may overtake you, to stand firm, and to be patient and enduring. Instead of repaying like with like, ye should requite opposition with the utmost benevolence and loving-kindness, and on no account attach importance to cruelties and injuries, but rather regard them as the wanton acts of children. For ultimately the radiance of the Kingdom will overwhelm the darkness of the world of being, and the holy, exalted character of your aims will become unmistakably apparent.[393]

*'Abdu'l-Bahá*

. . . the friends should persevere in their task and not let any obstacle, however great, hinder their onward march. In these days of sufferings and hardships, patience and hope are indispensable for the success of any idea or plan.[394]

*Written on behalf of Shoghi Effendi*

## Every night is followed by a day

Even as Jesus Christ forfeited His life, may you, likewise, offer yourselves in the threshold of sacrifice for the betterment of the world; and just as Bahá'u'lláh suffered severe ordeals and calamities nearly fifty years for you, may you be willing to undergo difficulties and withstand catastrophes for humanity in general. May you bear these trials and tests most willingly and joyously, for every night is followed by a day, and every day has a night. Every spring has an autumn, and every autumn has its spring.[395]

*'Abdu'l-Bahá*

## This will soon pass away

Let neither despondency nor despair becloud the serenity of thy life or restrain thy freedom. These days shall pass away. We will, please God, in the Abhá Kingdom and beneath the sheltering shadow of the Blessed Beauty, forget all these our earthly cares and will find each one of these base calumnies amply compensated by His expressions of praise and favour.

From the beginning of time sorrow and anxiety, regret and tribulation, have always been a lot of every loyal servant of God.[396]

*'Abdu'l-Bahá*


Should anyone at any time encounter hard and perplexing times, he must say to himself, 'This will soon pass.' Then he will be calm and quiet. In all my calamity and difficulties I used to say to myself, 'This will pass away.' Then I became patient. If anyone cannot be patient and cannot endure, and if he wishes to become a martyr, then let him arise in service to the Cause of God.[397]

*Attributed to 'Abdu'l-Bahá*


The Guardian is fully aware of the trials and tests through which you have passed. But he is confident that these sufferings, though sad and even unbearable in their immediate effects, will ultimately serve to invigorate and enrich your spiritual life.[398]

*Written on behalf of Shoghi Effendi*

*Solutions to Tests:*

# *Spiritual Transformation*

# Spiritual Transformation

O Son of Man! Sorrow not save that thou art far from Us. Rejoice not save that thou art drawing near and returning unto Us.[399]

*Bahá'u'lláh*

## We must desire to be transformed

Success or failure, gain or loss, must . . . depend upon man's own exertions. The more he striveth, the greater will be his progress.[400]

*Bahá'u'lláh*

All that which ye potentially possess can, however, be manifested only as a result of your own volition. Your own acts testify to this truth.[401]

*Bahá'u'lláh*

Indeed, if God willeth, He is potent to turn the stone into a mirror, but the person himself remaineth reconciled to his state. Had he wished to become a crystal, God would have made him to assume crystal form.[402]

*The Báb*

## That God may guide our steps through inspiration

I adjure Thee by Thy might, O my God! Let no harm beset me in times of tests, and in moments of heedlessness guide my steps aright through Thine inspiration. Thou art God, potent art Thou to do what Thou desirest. No one can withstand Thy Will or thwart Thy Purpose.[403]

*The Báb*

## We are worthy

Thy letter was received. Thou has written 'I am not worthy.' Who is worthier than thee? Hadst thou not been worthy, thou wouldst not have turned to God and wouldst not have wished to enter the Kingdom.

Thy worthiness has guided thee until this blessing and bounty have encompassed thee.[404]

*'Abdu'l-Bahá*

## We can choose our thoughts and emotions

I will no longer be sorrowful or grieved; I will be a happy and joyful being. O God! I will no longer be full of anxiety, nor will I let trouble harass me. I will not dwell on the unpleasant things of life.[405]

*'Abdu'l-Bahá*

I charge you all that each one of you concentrate all the thoughts of your heart on love and unity. When a thought of war comes, oppose it by a stronger thought of peace. A thought of hatred must be destroyed by a more powerful thought of love.[406]

*'Abdu'l-Bahá*

## Happiness is founded on spiritual behaviour

In a time to come, morals will degenerate to an extreme degree. It is essential that children be reared in the Bahá'í way, that they may find happiness both in this world and the next. If not, they shall be beset by sorrows and troubles, for human happiness is founded upon spiritual behaviour.[407]

*'Abdu'l-Bahá*

True happiness depends on spiritual good and having the heart ever open to receive the Divine Bounty.

If the heart turns away from the blessings God offers how can it hope for happiness? If it does not put its hope and trust in God's Mercy, where can it find rest? Oh, trust in God! for His Bounty is everlasting, and in His Blessings, for they are superb. Oh! put your faith in the Almighty, for He faileth not and His goodness endureth for ever! His Sun giveth Light continually, and the Clouds of His Mercy are full of the Waters of Compassion with which He waters the hearts of all who trust in Him.[408]

*'Abdu'l-Bahá*

## Joy gives us wings

Joy gives us wings! In times of joy our strength is more vital, our intellect keener, and our understanding less clouded. We seem better able to cope with the world and to find our sphere of usefulness. But when sadness visits us we become weak, our strength leaves us, our comprehension is dim and our intelligence veiled. The actualities of life seem to elude our grasp, the eyes of our spirits fail to discover the sacred mysteries, and we become even as dead beings.

There is no human being untouched by these two influences; but all the sorrow and the grief that exist come from the world of matter – the spiritual world bestows only the joy![409]

*'Abdu'l-Bahá*

## Day by day we must strive to become better

I cannot understand why people insist on the fact that one cannot give up a thing once he is accustomed to it. One can do it very easily if he makes up his mind fully, resolving to quit it forever. It is all a matter of character and determination.[410]

*Attributed to 'Abdu'l-Bahá*

Therefore I say that man must travel in the way of God. Day by day he must endeavour to become better, his belief must increase and become firmer, his good qualities and his turning to God must be greater, the fire of his love must flame more brightly; then day by day he will make progress, for to stop advancing is the means of going back. The bird when he flies soars ever higher and higher, for as soon as he stops flying he will come down. Every day, in the morning when arising you should compare today with yesterday and see in what condition you are. If you see your belief is stronger and your heart more occupied with God and your love increased and your freedom from the world greater then thank God and ask for the increase of these qualities. You must begin to pray and repent for all that you have done which is wrong and you must implore and ask for help and assistance that you may become better than yesterday so that you may continue to make progress.[411]

*'Abdu'l-Bahá*

## Man will ascend if the heavenly power is greater

I desire that each of you become so great that each may guide a nation. Now the friends must endeavour to attain such a station so as to teach the people of America. Divine qualities are unlimited. For this reason you must not be satisfied with one quality, but must try to attain all. Each of us must improve himself, that he may attain nothing short of the best. When one stops, he descends. A bird, when it is flying, soars; but as soon as it stops, it falls. While man is directed upward, he develops. As soon as he stops, he descends. Therefore I wish the beloved of God always to ascend and develop.

There exist in man two powers. One power uplifts him. This is divine attraction, which causes man's elevation. In all grades of existence he will develop through this power. This belongs to the spirit. The other power causes man to descend. This is the animal nature. The first attracts man to the Kingdom. The second brings him down to the contingent world.

Now we must consider which of these will gain more power. If the heavenly power overcome, man will become heavenly, enlightened, merciful; but if the worldly power overcome, he will be dark, satanic, and like the animal. Therefore he must develop continually. As long as the heavenly power is the great force, man will ascend.[412]

*Attributed to 'Abdu'l-Bahá*

## Effecting personal transformation

How great, therefore, how staggering the responsibility that must weigh upon the present generation of the American believers, at this early stage in their spiritual and administrative evolution, to weed out, by every means in their power, those faults, habits, and tendencies which they have inherited from their own nation, and to cultivate, patiently and prayerfully, those distinctive qualities and characteristics that are so indispensable to their effective participation in the great redemptive work of their Faith. Incapable as yet, in view of the restricted size of their community and the limited influence it now wields, of producing any marked effect on the great mass of their countrymen, let them focus their attention, for the present, on their own selves, their own individual needs, their own personal deficiencies and weaknesses, ever mindful that every intensification of effort on their part will better equip them for the time when they will be called upon to eradicate in their turn such evil tendencies from the lives and the hearts of the entire body of their fellow-citizens.[413]

*Shoghi Effendi*

## We must make an effort in order to be recreated

Effort is an inseparable part of man's life . . . Life is after all a struggle. Progress is attained through struggle, and without such a struggle life ceases to have a meaning; it becomes even extinct.[414]

*Written on behalf of Shoghi Effendi*

Our past is not the thing that matters so much in this world as what we intend to do with our future. The inestimable value of religion is that when a man is vitally connected with it, through a real and living belief in it and in the Prophet Who brought it, he receives a strength greater than his own which helps him to develop his good characteristics and overcome his bad ones. The whole purpose of religion is to change not only our thoughts but our acts; when we believe in God and His Prophet and His Teachings, we are growing, even though we perhaps thought ourselves incapable of growth and change![415]

*Written on behalf of Shoghi Effendi*

We should try to change, to let the Power of God help recreate us and make us true Bahá'ís in deed as well as in belief. But sometimes the process is slow, sometimes it never happens because the individual does not try hard enough.[416]

*Written on behalf of Shoghi Effendi*

## Be not content with relative distinction and excellence

... the chosen ones of God .. should not look at the depraved conditions of the society in which they live, nor at the evidences of moral degradation and frivolous conduct which the people around them display. They should not content themselves merely with relative distinction and excellence. Rather they should fix their gaze upon nobler heights by setting the counsels and exhortations of the pen of Glory as their supreme goal. Then it will be readily realized how numerous are the stages that still remain to be traversed and how far off the desired goal lies – a goal which is none other than exemplifying heavenly morals and virtues.[417]

*Shoghi Effendi*

## We must continue to develop

Life is a constant struggle, not only against forces around us, but above all against our own 'ego'. We can never afford to rest on our oars, for if we do, we soon see ourselves carried down stream again. Many of those who drift away from the Cause do so for the reason that they had ceased to go on developing. They became complacent, or indifferent, and consequently ceased to draw the spiritual strength and vitality from the Cause which they should have . . . Generally speaking nine-tenths of the friends' troubles are because they don't do the Bahá'í thing, in relation to each other, to the administrative bodies or in their personal lives.[418]

*Written on behalf of Shoghi Effendi*

The power of God can entirely transmute our characters and make of us beings entirely unlike our previous selves. Through prayer and supplication, obedience to the divine laws Bahá-'u'lláh has revealed, and ever-increasing service to His Faith, we can change ourselves.[419]

*Written on behalf of Shoghi Effendi*

He hopes that you will develop into Bahá'ís in character as well as in belief. The whole purpose of Bahá'u'lláh is that we should become a new kind of people, people who are upright, kind, intelligent, truthful, and honest and who live according to His great laws laid down for this new epoch in man's development. To call ourselves Bahá'ís is not enough, our inmost being must become ennobled and enlightened through living a Bahá'í life.[420]

*Written on behalf of Shoghi Effendi*

The only people who are truly free of the 'dross of self' are the Prophets, for to be free of one's ego is a hall-mark of perfection. We humans are *never* going to become perfect, for perfection belongs to a realm we are not destined to enter. However, we must constantly mount higher, seek to be more perfect. The ego is the animal in us, the heritage of the flesh which is full of selfish desires. By obeying the laws of God, seeking to live the life laid down in our teachings, and prayer and struggle, we can subdue our egos. We call people 'saints' who have achieved the highest degree of mastery over their egos.[421]

*Written on behalf of Shoghi Effendi*

## Spiritual growth is an indefinite journey

As we almost never attain any spiritual goal without seeing the next goal we must attain still beyond our reach, he urges you, who have come so far already on the path of spirituality, not to fret about the distance you still have to cover! It is an indefinite journey, and, no doubt in the next world the soul is privileged to draw closer to God than is possible when bound on this physical plane.[422]

*Written on behalf of Shoghi Effendi*

. . . the fundamental purpose of all religions – including our own – is to bring man nearer to God, and to change his character, which is of the utmost importance. Too much emphasis is often laid on the social and economic aspects of the Teachings; but the moral aspect cannot be over-emphasized.[423]

*Written on behalf of Shoghi Effendi*

Do not feel discouraged if your labours do not always yield an abundant fruitage. For a quick and rapidly-won success is not always the best and the most lasting. The harder you strive to attain your goal, the greater will be the confirmations of Bahá'u'lláh and the more certain you can feel to attain success. Be cheerful, therefore, and exert yourself with full faith and confidence.[424]

*Written on behalf of Shoghi Effendi*

. . . our struggles as individuals, often handicapped by the sense of our own inadequacy, are reinforced by the grace of Bahá'u'lláh, Who enables us to achieve the seemingly impossible![425]

*Written on behalf of Shoghi Effendi*

The Bahá'ís themselves as a body have one great advantage; they are sincerely convinced Bahá'u'lláh is right; they have a plan, and they are trying to follow it. But to pretend they are perfect, that the Bahá'ís of the future will not be a hundred times more mature, better balanced, more exemplary in their conduct, would be foolish.[426]

*Written on behalf of Shoghi Effendi*

## Bringing ourselves to account

His Holiness, the blessed Báb, mentions in His book that every one must consider at the end of each day what have been his actions. If he finds something which would please God, he must thank Him and pray to be strengthened to do this good act throughout his life; but if his actions have not been approvable or honest, he must earnestly ask God for strength to do better.[427]

*Attributed to 'Abdu'l-Bahá*

## We must honestly weigh our strengths and weaknesses

There is nothing more harmful to the individual – and also to society than false humility which is hypocritical, and hence unworthy of a true Bahá'í. The true believer is one who is conscious of his strength as well as of his weakness, and who, fully availing himself of the manifold opportunities and blessings which God gives him, strives to overcome his defects and weaknesses and this by means of a scrupulous adherence to all the laws and commandments revealed by God through His Manifestation.[428]

*Written on behalf of Shoghi Effendi*

We should not be occupied with our failings and weaknesses, but concern ourselves with the will of God so that it may flow through us, thereby healing these human infirmities.[429]

'Abdu'l-Bahá

## Concentrate on the Faith, not on personal failures

Regarding your own condition: He strongly urges you not to dwell on yourself. Each one of us, if we look into our failures, is sure to feel unworthy and despondent, and this feeling only frustrates our constructive efforts and wastes time. The thing for us to focus on is the glory of the Cause and the Power of Bahá'u'lláh which can make of a mere drop a surging sea! You certainly have no right to feel negative; you have embraced this glorious Faith and arisen with devotion to serve it, and your labours are greatly appreciated by both the Guardian and your fellow-Bahá'ís. With something as positive as the Faith and all it teaches behind you, you should be a veritable lion of confidence, and he will pray that you may become so.[430]

Written on behalf of Shoghi Effendi

Let no excessive self-criticism or any feeling of inadequacy, inability or inexperience hinder you or cause you to be afraid. Bury your fears in the assurances of Bahá'u'lláh. Has He not asserted that upon anyone who mentions His Name will descend the 'hosts of Divine inspiration' and that on such a one will also descend the 'Concourse on high, each bearing aloft a chalice of pure light'?[431]

The Universal House of Justice

He urges you to persevere and add up your accomplishments, rather than to dwell on the dark side of things. Everyone's life has both a dark and bright side. The Master said: turn your back to the darkness and your face to Me.[432]

Written on behalf of Shoghi Effendi

# Struggle against pessimism and depression

Yield not to grief and sorrow; they cause the greatest misery.[433]

'Abdu'l-Bahá

He [Shoghi Effendi] was very sorry to hear of the condition of your dear sister. He would advise her to turn her thoughts determinedly and intelligently – by that I mean unemotionally – to God, realizing that He is forgiving, that in one moment He can, through His Blessed Mercy, take away our sense of failure and help us to do better in the future – if we sincerely wish to; to turn to Him in prayer and seek to draw closer to Him; and to accept His Will and submit her own desires and opinions to His Wish and plan for her.

There is a tremendous darkness in the world today, the darkness caused by mankind's going against the Laws of God and giving way to the animal side of human nature. People must recognize this fact, and consciously struggle against pessimism and depression.[434]

Written on behalf of Shoghi Effendi

. . . a pessimistic and critical approach (although perhaps fully justified by the situation) produces no results. We, having the power of the Faith to draw on, must always be constructive in our efforts, as this will produce results and attract Divine blessings upon them.[435]

Written on behalf of Shoghi Effendi

## Overcoming fear

He will certainly pray that you may entirely overcome your fear-complex. When you concentrate your thoughts on realizing that you now belong to Bahá'u'lláh, are His servant whom He loves and will always help, if you ask Him to, and that the great spiritual strength of the Cause of God is behind you for you to draw upon, you will soon sce your fears melting away.[436]

Written on behalf of Shoghi Effendi

## Fear not; God will compensate the innocent

He [Shoghi Effendi] does not feel that fear – for ourselves or for others – solves any problem, or enables us to better meet it if it ever does arise. We do not know what the future holds exactly, or how soon we may all pass through another ordeal worse than the last one.

But what we do know is that all we can do as Bahá'ís is to teach and to exemplify the Faith. We cannot bear the burden of suffering of others, and we should not try to. All men are in God's hands, and even if they do get killed we know there is another life beyond this that can hold great hope and happiness for the soul.

No matter what happens, nothing is as important as our feeling of trust in God, our inner peacefulness and faith that all, in the end, in spite of the severity of the ordeals we may pass through will come out as Bahá'u'lláh has promised.

He urges you to put these dark thoughts from your mind, and remember that if God, the Creator of all men, can bear to see them suffer so, it is not for us to question His wisdom. He can compensate the innocent, in His own way, for the afflictions they bear.[437]

*Written on behalf of Shoghi Effendi*

## Peace of mind

Peace of mind is gained by the centering of the spiritual consciousness on the Prophet of God; therefore you should study the spiritual Teachings, and receive the Water of Life from the Holy Utterances. Then by translating these high ideals into action, your entire character will be changed, and your mind will not only find peace, but your entire being will find joy and enthusiasm.[438]

*Written on behalf of Shoghi Effendi*

# Do no be affected by the negative forces of the world

The friends must realize the Power of the Holy Spirit which is manifest and quickening them at this time through the appearance of Bahá'u'lláh. There is no force of heaven or earth which can affect them if they place themselves wholly under the influence of the Holy Spirit and under its guidance. Such individuals who are subject to the negative influences of the world are those who are not properly consecrated in the Faith.[439]

*Written on behalf of Shoghi Effendi*

## Be patient with others and our own selves

We must not only be patient with others, infinitely patient!, but also with our own poor selves, remembering that even the Prophets of God sometimes got tired and cried out in despair![440]

*Written on behalf of Shoghi Effendi*

## The necessity of rest and relaxation

. . . you should not neglect your health, but consider it the means which enables you to serve. It – the body – is like a horse which carries the personality and spirit, and as such should be well cared for so it can do its work! You should certainly safeguard your nerves, and force yourself to take time, and not only for prayer and meditation, but for real rest and relaxation.[441]

*Written on behalf of Shoghi Effendi*

## Greatest of all battles is the spiritual battle

If we could perceive the true reality of things we would see that the greatest of all battles raging in the world today is the spiritual battle. If the believers like yourself, young and eager and full of life, desire to win laurels for true and undying heroism, then let them join in the spiritual battle – whatever their physical occupation may be – which involves the very soul of man. The hardest and the noblest task in the world today is to be a true Bahá'í; this requires that we defeat not only the current evils prevailing all over the world, but the weaknesses, attachments to the past, prejudices, and selfishnesses that may be inherited and acquired within our own characters; that we give forth a shining and incorruptible example to our fellow-men.[442]

*Written on behalf of Shoghi Effendi*

## The responsibility of young believers is very great

The responsibility of young believers is very great, as they must not only fit themselves to inherit the work of the older Bahá'ís and carry on the affairs of the Cause in general, but the world which lies ahead of them – as promised by Bahá'u'lláh – will be a world chastened by its sufferings, ready to listen to His Divine Message at last; and consequently a very high character will be expected of the exponents of such a religion. To deepen their knowledge, to perfect themselves in the Bahá'í standards of virtue and upright conduct, should be the paramount duty of every young Bahá'í.[443]

*Written on behalf of Shoghi Effendi*

## The importance of transforming the Bahá'í world

The tasks facing the believers everywhere are great, for they see only too clearly that the only permanent remedy for the many afflictions the world is suffering from, is a change of heart and a new pattern of not only thought but personal conduct.[444]

*Written on behalf of Shoghi Effendi*

The divergence between the ways of the world and of the Cause of God becomes ever wider. And yet the two must come together. The Bahá'í community must demonstrate in ever-increasing measure its ability to redeem the disorderliness, the lack of cohesion, the permissiveness, the godlessness of modern society; the laws, the religious obligations, the observances of Bahá'í life, Bahá'í moral principles and standards of dignity, decency and reverence, must become deeply implanted in Bahá'í consciousness and increasingly inform and characterize this community.[445]

*The Universal House of Justice*

## The ability to effect personal transformation

There are . . . innumerable examples of individuals who have been able to effect drastic and enduring changes in their behaviour, through drawing on the spiritual powers available by the bounty of God.[446]

*Written on behalf of the Universal House of Justice*

## Transformation is the essential purpose of the cause

It is not enough to proclaim the Bahá'í message, essential as that is. It is not enough to expand the rolls of Bahá'í membership, vital as that is. Souls must be transformed, communities thereby consolidated, new models of life thus attained. Transformation is the essential purpose of the Cause of Bahá'u'lláh, but it lies in the will and effort of the individual to achieve it in obedience to the Covenant. Necessary to the progress of this life-fulfilling transformation is knowledge of the will and purpose of God through regular reading and study of the Holy Word.[447]

*The Universal House of Justice*

*Solutions to Tests:*

# *Apologize for Oneself and Forgive Others*

# Apologize for Oneself and Forgive Others

O Son of Man! Breathe not the sins of others so long as thou art thyself a sinner. Shouldst thou transgress this command, accursed wouldst thou be, and to this I bear witness.[448]

O Emigrants! The tongue I have designed for the mention of Me, defile it not with detraction. If the fire of self overcome you, remember your own faults and not the faults of My creatures, inasmuch as every one of you knoweth his own self better than he knoweth others.[449]

*Bahá'u'lláh*

## The effect of words can last a century

For the tongue is a smouldering fire, and excess of speech a deadly poison. Material fire consumeth the body, whereas the fire of the tongue devoureth both heart and soul. The force of the former lasteth but for a time, whilst the effects of the latter endure a century.[450]

*Bahá'u'lláh*

## The most great sin

Ye have been forbidden to commit murder or adultery, or to engage in backbiting or calumny; shun ye, then, what hath been prohibited in the holy Books and Tablets.[451]

*Bahá'u'lláh*

That seeker should also regard backbiting as grievous error, and keep himself aloof from its dominion, inasmuch as backbiting quencheth the light of the heart, and extinguisheth the life of the soul.[452]

*Bahá'u'lláh*

. . . the worst human quality and the most great sin is backbiting; more especially when it emanates from the tongues of the believers of God. If some means were devised so that the doors of backbiting could be shut eternally and each one of the believers of God unsealed his tongue in the praise of the other, then the teachings of His Holiness Bahá'u'lláh would be spread, the hearts illuminated, the spirits glorified and the human world would attain to everlasting felicity.[453]

*'Abdu'l-Bahá*

O beloved of the Lord! If any soul speak ill of an absent one, the only result will clearly be this: he will dampen the zeal of the friends and tend to make them indifferent. For backbiting is divisive, it is the leading cause among the friends of a disposition to withdraw. If any individual should speak ill of one who is absent, it is incumbent on his hearers, in a spiritual and friendly manner, to stop him, and say in effect: would this detraction serve any useful purpose? Would it please the Blessed Beauty, contribute to the lasting honour of the friends, promote the holy Faith, support the Covenant, or be of any possible benefit to any soul? No, never! On the contrary, it would make the dust to settle so thickly on the heart that the ears would hear no more, and the eyes would no longer behold the light of truth.[454]

*'Abdu'l-Bahá*

Never speak disparagingly of others, but praise without distinction. Pollute not your tongues by speaking evil of another.[455]

*'Abdu'l-Bahá*

In this sacred Dispensation, conflict and contention are in no wise permitted. Every aggressor deprives himself of God's grace. It is incumbent upon everyone to show the utmost love, rectitude of conduct, straightforwardness and sincere kindliness unto all the peoples and kindreds of the world, be they friends or strangers.[456]

*'Abdu'l-Bahá*

On no subject are the Bahá'í teachings more emphatic than on the necessity to abstain from fault-finding and backbiting while being ever eager to discover and root out our own faults and overcome our own failings.

If we profess loyalty to Bahá'u'lláh, to our Beloved Master and our dear Guardian, then we must show our love by obedience to these explicit teachings. Deeds not words are what they demand, and no amount of fervour in the use of expressions of loyalty and adulation will compensate for failure to live in the spirit of the teachings.[457]

*Written on behalf of Shoghi Effendi*

## We must also stop listening to backbiting

The friends should also understand that they should not only cease backbiting and gossiping, but should cease listening to others who fall into this sin. Ignoring gossip and slander is a positive, constructive and healing action helpful to the community, the gossiper and to the persons slandered.[458]

*The Universal House of Justice*

## Discussing a problem without backbiting

You ask in your letter for guidance on the implications of the prohibitions on backbiting and more specifically whether, in moments of anger or depression, the believer is permitted to turn to his friends to unburden his soul and discuss his problem in human relations. Normally, it is possible to describe the situation surrounding a problem and seek help and advice in resolving it, without necessarily mentioning names. The individual believer should seek to do this, whether he is consulting a friend, Bahá'í or non-Bahá'í, or whether the friend is consulting him.

'Abdu'l-Bahá does not permit adverse criticism of individuals by name in discussion among the friends, even if the one criticizing believes that he is doing so to protect the interests of the Cause.

If the situation is of such gravity as to endanger the interests of the Faith, the complaint, as your National Spiritual Assembly has indicated, should be submitted to the Local Spiritual Assembly, or as you state to a representative of the institution of the Counsellors, for consideration and action. In such cases, of course, the name of the person or persons involved will have to be mentioned.[459]

*Written on behalf of the Universal House of Justice*

## No greater harm to the Cause than dissension and strife

He, Who is the Eternal Truth, beareth Me witness! Nothing whatever can, in this Day, inflict a greater harm upon this Cause than dissension and strife, contention, estrangement and apathy, among the loved ones of God. Flee them, through the power of God and His sovereign aid, and strive ye to knit together the hearts of men, in His Name, the Unifier, the All-Knowing, the All-Wise.[460]

*Bahá'u'lláh*

In brief, O ye believers of God! The text of the Divine Book is this: If two souls quarrel and contend about a question of the Divine questions, differing and disputing, *both are wrong*. The wisdom of this incontrovertible law of God is this: That between two souls from amongst the believers of God, no contention and dispute may arise; that they may speak with each other with infinite amity and love. Should there appear the least trace of controversy, they must remain silent, and both parties must continue their discussions no longer, but ask the reality of the question from the Interpreter. This is the irrefutable command![461]

'Abdu'l-Bahá

Endeavour, therefore, that ye may scatter and disperse the army of doubt and of error with the power of the holy utterances. This is my exhortation and this is my counsel. Do not quarrel with anybody, and shun every form of dispute. Utter the Word of God. If he accepteth it the desired purpose is attained, and if he turneth away leave him to himself and trust to God.

Such is the attribute of those who are firm in the Covenant.[462]

'Abdu'l-Bahá

As long as the friends quarrel amongst themselves their efforts will not be blessed for they are disobeying God.[463]

Written on behalf of Shoghi Effendi

## We should not judge others

All religions teach that we should love one another; that we should seek out our own shortcomings before we presume to condemn the faults of others, that we must not consider ourselves superior to our neighbours! We must be careful not to exalt ourselves lest we be humiliated.

Who are *we* that we should judge? How shall we know who, in the sight of God, is the most upright man? God's thoughts are not like our thoughts! How many men who have seemed saint-like to their friends have fallen into the greatest humiliation. Think of Judas Iscariot; he began well, but remember his end! On the other hand, Paul, the Apostle, was in his early life an enemy of Christ, whilst later he became His most faithful servant. How then can we flatter ourselves and despise others?

Let us therefore be humble, without prejudices, preferring others' good to our own! Let us never say, 'I am a believer but he is an infidel', 'I am near to God, whilst he is an outcast'. We can never know what will be the final judgement! Therefore let us help all who are in need of any kind of assistance.

Let us teach the ignorant, and take care of the young child until he grows to maturity. When we find a person fallen into the depths of misery or sin we must be kind to him, take him by the hand, help him to regain his footing, his strength; we must guide him with love and tenderness, treat him as a friend not as an enemy.

We have no right to look upon any of our fellow-mortals as evil.[464]

*'Abdu'l-Bahá*

[Shoghi Effendi] was very sorry to hear that you have had so many tests in your Bahá'í life. There is no doubt that many of them are due to our own nature. In other words, if we are very sensitive, or if we are in some way brought up in a different environment from the Bahá'ís amongst whom we live, we naturally see things differently and may feel them more acutely; and the other side of it is that the imperfections of our fellow-Bahá'ís can be a great trial to us.

We must always remember that in the cesspool of material-ism, which is what modern civilization has to a certain extent become, Bahá'ís – that is some of them – are still to a certain extent affected by the society from which they have sprung. In other words, they have recognized the Manifestation of God, but they have not been believers long enough, or perhaps not tried hard enough, to become 'a new Creation'.

All we can do in such cases is to do our duty; and the Guard-ian feels very strongly that your duty is towards Bahá'u'lláh and the Faith you love so dearly; and certainly not to take the weaker course and sever yourself from the Bahá'í Community.

He feels that, if you close your eyes to the failings of others, and fix your love and prayers upon Bahá'u'lláh, you will have the strength to weather this storm, and will be much better for it in the end, spiritually. Although you suffer, you will gain a maturity that will enable you to be of greater help to both your fellow-Bahá'ís and your children.[465]

*Written on behalf of Shoghi Effendi*

## Suppress every critical thought and harsh word

When criticism and harsh words arise within a Bahá'í community, there is no remedy except to put the past behind one, and persuade all concerned to turn over a new leaf, and for the sake of God and His Faith refrain from mentioning the subjects which have led to misunderstanding and inharmony. The more the friends argue back and forth and maintain, each side, that their point of view is the right one, the worse the whole situation becomes.

When we see the condition the world is in today, we must surely forget these utterly insignificant internal disturbances, and rush, unitedly, to the rescue of humanity. You should urge your fellow-Bahá'ís to take this point of view, and to support you in a strong effort to suppress every critical thought and every harsh word, in order to let the spirit of Bahá'u'lláh flow into the entire community, and unite it in His love and in His service.[466]

*Written on behalf of Shoghi Effendi*

If ye become aware of a sin committed by another, conceal it, that God may conceal your own sin.[467]

*Bahá'u'lláh*

## Apologize for oneself, forgive and forget

He [Shoghi Effendi] feels that the present inharmony prevailing amongst you . . . is very detrimental to the advancement of the Cause, and can only lead to disruption and the chilling of the interest of new believers. You . . . should forget about your personal grievances, and unite for the protection of the Faith which he well knows you are all loyally devoted to and ready to sacrifice for.

Perhaps the greatest test Bahá'ís are ever subjected to is from each other; but for the sake of the Master they should be ever ready to overlook each other's mistakes, apologize for harsh words they have uttered, forgive and forget. He strongly recommends to you this course of action.[468]

*Written on behalf of Shoghi Effendi*

## Do not complain of others

Pollute not your tongues by speaking evil of another. Recognize your enemies as friends, and consider those who wish you evil as the wishers of good. You must not see evil as evil and then compromise with your opinion, for to treat in a smooth, kindly way one whom you consider evil or an enemy is hypocrisy, and this is not worthy or allowable. You must consider your enemies as your friends, look upon your evil-wishers as your well-wishers and treat them accordingly. Act in such a way that your heart may be free from hatred. Let not your heart be offended with anyone. If some one commits an error and wrong toward you, you must instantly forgive him. Do not complain of others. Refrain from reprimanding them, and if you wish to give admonition or advice, let it be offered in such a way that it will not burden the bearer. Turn all your thoughts toward bringing joy to hearts. Beware! Beware! lest ye offend any heart. Assist the world of humanity as much as possible. Be the source of consolation to every sad one, assist every weak one, be helpful to every indigent one, care for every sick one, be the cause of glorification to every lowly one, and shelter those who are overshadowed by fear.[469]

*'Abdu'l-Bahá*


Petty bickerings and jealousies make one to lose all traces of spirituality, excommunicate a person from the divine company of the worthy ones, submerge one in the sea of phantasms, suffer one to become cold and pessimistic and throw him headlong into the depths of despair and hopelessness! You must not listen to anyone speaking about another; because no sooner do you listen to one than you must listen to someone else and thus the circle will be enlarged endlessly![470]

*Attributed to 'Abdu'l-Bahá*

# Overlook the shortcomings of others

You ask how to deal with anger. The House of Justice suggests that you call to mind the admonitions found in our Writings on the need to overlook the shortcomings of others; to forgive and conceal their misdeeds, not to expose their bad qualities, but to search for and affirm their praiseworthy ones, and to endeavour to be always forbearing, patient, and merciful.[471]

*Written on behalf of the Universal House of Justice*


The Bahá'ís are not perfect, but they have made a great step forward by embracing the Faith of God. We must be patient with each other, and realize that each one of us has some faults to overcome, of one kind or another.[472]

*Written on behalf of Shoghi Effendi*


## We must overcome the desire to take sides

The Bahá'ís must learn to forget personalities and to overcome the desire – so natural in people – to take sides and fight about it. They must also learn to really make use of the great principle of consultation.[473]

*Written on behalf of Shoghi Effendi*


The world is full of evil and dark forces and the friends must not permit these forces to get hold of them by thinking and feeling negatively towards each other.[474]

*Written on behalf of Shoghi Effendi*


## We must be patient with each other

We must be patient with each other's shortcomings, and always strive to create love and unity among the believers, who, after all, are still immature in many ways and far from perfect. The Faith itself is the great thing, and the Bahá'ís must strive to become ever more perfect instruments for Bahá'u'lláh to use and to accomplish His purpose through.[475]

*Written on behalf of Shoghi Effendi*

The friends must be patient with each other and must realize
that the Cause is still in its infancy and its institutions are not
yet functioning perfectly. The greater the patience, the loving
understanding and the forbearance the believers show towards
each other and their shortcomings, the greater will be the
progress of the whole Bahá'í community at large.[476]

*Written on behalf of Shoghi Effendi*

## Our patience can be transformed into virtues

As to the inconveniences you have experienced during the last
ten years, the best consolation I can imagine for you is your
own quotation of the *Hidden Words*, 'My calamity is my providence.' We must bear with one another. It is only through
suffering that the nobility of character can make itself manifest.
The energy we expend in enduring the intolerance of some
individuals of our community is not lost. It is transformed into
fortitude, steadfastness and magnanimity. The lives of Bahá-
'u'lláh and 'Abdu'l-Bahá are the best examples for this. Sacrifices in the path of one's religion produce always immortal
results, 'Out of the ashes rises the phoenix.'[477]

*Written on behalf of Shoghi Effendi*

## Create greater love and harmony

So many misunderstandings arise from the passionate attachment of the friends to the Faith and also their immaturity. We
must therefore be very patient and loving with each other and
try to establish unity in the Bahá'í family. The differences . . .
which you describe in your letter he feels are caused by the
above and not by enmity to the Faith or insincerity.[478]

*Written on behalf of Shoghi Effendi*

# Dwell on our own development

Let your thoughts dwell on your own spiritual development, and close your eyes to the deficiencies of other souls. Act ye in such wise, showing forth pure and goodly deeds, and modesty and humility, that ye will cause others to be awakened.[479]

*'Abdu'l-Bahá*

Strive with all your power to be free from imperfections. Heedless souls are always seeking faults in others. What can the hypocrite know of others' faults when he is blind to his own? This is the meaning of the words in the *Seven Valleys*. It is a guide for human conduct. As long as a man does not find his own faults, he can never become perfect. Nothing is more fruitful for man than the knowledge of his own shortcomings. The Blessed Perfection says, 'I wonder at the man who does not find his own imperfections.'[480]

*'Abdu'l-Bahá*

Those souls who consider themselves as imperfect, they are the people of the Kingdom. Those persons who prefer themselves above others are egotists and worshippers of self; they are deprived of the graces of the Lord of mankind.[481]

*Attributed to 'Abdu'l-Bahá*

Bahá'u'lláh also recognizes that human beings are fallible. He knows that, in our weakness, we shall repeatedly stumble when we try to walk in the path He has pointed out to us.

If all human beings became perfect the moment they accepted the call of Bahá'u'lláh this world would be another world. It is in light of our frailty that 'Abdu'l-Bahá appealed to the friends everywhere to love each other and stressed the emphatic teaching of Bahá'u'lláh that each of us should concentrate upon improving his or her own life and ignore the faults of others.

How many times the Master stressed the need for unity, for without it His Father's Cause could not go forward.[482]

*The Universal House of Justice*

In order to achieve this cordial unity one of the first essentials insisted on by Bahá'u'lláh and 'Abdu'l-Bahá is that we resist the natural tendency to let our attention dwell on the faults and failings of others rather than on our own. Each of us is responsible for one life only, and that is our own. Each of us is immeasurably far from being 'perfect as our heavenly father is perfect' and the task of perfecting our own life and character is one that requires all our attention, our will-power and energy. If we allow our attention and energy to be taken up in efforts to keep others right and remedy their faults, we are wasting precious time. We are like ploughmen each of whom has his team to manage and his plough to direct, and in order to keep his furrow straight he must keep his eye on his goal and concentrate on his own task. If he looks to this side and that to see how Tom and Harry are getting on and to criticize their ploughing, then his own furrow will assuredly become crooked.[483]

*Written on behalf of Shoghi Effendi*

We can never exert the influence over others which we can exert over ourselves. If we are better, if we show love, patience, and understanding of the weakness of others, if we seek to never criticize but rather encourage others will do likewise, and we can really help the Cause through our example and spiritual strength.[484]

*Written on behalf of Shoghi Effendi*

## Ignore any rebuffs we may receive

We must never dwell too much on the attitudes and feelings of our fellow believers towards us. What is most important is to foster love and harmony and ignore any rebuffs we may receive; in this way the weakness of human nature and the peculiarity or attitude of any particular person is not magnified, but pales into insignificance in comparison with our joint service to the Faith we all love.[485]

*Written on behalf of Shoghi Effendi*


You should not allow the remarks made by the Bahá'ís to hurt or depress you, but should forget the personalities, and arise to do all you can, yourself, to teach the Faith.[486]

*Written on behalf of Shoghi Effendi*


## *Return kindness to those who wish you ill*

If others hurl their darts against you, offer them milk and honey in return; if they poison your lives, sweeten their souls; if they injure you, teach them how to be comforted; if they inflict a wound upon you, be a balm to their sores; if they sting you, hold to their lips a refreshing cup.[487]

*'Abdu'l-Bahá*


O ye friends of God! Show ye an endeavour that all the nations and communities of the world, even the enemies, put their trust, assurance and hope in you; that if a person falls into errors for a hundred-thousand times he may yet turn his face to you, hopeful that you will forgive his sins; for he must not become hopeless, neither grieved nor despondent. This is the conduct and the manner of the people of Bahá.[488]

*'Abdu'l-Bahá*


The truth is, nothing is sweeter for a man than doing good to someone who has done evil to him. Whenever he remembers having been kind to his enemies, his heart will rejoice.[489]

*Attributed to 'Abdu'l-Bahá*

## *If we love God, we can love all people*

We must love God, and in this state, a general love for all men becomes possible. We cannot love each human being for himself but our feeling towards humanity should be motivated by our love for the Father who created all men.[490]

*Written on behalf of Shoghi Effendi*

## *Overcoming racial prejudice*

A tremendous effort is required by both races if their outlook, their manners, and conduct are to reflect, in this darkened age, the spirit and teachings of the Faith of Bahá'u'lláh. Casting away once and for all the fallacious doctrine of racial superiority, with all its attendant evils, confusion, and miseries, and welcoming and encouraging the intermixture of races, and tearing down the barriers that now divide them, they should each endeavour, day and night, to fulfil their particular responsibilities in the common task which so urgently faces them. Let them, while each is attempting to contribute its share to the solution of this perplexing problem, call to mind the warnings of 'Abdu'l-Bahá, and visualize, while there is yet time, the dire consequences that must follow if this challenging and unhappy situation that faces the entire American nation is not definitely remedied.

Let the white make a supreme effort in their resolve to contribute their share to the solution of this problem, to abandon once for all their usually inherent and at times subconscious sense of superiority, to correct their tendency towards revealing a patronizing attitude towards the members of the other race, to persuade them through their intimate, spontaneous and informal association with them of the genuineness of their friendship and the sincerity of their intentions, and to master their impatience of any lack of responsiveness on the part of a people who have received, for so long a period, such grievous and slow-healing wounds. Let the Negroes, through a corresponding effort on their part, show by every means in their power the warmth of their response, their readiness to forget the past, and their ability to wipe out every trace of suspicion that may still linger in their hearts and minds. Let neither think that the solution of so vast a problem is a matter that exclusively concerns the other. Let neither think that such a problem can either easily or immediately be resolved. Let neither think that they can wait confidently for the solution of this problem until the initiative has been taken, and the favourable circumstances created, by agencies that stand outside the orbit of their Faith. Let neither think that anything short of genuine love, extreme patience, true humility, consummate tact, sound initiative, mature wisdom, and deliberate, persistent, and prayerful effort, can succeed in blotting out the stain which this patent evil has left on the fair name of their common country. Let them rather believe, and be firmly convinced, that on their mutual understanding, their amity, and sustained cooperation, must depend, more than on any other force or organization operating outside the circle of their Faith, the deflection of that dangerous course so greatly feared by 'Abdu'l-Bahá, and the materialization of the hopes He cherished for their joint contribution to the fulfilment of that country's glorious destiny.[491]

*Shoghi Effendi*

## Unity overcomes all obstacles

The increase in membership in the Canadian Bahá'í Community this past year was also most encouraging. It shows that there is, primarily, unity among the believers, for where this fundamental quality is lacking in a Bahá'í community any real growth is impossible. That is why the beloved Master so constantly admonished the friends to be as one soul in different bodies, for this love and unity constitutes their spiritual health and gives them the strength to overcome all obstacles in their path.[492]

*Written on behalf of Shoghi Effendi*

. . .the friends should unite, should become really keenly conscious of the fact that they are one spiritual family, held together by bonds more sacred and eternal than those physical ties which make people of the same family. If the friends will forget all personal differences and open their hearts to a great love for each other for the sake of Baha'u'llah, they will find that their powers are vastly increased; they will attract the heart of the public, and will witness a rapid growth of the Holy Faith.[493]

*Written on behalf of Shoghi Effendi*

We Bahá'ís can always, with the aid of Bahá'u'lláh, Who is ever ready to strengthen and assist us, turn our stumbling blocks into stepping stones, and utilize the often violent forces released by sincere but perhaps misguided friends, as a positive stream of power by turning them into productive channels instead of destructive ones.[494]

*Written on behalf of Shoghi Effendi*

## The transforming power of love

Love is, indeed, a most potent elixir that can transform the vilest and meanest of people into heavenly souls. May your example serve to further confirm the truth of this beautiful teaching of our Faith.[495]

*Written on behalf of Shoghi Effendi*

## The Secret of Universal Participation

The real secret of universal participation lies in the Master's oft expressed wish that the friends should love each other, constantly encourage each other, work together, be as one soul in one body, and in so doing become a true, organic, healthy body animated and illumined by the spirit. In such a body all will receive spiritual health and vitality from the organism itself, and the most perfect flowers and fruits will be brought forth.[496]

*The Universal House of Justice*

*Solutions to Tests:*

# *Teach the Cause*

# Teach the Cause

Arise to serve the Cause of God, in such wise that the cares and sorrows caused by them that have disbelieved in the Dayspring of the Signs of God may not afflict you.[497]

*Bahá'u'lláh*

## Raise up a new creation

Darkness hath encompassed every land, O my God, and caused most of Thy servants to tremble. I beseech Thee, by Thy Most Great Name, to raise in every city a new creation that shall turn towards Thee, and shall remember Thee amidst Thy servants, and shall unfurl by virtue of their utterances and wisdom the ensigns of Thy victory, and shall detach themselves from all created things.[498]

*Bahá'u'lláh*

## Confirmations come through teaching

O ye servants of the Blessed Beauty! . . . It is clear that in this day, confirmations from the unseen world are encompassing all those who deliver the divine Message. Should the work of teaching lapse, these confirmations would be entirely cut off, since it is impossible for the loved ones of God to receive assistance unless they teach.[499]

*'Abdu'l-Bahá*

When the friends do not endeavour to spread the message, they fail to remember God befittingly, and will not witness the tokens of assistance and confirmation from the Abhá Kingdom nor comprehend the divine mysteries. However, when the tongue of the teacher is engaged in teaching, he will naturally himself be stimulated, will become a magnet attracting the divine aid and bounty of the Kingdom, and will be like unto the bird at the hour of dawn, which itself becometh exhilarated by its own singing, its warbling and its melody.[500]

*'Abdu'l-Bahá*

The teaching work should under all conditions be actively pursued by the believers because divine confirmations are dependent upon it. Should a Bahá'í refrain from being fully, vigorously and wholeheartedly involved in the teaching work he will undoubtedly be deprived of the blessings of the Abhá Kingdom.[501]

*'Abdu'l-Bahá*

The sustaining strength of Bahá'u'lláh Himself, the Founder of the Faith, will be withheld from every and each individual who fails in the long run to arise and play his part.

. . . The unseen legions, standing rank upon rank, and eager to pour forth from the Kingdom on high the full measure of their celestial strength on the individual participants of this incomparably glorious Crusade, are powerless unless and until each potential crusader decides for himself, and perseveres in his determination, to rush into the arena of service ready to sacrifice his all for the Cause he is called upon to champion.[502]

*Shoghi Effendi*

Though the ultimate blessings that must crown the consummation of your mission be undoubted, and the Divine promises given you firm and irrevocable, yet the measure of the goodly reward which every one of you is to reap must depend on the extent to which your daily exertions will have contributed to the expansion of that mission and the hastening of its triumph.[503]

*Shoghi Effendi*

## However great the perils

I appeal on this solemn occasion, rendered doubly sacred through the approaching hundredth anniversary of the most devastating holocaust in the annals of the Faith, at this anxious hour in the fortunes of this travailing age, to the entire body of the American believers . . . to rededicate themselves and resolve, no matter how great the perils confronting their sister communities on the European, Asiatic, African and Australian continents, however sombre the situation facing both the cradle of the Faith and its World Centre, however grievous the vicissitudes they themselves may eventually suffer, to hold aloft unflinchingly the torch of the Faith impregnated with the blood of innumerable martyrs and transmit it unimpaired so that it may add lustre to future generations destined to labour after them.[504]

*Shoghi Effendi*

## To overcome community problems

He was very sorry to learn of the inharmony amongst the friends there; and he feels that the only wise course of action is for all the believers to devote themselves to teaching the Faith and co-operating with their National Body.

Often these trials and tests which *all* Bahá'í communities inevitably pass through seem terrible, at the moment, but in retrospect we understand that they were due to the frailty of human nature, to misunderstandings, and to the growing pains which every Bahá'í community must experience.[505]

*Written on behalf of Shoghi Effendi*

## Today the Cause needs teachers, not martyrs

Every day has certain needs. In those early days the Cause needed Martyrs, and people who would stand all sorts of torture and persecution in expressing their faith and spreading the message sent by God. Those days are, however, gone.

The Cause at present does not need martyrs who would die for their faith, but servants who desire to teach and establish the Cause throughout the world. To live to teach in the present day is like being martyred in those early days. It is the spirit that moves us that counts, not the act through which that spirit expresses itself; and that spirit is to serve the Cause of God with our heart and soul.[506]

*Written on behalf of Shoghi Effendi*

## Prayer, meditation and action

Teaching is the source of Divine Confirmation. It is not sufficient to pray diligently for guidance, but this prayer must be followed by meditation as to the best methods of action and then action itself. Even if the action should not immediately produce results, or perhaps not be entirely correct, that does not make so much difference, because prayers can only be answered through action and if someone's action is wrong, God can use that method of showing the pathway which is right.[507]

*Written on behalf of Shoghi Effendi*

## Seek out jewel-like souls

His hope and prayer is that during these times of danger, stress, and misery, the Bahá'ís will seek out amidst their fellow-countrymen those jewel-like souls that belong to Bahá'u'lláh and bring them the blessing and comfort of His Faith.[508]

*Written on behalf of Shoghi Effendi*

## Service brings assistance of Supreme Concourse

An individual must centre his whole heart and mind on service to the Cause, in accordance with the high standards set by Bahá'u'lláh. When this is done, the hosts of the Supreme Concourse will come to the assistance of the individual, and every difficulty and trial will gradually be overcome.[509]

*Written on behalf of Shoghi Effendi*

There is nothing that brings success in the Faith like service. Service is the magnet which draws the Divine Confirmations. Thus, when a person is active, they are blessed by the Holy Spirit. When they are inactive, the Holy Spirit cannot find a repository in their being, and thus they are deprived of its healing and quickening rays.[510]

*Written on behalf of Shoghi Effendi*

No one can, of course, foresee the course of future events. But we do know that whatever of trial and suffering we may have to pass through is utterly insignificant in comparison with our infinite blessing of being the people bearing His Name and serving His Cause in these tremendous, history-making days.[511]

*Written on behalf of Shoghi Effendi*

## Teaching brings us happiness

To express our deep appreciation for this gift bestowed by God we should arise and spread this message of hope to the suffering humanity around us. Such is the nature of this gift that the more we give from it to others the greater will be our remaining share. For what pleasure can compare the pleasure of bringing joy and hope to other hearts. The more we make others happy the greater will be our own happiness and the deeper our sense of having served humanity.[512]

*Written on behalf of Shoghi Effendi*

## Our actions will point the way for humanity

The Master longed so to see the believers perfect their faith in living. Now is the supreme hour of test applied, not only to the whole world, but to the Bahá'ís too; how they act, to the degree they adhere to the spirit and the letter of their Faith, will point the way to watching humanity and demonstrate the worth of being a follower of Bahá'u'lláh.[513]

*Written on behalf of Shoghi Effendi*

The dark horizon faced by a world which has failed to recognize the Promised One, the Source of its salvation, acutely affects the outlook of the younger generations; their distressing lack of hope and their indulgence in desperate but futile and even dangerous solutions make a direct claim on the remedial attention of Bahá'í youth, who, through their knowledge of that Source and the bright vision with which they have thus been endowed, cannot hesitate to impart to their despairing fellow youth the restorative joy, the constructive hope, the radiant assurances of Bahá'u'lláh's stupendous Revelation.[514]

*The Universal House of Justice*

## Anguish over the world can be overcome by prayer and teaching

. . . the mental anguish which the prevailing situation induces can and must be overcome through prayer and a conscious attention to teaching the Cause and living the Bahá'í life with a world-embracing vision.[515]

*The Universal House of Justice*

## The world can only change through the Cause

. . . Bahá'ís are often accused of holding aloof from the 'real problems' of their fellow-men. But when we hear this accusation let us not forget that those who make it are usually idealistic materialists to whom material good is the only 'real' good, whereas we know that the working of the material world is merely a reflection of spiritual conditions and until the spiritual conditions can be changed there can be no lasting change for the better in material affairs.

We should also remember that most people have no clear concept of the sort of world they wish to build, nor how to go about building it. Even those who are concerned to improve conditions are therefore reduced to combatting every apparent evil that takes their attention. Willingness to fight against evils, whether in the form of conditions or embodied in evil men, has thus become for most people the touchstone by which they judge a person's moral worth. Bahá'ís, on the other hand, know the goal they are working towards and know what they must do, step by step, to attain it. Their whole energy is directed towards the building of the good, a good which has such a positive strength that in the face of it the multitude of evils – which are in essence negative – will fade away and be no more. To enter into the quixotic tournament of demolishing one by one the evils in the world is, to a Bahá'í, a vain waste of time and effort. His whole life is directed towards proclaiming the Message of Bahá'u'lláh, reviving the spiritual life of his fellow-men, uniting them in a Divinely-created World Order, and then, as that Order grows in strength and influence, he will see the power of that Message transforming the whole of human society and progressively solving the problems and removing the injustice which have so long bedevilled the world.[516]

*Written on behalf of the Universal House of Justice*

*Solutions to Tests:*

*Meditate on
Bahá'u'lláh's Sufferings*

# Meditate on Bahá'u'lláh's Sufferings

If tribulation touch thee for My sake, call thou to mind My ills and troubles, and remember My banishment and imprisonment. Thus do We devolve on thee what hath descended upon Us from Him Who is the All-Glorious, the All-Wise.[517]

*Bahá'u'lláh*

O Aḥmad! Forget not My bounties while I am absent. Remember My days during thy days, and My distress and banishment in this remote prison. And be thou so steadfast in My love that thy heart shall not waver, even if the swords of the enemies rain blows upon thee and all the heavens and the earth arise against thee.[518]

*Bahá'u'lláh*

Recall thou to mind My sorrows, My cares and anxieties, My woes and trials, the state of My captivity, the tears that I have shed, the bitterness of Mine anguish, and now My imprisonment in this far-off land. God, O Muṣṭafá, beareth Me witness. Couldst thou be told what hath befallen the Ancient Beauty, thou wouldst flee into the wilderness, and weep with a great weeping. In thy grief, thou wouldst smite thyself on the head, and cry out as one stung by the sting of the adder. Be thou grateful to God, that We have refused to divulge unto thee the secrets of those unsearchable decrees that have been sent down unto Us from the heaven of the Will of thy Lord, the Most Powerful, the Almighty.[519]

*Bahá'u'lláh*

## Countless afflictions massed behind His door

By the righteousness of God! Every morning I arose from My bed, I discovered the hosts of countless afflictions massed behind My door; and every night when I lay down, lo! My heart was torn with agony at what it had suffered from the fiendish cruelty of its foes. With every piece of bread the Ancient Beauty breaketh is coupled the assault of a fresh affliction, and with every drop He drinketh is mixed the bitterness of the most woeful of trials. He is preceded in every step He taketh by an army of unforeseen calamities, while in His rear follow legions of agonizing sorrows.

Such is My plight, wert thou to ponder it in thine heart. Let not, however, thy soul grieve over that which God hath rained down upon Us. Merge thy will in His pleasure, for We have, at no time, desired anything whatsoever except His Will, and have welcomed each one of His irrevocable decrees. Let thine heart be patient, and be thou not dismayed. Follow not in the way of them that are sorely agitated.[520]

*Bahá'u'lláh*

## Bahá'u'lláh never guarded Himself against trials

Praise be to Thee, O Thou Who art the Well-Beloved of all that have known Thee, and the Desire of the hearts of such as are devoted to Thee, inasmuch as Thou hast made me a target for the ills that I suffer in my love for Thee, and the object of the assaults launched against me in Thy path. Thy glory beareth me witness! I can, on no account, feel impatient of the adversities that I have borne in my love for Thee. From the very day Thou didst reveal Thyself unto me, I have accepted for myself every manner of tribulation. Every moment of my life my head crieth out to Thee and saith: 'Would, O my Lord, that I could be raised on the spear-point in Thy path!' while my blood entreateth Thee saying: 'Dye the earth with me, O my God, for the sake of Thy love and Thy pleasure!' Thou knowest that I have, at no time, sought to guard my body against any affliction, nay rather I have continually anticipated the things Thou didst ordain for me in the Tablet of Thy decree.[521]

*Bahá'u'lláh*

## Bahá'u'lláh thanked God for tribulations

Glorified art Thou, O Lord my God! I yield Thee thanks for that Thou hast made me the target of divers tribulations and the mark of manifold trials, in order that Thy servants may be endued with new life and all Thy creatures may be quickened.

I swear by Thy glory, O Thou the Best Beloved of the worlds and the Desire of all such as have recognized Thee! The one reason I wish to live is that I may reveal Thy Cause, and I seek the continuance of life only that I may be touched by adversity in Thy path.[522]

*Bahá'u'lláh*

How sweet to my taste is the bitterness of death suffered in Thy path, and how precious in my estimation are the shafts of Thine enemies when encountered for the sake of the exaltation of Thy word! Let me quaff in Thy Cause, O my God, whatsoever Thou didst desire, and send down upon me in Thy love all Thou didst ordain. By Thy glory! I wish only what Thou wishest, and cherish what Thou cherishest. In Thee have I, at all times, placed my whole trust and confidence.[523]

*Bahá'u'lláh*

But for the tribulations that have touched Me in the path of God, life would have held no sweetness for Me, and My existence would have profited Me nothing.[524]

*Bahá'u'lláh*

## Bahá'u'lláh served God throughout His trials

How many the days, O my God, which I have spent in utter loneliness with the transgressors amongst Thy servants, and how many the nights, O my Best-Beloved, during which I lay a captive in the hands of the wayward amidst Thy creatures! In the midst of my troubles and tribulations I have continued to celebrate Thy praise before all who are in Thy heaven and on Thy earth, and have not ceased to extol Thy wondrous glory in the kingdoms of Thy Revelation and of Thy creation, though all that I have been capable of showing forth hath fallen short of the greatness and the majesty of Thy oneness, and is unworthy of Thine exaltation and of Thine omnipotence.[525]

*Bahá'u'lláh*


Glory to Thee, O Thou Who art the Lord of all worlds, and the Beloved of all such as have recognized Thee! Thou seest me sitting under a sword hanging on a thread, and art well aware that in such a state I have not fallen short of my duty towards Thy Cause, nor failed to shed abroad Thy praise, and declare Thy virtues, and deliver all Thou hadst prescribed unto me in Thy Tablets. Though the sword be ready to fall on my head, I call Thy loved ones with such a calling that the hearts are carried away towards the horizon of Thy majesty and grandeur.[526]

*Bahá'u'lláh*


## To endure with patience our own sorrows

Thus have We disclosed to thee a glimmer of the woes that have come upon us, that thou mayest be made aware of Our sufferings, and patiently endure thy sorrows.[527]

*Bahá'u'lláh*


. . . to outward seeming, the human condition of the Holy Manifestations is subjected to tests, and when Their strength and endurance have by this means been revealed in the plenitude of power, other men receive instruction therefrom, and are made aware of how great must be their own steadfastness and endurance under tests and trials. For the Divine Educator must teach by word and also by deed, thus revealing to all the straight pathway of truth.[528]

'Abdu'l-Bahá

## Abdu'l-Bahá speaks of the sufferings of Bahá'u'lláh

The Abhá Beauty Himself – may the spirit of all existence be offered up for His loved ones – bore all manner of ordeals, and willingly accepted for Himself intense afflictions. No torment was there left that His sacred form was not subjected to, no suffering that did not descend upon Him. How many a night, when He was chained, did He go sleepless because of the weight of His iron collar; how many a day the burning pain of the stocks and fetters gave Him no moment's peace. From Níyávarán to Ṭihrán they made Him run – He, that embodied spirit, He Who had been accustomed to repose against cushions of ornamented silk – chained, shoeless, His head bared; and down under the earth, in the thick darkness of that narrow dungeon, they shut Him up with murderers, rebels and thieves. Ever and again they assailed Him with a new torment, and all were certain that from one moment to the next He would suffer a martyr's death. After some time they banished Him from His native land, and sent Him to countries alien and far away. During many a year in 'Iráq, no moment passed but the arrow of a new anguish struck His holy heart; with every breath a sword came down upon that sacred body, and He could hope for no moment of security and rest. From every side His enemies mounted their attack with unrelenting hate; and singly and alone He withstood them all. After all these tribulations, these body blows, they flung Him out of 'Iráq in the continent of Asia, to the continent of Europe, and in that place of bitter exile, of wretched hardships, to the wrongs that were heaped upon Him by the people of the Qur'án were now added the virulent persecutions, the powerful attacks, the plottings, the slanders, the continual hostilities, the hate and malice, of the people of the Bayán. My pen is powerless to tell it all; but ye have surely been informed of it. Then, after twenty-four years in this, the Most Great Prison, in agony and sore affliction, His days drew to a close.

To sum it up, the Ancient Beauty was ever, during His sojourn in this transitory world, either a captive bound with chains, or living under a sword, or subjected to extreme suffering and torment, or held in the Most Great Prison. Because of His physical weakness, brought on by His afflictions, His blessed body was worn away to a breath; it was light as a cobweb from long grieving. And His reason for shouldering this heavy load and enduring all this anguish, which was even as an ocean that hurleth its waves to high heaven – His reason for putting on the heavy iron chains and for becoming the very embodiment of utter resignation and meekness, was to lead every soul on earth to concord, to fellow-feeling, to oneness; to make known amongst all peoples the sign of the singleness of God, so that at last the primal oneness deposited at the heart of all created things would bear its destined fruit, and the splendour of 'No difference canst thou see in the creation of the God of Mercy' [Qur'án 67:3] would cast abroad its rays.[529]

'Abdu'l-Bahá

When Bahá'u'lláh had such persecutions to bear, God forbid that we should look for anything but suffering, hardship and pain.[530]

Attributed to 'Abdu'l-Bahá

Let not obstacles and disappointments, which are inevitable, dishearten you and whenever you are faced with trials recall our Beloved's innumerable sufferings.[531]

Shoghi Effendi

## The sufferings of Bahá'u'lláh

How grievously Bahá'u'lláh suffered to regenerate the world!

Wrongly accused, imprisoned, beaten, chained, banished from country to country, betrayed, poisoned, stripped of material possession, and 'at every moment tormented with a fresh torment': such was the cruel reception that greeted the Everlasting Father, Him Who is the Possessor of all Names and Attributes. For two score years, until the end of His earthly days, He remained a prisoner and exile – persecuted unceasingly by the rulers of Persia and the Ottoman Empire, opposed relentlessly by a vicious and scheming clergy, neglected abjectly by other sovereigns to whom He addressed potent letters imparting to them that which, in His truth-bearing words, 'is the cause of the well-being, the unity, the harmony, and the reconstruction of the world, and of the tranquillity of the nations'. 'My grief', He once lamented, 'exceedeth all the woes to which Jacob gave vent, and all the afflictions of Job are but a part of My sorrows.'

The voice halts for shame from continuing so deplorable a recitation, the heart is torn by mere thought of the Divine Target of such grief – grief no ordinary mortal could endure. But lest we give way to feelings of gloom and distress, we take recourse in the tranquil calm He induces with such meaningful words as these: 'We have borne it all with the utmost willingness and resignation, so that the souls of men may be edified, and the Word of God be exalted.' Thus, the Wronged One, patient beyond measure, preserved a majestic composure, revealing His true Self as the Merciful, the Loving, the Incomparable Friend. Concentrating His energies on the pivotal purpose of His Revelation, He transmuted His tribulations into instruments of redemption and summoned all peoples to the banner of unity . . .[532]

*The Universal House of Justice*

*Solutions to Tests:*

# Consultation

# Consultation

The Great Being saith: The heaven of divine wisdom is illumined with the two luminaries of consultation and compassion. Take ye counsel together in all matters, inasmuch as consultation is the lamp of guidance which leadeth the way, and is the bestower of understanding.[533]

*Bahá'u'lláh*

No welfare and no well-being can be attained except through consultation.[534]

*Bahá'u'lláh*

Consultation bestoweth greater awareness and transmuteth conjecture into certitude. It is a shining light which, in a dark world, leadeth the way and guideth. For everything there is and will continue to be a station of perfection and maturity. The maturity of the gift of understanding is made manifest through consultation.[535]

*Bahá'u'lláh*

## Take no important step without consultation

Settle all things, both great and small, by consultation. Without prior consultation, take no important step in your own personal affairs.[536]

*'Abdu'l-Bahá*

Regarding thy question about consultation of a father with his son, or a son with his father, in matters of trade and com-

merce, consultation is one of the fundamental elements of the
foundation of the Law of God. Such consultation is assuredly
acceptable, whether between father and son, or with others.
There is nothing better than this. Man must consult in all
things for this will lead him to the depths of each problem and
enable him to find the right solution.[537]

'Abdu'l-Bahá

## Consult with others to devise solutions

The question of consultation is of the utmost importance, and
is one of the most potent instruments conducive to the tranquillity and felicity of the people. For example, when a believer
is uncertain about his affairs, or when he seeketh to pursue a
project or trade, the friends should gather together and devise
a solution for him. He, in his turn, should act accordingly.
Likewise in larger issues, when a problem ariseth, or a difficulty occurreth, the wise should gather, consult, and devise a
solution. They should then rely upon the one true God, and
surrender to His Providence, in whatever way it may be revealed, for divine confirmations will undoubtedly assist. Consultation, therefore, is one of the explicit ordinances of the
Lord of mankind.[538]

'Abdu'l-Bahá

## The views of several preferable to one

The purpose of consultation is to show that the views of several
individuals are assuredly preferable to one man, even as the
power of a number of men is of course greater than the power
of one man.[539]

'Abdu'l-Bahá

## Consult with friends and spiritual assemblies

We are often told by the Master that under such circumstances
we should consult our friends, especially the Assemblies, and

seek their advice. It would be nice if you should follow that advice and take some of the friends into your confidence. Maybe God's will is best attained through consultation.[540]

*Written on behalf of Shoghi Effendi*

With proper consultation some method is sure to be found. There is no need to wait until an Assembly is constituted to start consulting. The view of two earnest souls is always better than one.[541]

*Written on behalf of Shoghi Effendi*

## Consult with professionals

The Guardian advises that you should refer to other doctors, and follow the majority vote.[542]

*Written on behalf of Shoghi Effendi*

As you know Bahá'u'lláh has ordained that in case of illness we should always consult the most competent physicians. And this is exactly what the Guardian strongly advises you to do. For prayer alone is not sufficient. To render it more effective we have to make use of all the physical and material advantages which God has given us. Healing through purely spiritual forces is undoubtedly as inadequate as that which materialist physicians and thinkers vainly seek to obtain by resorting entirely to mechanical devices and methods. The best result can be obtained by combining the two processes, spiritual and physical.[543]

*Written on behalf of Shoghi Effendi*

## Consult with psychiatrists

Psychiatric treatment in general is no doubt an important contribution to medicine, but we must believe it is still a growing rather than a perfected science. As Bahá'u'lláh has urged us to avail ourselves of the help of good physicians Bahá'ís are certainly not only free to turn to psychiatry for assistance but should, when advisable, do so. This does not mean psychiatrists are always wise or always right, it means we are free to avail ourselves of the best medicine has to offer us.[544]

*Written on behalf of Shoghi Effendi*

Psychology is still a very young and inexact science, and as the years go by Bahá'í psychologists, who know from the teachings of Bahá'u'lláh the true pattern of human life, will be able to make great strides in the development of this science, and will help profoundly in the alleviation of human suffering.[545]

*The Universal House of Justice*

## Consult professional counsellors

The House of Justice is distressed to learn that you and your husband are continuing to experience marital difficulties. It has frequently advised believers in such situations to turn to the Spiritual Assemblies for advice and counsel, and to follow this advice in their efforts to preserve the unity of their marital relationship. It has been found useful in many instances to also seek the assistance of competent professional marriage counsellors, who can provide useful insights and guidance in the use of constructive measures to bring about a greater degree of unity.[546]

*Written on behalf of the Universal House of Justice*

Neither you nor your husband should hesitate to continue consulting professional marriage counsellors, individually and together if possible, and also to take advantage of the supportive counselling which can come from wise and mature friends. Non-Bahá'í counselling can be useful but it is usually necessary to temper it with Bahá'í insight.[547]

*Written on behalf of the Universal House of Justice*

## The options that are available to us

A Bahá'í who has a problem may wish to make his own decision upon it after prayer and after weighing all the aspects of it in his own mind; he may prefer to seek the counsel of individual friends or of professional counsellors such as his doctor or lawyer so that he can consider such advice when making his decision; or in a case where several people are involved, such as a family situation, he may want to gather together those who are affected so that they may arrive at a collective decision.[548]

*Written on behalf of the Universal House of Justice*

*Solutions to Tests:*

*Ask Forgiveness from God*

# Ask Forgiveness from God

O Son of Being! Bring thyself to account each day ere thou art summoned to a reckoning; for death, unheralded, shall come upon thee and thou shalt be called to give account for thy deeds.[549]

*Bahá'u'lláh*

## God's mercy surpasses His wrath

. . . return ye to God and repent, that He, through His grace, may have mercy upon you, may wash away your sins, and forgive your trespasses. The greatness of His mercy surpasseth the fury of His wrath, and His grace encompasseth all who have been called into being and been clothed with the robe of life, be they of the past or of the future.[550]

*Bahá'u'lláh*

He Who is the Eternal Truth knoweth well what the breasts of men conceal. His long forbearance hath emboldened His creatures, for not until the appointed time is come will He rend any veil asunder. His surpassing mercy hath restrained the fury of His wrath, and caused most people to imagine that the one true God is unaware of the things they have privily committed. By Him Who is the All-Knowing, the All-Informed! The mirror of His knowledge reflecteth, with complete distinctness, precision and fidelity, the doings of all men. Say: Praise be to Thee, O Concealer of the sins of the weak and helpless! Magnified be Thy name, O Thou that forgivest the heedless ones that trespass against Thee![551]

*Bahá'u'lláh*

## We must bring ourselves to account before God

Set before thine eyes God's unerring Balance and, as one standing in His Presence, weigh in that Balance thine actions every day, every moment of thy life. Bring thyself to account ere thou art summoned to a reckoning, on the Day when no man shall have strength to stand for fear of God, the Day when the hearts of the heedless ones shall be made to tremble.[552]

*Bahá'u'lláh*

## God's distress over our sins

Every time My name 'the All-Merciful' was told that one of My lovers had breathed a word that runneth counter to My wish, it repaired, grief-stricken and disconsolate to its abode; and whenever My name 'the Concealer' discovered that one of My followers had inflicted any shame or humiliation on his neighbour, it, likewise, turned back chagrined and sorrowful to its retreats of glory, and there wept and mourned with a sore lamentation. And whenever My name 'the Ever-Forgiving' perceived that any one of My friends had committed any transgression, it cried out in its great distress, and, overcome with anguish, fell upon the dust, and was borne away by a company of the invisible angels to its habitation in the realms above.

. . . Every time the sin committed by any one amongst them was breathed in the Court of His Presence, the Ancient Beauty would be so filled with shame as to wish He could hide the glory of His countenance from the eyes of all men, for He hath, at all times, fixed His gaze on their fidelity, and observed its essential requisites.[553]

*Bahá'u'lláh*

## A special prayer for forgiveness

When the sinner findeth himself wholly detached and freed from all save God, he should beg forgiveness and pardon from

Him . . . The sinner should, between himself and God, implore mercy from the Ocean of mercy, beg forgiveness from the Heaven of generosity and say:

O God, my God! I implore Thee by the blood of Thy true lovers who were so enraptured by Thy sweet utterance that they hastened unto the Pinnacle of Glory, the site of the most glorious martyrdom, and I beseech Thee by the mysteries which lie enshrined in Thy knowledge and by the pearls that are treasured in the ocean of Thy bounty to grant forgiveness unto me and unto my father and my mother. Of those who show forth mercy, Thou art in truth the Most Merciful. No God is there but Thee, the Ever-Forgiving, the All-Bountiful.

O Lord! Thou seest this essence of sinfulness turning unto the ocean of Thy favour and this feeble one seeking the kingdom of Thy divine power and this poor creature inclining himself towards the day-star of Thy wealth. By Thy mercy and Thy grace, disappoint him not, O Lord, nor debar him from the revelations of Thy bounty in Thy days, nor cast him away from Thy door which Thou hast opened wide to all that dwell in Thy heaven and on Thine earth.

Alas! Alas! My sins have prevented me from approaching the Court of Thy holiness and my trespasses have caused me to stray far from the Tabernacle of Thy majesty. I have committed that which Thou didst forbid me to do and have put away what Thou didst order me to observe.

I pray Thee by Him Who is the sovereign Lord of Names to write down for me with the Pen of Thy bounty that which will enable me to draw nigh unto Thee and will purge me from my trespasses which have intervened between me and Thy forgiveness and Thy pardon.

Verily, Thou art the Potent, the Bountiful. No God is there but Thee, the Mighty, the Gracious.[554]

*Bahá'u'lláh*

## God has forgiven what is past

We exhort you, O peoples of the world, to observe that which will elevate your station. Hold fast to the fear of God and firmly adhere to what is right. Verily I say, the tongue is for mentioning what is good, defile it not with unseemly talk. God hath forgiven what is past. Henceforward everyone should utter that which is meet and seemly, and should refrain from slander, abuse and whatever causeth sadness in men.[555]

*Bahá'u'lláh*

## That God may conceal our sins

If ye become aware of a sin committed by another, conceal it, that God may conceal your own sin.[556]

*Bahá'u'lláh*

## The greatness of God's mercy

My God, my God! If none be found to stray from Thy path, how, then, can the ensign of Thy mercy be unfurled, or the banner of Thy bountiful favour be hoisted? And if iniquity be not committed, what is it that can proclaim Thee to be the Concealer of men's sins, the Ever-Forgiving, the Omniscient, the All-Wise? May my soul be a sacrifice to the trespasses of them that trespass against Thee, for upon such trespasses are wafted the sweet savours of the tender mercies of Thy Name, the Compassionate, the All-Merciful. May my life be laid down for the transgressions of such as transgress against Thee, for through them the breath of Thy grace and the fragrance of Thy loving-kindness are made known and diffused amongst men. May my inmost being be offered up for the sins of them that have sinned against Thee, for it is as a result of such sins that the Day Star of Thy manifold favours revealeth itself above the horizon of Thy bounty, and the clouds of Thy never-failing providence rain down their gifts upon the realities of all created things.[557]

*Bahá'u'lláh*

O Thou forgiving Lord! Thou art the shelter of all these Thy servants. Thou knowest the secrets and art aware of all things.

We are all helpless, and Thou art the Mighty, the Omnipotent. We are all sinners, and Thou art the Forgiver of sins, the Merciful, the Compassionate. O Lord! Look not at our shortcomings. Deal with us according to Thy grace and bounty. Our shortcomings are many, but the ocean of Thy forgiveness is boundless. Our weakness is grievous, but the evidences of Thine aid and assistance are clear.[558]

*'Abdu'l-Bahá*

*Solutions to Tests:*

# *Develop the Fear of God*

# Develop the Fear of God

Verily I say: The fear of God hath ever been a sure defence and a safe stronghold for all the peoples of the world. It is the chief cause of the protection of mankind, and the supreme instrument for its preservation. Indeed, there existeth in man a faculty which deterreth him from, and guardeth him against, whatever is unworthy and unseemly, and which is known as his sense of shame. This, however, is confined to but a few; all have not possessed and do not possess it.[559]

*Bahá'u'lláh*

In formulating the principles and laws a part hath been devoted to penalties which form an effective instrument for the security and protection of men. However, dread of the penalties maketh people desist only outwardly from committing vile and contemptible deeds, while that which guardeth and restraineth man both outwardly and inwardly hath been and still is the fear of God. It is man's true protector and his spiritual guardian. It behoveth him to cleave tenaciously unto that which will lead to the appearance of this supreme bounty.[560]

*Bahá'u'lláh*

O Jalíl! Admonish men to fear God. By God! This fear is the chief commander of the army of thy Lord. Its hosts are a praiseworthy character and goodly deeds. Through it have the cities of men's hearts been opened throughout the ages and centuries, and the standards of ascendancy and triumph raised above all other standards.[561]

*Bahá'u'lláh*

Verily I say, fear of God is the greatest commander that can render the Cause of God victorious, and the hosts which best befit this commander have ever been and are an upright character and pure and goodly deeds.[562]

*Bahá'u'lláh*

In truth, religion is a radiant light and an impregnable stronghold for the protection and welfare of the peoples of the world, for the fear of God impelleth man to hold fast to that which is good, and shun all evil.[563]

*Bahá'u'lláh*

## Be afraid of none but God

Whoso hath known God shall know none but Him, and he that feareth God shall be afraid of no one except Him, though the powers of the whole earth rise up and be arrayed against him.[564]

*Bahá'u'lláh*

Verily, the wayfarer who journeyeth unto God, unto the Crimson Pillar in the snow-white path, will never reach unto his heavenly goal unless he abandoneth all that men possess: 'And if he feareth not God, God will make him to fear all things; whereas all things fear him who feareth God.'[565]

*Bahá'u'lláh*

## The importance of the fear of God

You ask him about the fear of God: perhaps the friends do not realize that the majority of human beings need the element of fear in order to discipline their conduct? Only a relatively very highly evolved soul would always be disciplined by love alone. Fear of punishment, fear of the anger of God if we do evil, are needed to keep people's feet on the right path. Of course we should love God – but we must fear Him in the sense of a child fearing the righteous anger and chastisement of a parent; not cringe before Him as before a tyrant, but know His Mercy exceeds His Justice![566]

*Written on behalf of Shoghi Effendi*

As regards the passages in the sacred writings indicating the wrath of God; Shoghi Effendi says that the Divinity has many attributes:  He is loving and merciful but also just. Just as reward and punishment, according to Bahá'u'lláh, are the pillars upon which society rests, so mercy and justice may be considered as their counterpart in the world to come. Should we disobey God and work against His commands He will view our acts in the light of justice and punish us for it. That punishment may not be in the form of fire, as some believe, but in the form of spiritual deprivation and degradation. This is why we read so often in the prayers statements such as 'God do not deal with us with justice, but rather through thy infinite mercy.' The wrath of God is in the administration of His justice, both in this world and in the world to come. A God that is only loving or only just is not a perfect God. The divinity has to possess both of these aspects as every father ought to express both in his attitude towards his children. If we ponder a while, we will see that our welfare can be insured only when both of these divine attributes are equally emphasized and practised.[567]

*Written on behalf of Shoghi Effendi*

## Understanding the fear of God

In explaining the fear of God to children, there is no objection to teaching it as 'Abdu'l-Bahá so often taught everything, in the form of parables. Also the child should be made to understand that we don't fear God because He is cruel, but we fear

Him because He is Just, and, if we do wrong and deserve to be punished, then in His Justice He may see fit to punish us. We must both love God and fear Him.[568]

*Written on behalf of Shoghi Effendi*

*Readings for Comfort during Illness*

# Readings for Comfort during Illness

Thy name is my healing, O my God, and remembrance of Thee is my remedy. Nearness to Thee is my hope, and love for Thee is my companion. Thy mercy to me is my healing and my succor in both this world and the world to come. Thou, verily, art the All-Bountiful, the All-Knowing, the All-Wise.[569]

*Bahá'u'lláh*

. . . the remembrance of Thee is a healing medicine to the hearts of such as have drawn nigh unto Thy court . . . [570]

*Bahá'u'lláh*

## The soul is exalted above illness

Know thou that the soul of man is exalted above, and is independent of all infirmities of body or mind. That a sick person showeth signs of weakness is due to the hindrances that interpose themselves between his soul and his body, for the soul itself remaineth unaffected by any bodily ailments.[571]

*Bahá'u'lláh*

## The power of the long healing prayer

. . . protect the bearer of this blessed Tablet, and whoso reciteth it, and whoso cometh upon it, and whoso passeth around the house wherein it is. Heal Thou, then, by it every sick, diseased and poor one, from every tribulation and distress, from every loathsome affliction and sorrow, and guide Thou by it whosoever desireth to enter upon the paths of Thy guidance, and the ways of Thy forgiveness and grace.[572]

*Bahá'u'lláh*

## Ill health is an unavoidable condition

Although ill health is one of the unavoidable conditions of man, truly it is hard to bear. The bounty of good health is the greatest of all gifts.[573]

*'Abdu'l-Bahá*

O thou maid-servant of God!

Although in body thou art weak and ill and, like unto Job, the object of many trials, yet (Praise be to God!) thou art strong in spirit and in the utmost health and joyousness. The peculiarities of this physical world are illness and diseases, and the essences of the universe of God are health and vigour. The body is like unto the lamp and the spirit is like unto the light. Praise be to God, that the light is in the utmost brilliancy no matter if the lamp is somewhat affected.[574]

*'Abdu'l-Bahá*

## Illnesses do not affect the spirit

Often physical sickness draws man nearer unto his Maker, suffers his heart to be made empty of all worldly desires until it becomes tender and sympathetic toward all sufferers and compassionate to all creatures. Although physical diseases cause man to suffer temporarily, yet they do not touch his spirit. Nay, rather, they contribute toward the divine purpose; that is, spiritual susceptibilities will be created in his heart.[575]

*Attributed to 'Abdu'l-Bahá*

## Unless the spirit is healed

Unless the spirit be healed, the cure of the body is worth nothing. All is in the hands of God, and without Him there can be no health in us![576]

*'Abdu'l-Bahá*

## Physical and spiritual healing

Illnesses which occur by reason of physical causes should be treated by doctors with medical remedies; those which are due to spiritual causes disappear through spiritual means. Thus an illness caused by affliction, fear, nervous impressions, will be healed more effectively by spiritual rather than by physical treatment. Hence, both kinds of treatment should be followed; they are not contradictory. Therefore thou shouldst also accept physical remedies inasmuch as these too have come from the mercy and favour of God, Who hath revealed and made manifest medical science so that His servants may profit from this kind of treatment also. Thou shouldst give equal attention to spiritual treatments, for they produce marvellous effects.[577]

*'Abdu'l-Bahá*

With regard to your question concerning spiritual healing. Such a healing constitutes, indeed, one of the most effective methods of relieving a person from either his mental or physical pains and sufferings. 'Abdu'l-Bahá has in His *Paris Talks* emphasized its importance by stating that it should be used as an essential means for effecting a complete physical cure. Spiritual healing, however, is not and cannot be a substitute for material healing, but it is a most valuable adjunct to it. Both are, indeed, essential and complementary.[578]

*Written on behalf of Shoghi Effendi*

With reference to your question concerning spiritual healing: Its importance, as you surely know, has been greatly emphasized by 'Abdu'l-Bahá, Who considered it, indeed, as an essential part of physical processes of healing. Physical healing cannot be complete and lasting unless it is reinforced by spiritual healing. And this last one can be best obtained through obedience to the laws and commandments of God as revealed to us through His Manifestations. Individual believers, however, can also help by imparting healing to others. But the success of their efforts depends entirely on their strict adherence to the Teachings, and also on the manner in which they impart them to others. According to Bahá'u'lláh man cannot obtain full guidance directly from God. He must rather seek it through His Prophets.[579]

*Written on behalf of Shoghi Effendi*

## Sometimes healing may not be right for the patient

The prayers which were revealed to ask for healing apply both to physical and spiritual healing. Recite them, then, to heal both the soul and the body. If healing is right for the patient, it will certainly be granted; but for some ailing persons, healing would only be the cause of other ills, and therefore wisdom doth not permit an affirmative answer to the prayer.[580]

*'Abdu'l-Bahá*

## Consult a competent physician

According to the explicit decree of Bahá'u'lláh one must not turn aside from the advice of a competent doctor. It is imperative to consult one even if the patient himself be a well-known and eminent physician. In short, the point is that you should maintain your health by consulting a highly-skilled physician.[581]

*'Abdu'l-Bahá*

It is incumbent upon everyone to seek medical treatment and to follow the doctor's instructions, for this is in compliance with the divine ordinance, but, in reality, He Who giveth healing is God.[582]

*'Abdu'l-Bahá*

## Happiness is a great healer

We should all visit the sick. When they are in sorrow and

suffering, it is a real help and benefit to have a friend come. Happiness is a great healer to those who are ill. In the East it is the custom to call upon the patient often and meet him individually. The people in the East show the utmost kindness and compassion to the sick and suffering. This has greater effect than the remedy itself. You must always have this thought of love and affection when you visit the ailing and afflicted.[583]

*'Abdu'l-Bahá*

You must be happy always. You must be counted among the people of joy and happiness and must be adorned with divine morals. In a large measure happiness keeps our health while depression of spirit begets disease.[584]

*Attributed to 'Abdu'l-Bahá*

## We have the Faith to sustain us

Cancer is such a terrible scourge in the world today! But when the believers are called upon to go through such bitter ordeals they have the Faith to sustain them, the love of their Bahá'í friends to comfort them, and the glorious words of Bahá'u'lláh regarding immortality to give them confidence and courage. Blessed are we, indeed, even, in the midst of our greatest trials.[585]

*Written on behalf of Shoghi Effendi*

## Do not take a defeatist attitude

There are a great many as you know mental diseases and troubles at present, and the one thing Bahá'ís must not do is take a defeatist attitude toward them. The power in the Faith is such that it can sustain us on a much higher level in spite of whatever our ailments might be, than other people who are denied it. This however does not mean that we should ignore medical opinion and treatment. On the contrary, we should do our best to procure the opinion of specialists and competent doctors.[586]

*Written on behalf of Shoghi Effendi*

## Illness has no effect on the spirit

It is very hard to be subject to any illness, particularly a mental one. However, we must always remember these illnesses have nothing to do with our spirit or our inner relation to God. It is a great pity that as yet so little is really known of the mind, its workings and the illnesses that afflict it; no doubt, as the world becomes more spiritually minded and scientists understand the true nature of man, more humane and permanent cures for mental diseases will be found.

. . . You must always remember, no matter how much you or others may be afflicted with mental troubles and the crushing environment of these State Institutions, that your spirit is healthy, near to our Beloved, and will in the next world enjoy a happy and normal state of soul. Let us hope in the meantime scientists will find better and permanent cures for the mentally afflicted. But in this world such illness is truly a heavy burden to bear![587]

*Written on behalf of Shoghi Effendi*

## Do not feel inferior because of a disability

He [the Guardian] does not feel you should permit your speech impediment to give you a sense of inferiority. Moses stammered! And what you are and what you believe as a Bahá'í give you a tremendous advantage over others. This does not mean that you should not make every effort to overcome it, and go to doctors for advice and assistance. He also assures you he will pray that you may overcome this difficulty entirely, also that wherever you are the way will open for you to teach and serve the Faith.[588]

*Written on behalf of Shoghi Effendi*

## Physical pain is unavoidable but there is wisdom in suffering

As to your question concerning the meaning of physical suffering and its relation to mental and spiritual healing. Physical pain is a necessary accompaniment of all human existence, and as such is unavoidable. As long as there will be life on earth, there will be also suffering, in various forms and degrees. But suffering, although an inescapable reality, can nevertheless be utilized as a means for the attainment of happiness. This is the interpretation given to it by all the prophets and saints who, in the midst of severe tests and trials, felt happy and joyous and experienced what is best and holiest in life. Suffering is both a reminder and a guide. It stimulates us better to adapt ourselves to our environmental conditions, and thus leads the way to self improvement. In every suffering one can find a meaning and a wisdom. But it is not always easy to find the secret of that wisdom. It is sometimes only when all our suffering has passed that we become aware of its usefulness. What man considers to be evil turns often to be a cause of infinite blessings. And this is due to his desire to know more than he can. God's wisdom is, indeed, inscrutable to us all, and it is no use pushing too far trying to discover that which shall always remain a mystery to our mind.[589]

*Written on behalf of Shoghi Effendi*

## Illness may be for the development of ourselves or others

The Beloved Guardian has asked me to assure you and the parents of the dear baby of his prayers for his healing, both material and spiritual.

It is difficult for us to understand these calamities when they come to us. Those who are firm in the Faith, know that the Hand of God protects them, and if something of this nature comes upon them, it is for some reason, which may have to do with the spiritual development of the one affected, or the spiritual development and welfare of the loved ones; or even for the melting of the hearts of non-Bahá'ís, who will be affected by the Divine Spirit, through the manner in which the Bahá'í meets such an ordeal.[590]

*Written on behalf of Shoghi Effendi*

## Concerning mental illness

It is not easy to be burdened with long years of mental illness such as you describe. And plainly you have sought aid from many persons of scientific and non-scientific training backgrounds, apparently to little avail over the years of your prolonged illness. Possibly you should consider, if it is feasible, consulting the best specialists in a medical centre in one of the major cities, where the most advanced diagnosis and treatment can be obtained. The science of the mind, of normality and of the disabilities from which it may suffer, is in its relative infancy, but much may be possible to aid you to minimize your suffering and make possible an active life. The last ten years in the therapy of mental disorders has seen important advances from which you may well benefit.

Your discovery of the Faith, of its healing Writings and its great purposes for the individual and for all mankind, have indeed brought to you a powerful force toward a healthy life which will sustain you on a higher level, whatever your ailment may be. The best results for the healing process are to combine the spiritual with the physical, for it should be possible for you to overcome your illness through the combined and sustained power of prayer and of determined effort.[591]

*Written on behalf of the Universal House of Justice*

. . . mental illness is not spiritual, although its effects may indeed hinder and be a burden in one's striving toward spiritual progress. In a letter written on behalf of the Guardian to a believer there is this further passage: 'Such hindrances (i.e. illness and outer difficulties), no matter how severe and insuperable they may at first seem, can and should be effectively overcome through the combined and sustained power of prayer and of determined and continued effort.'

That effort can include the counsel of wise and experienced physicians, including psychiatrists. Working for the Faith, serving others who may need you, and giving of yourself can aid you in your struggle to overcome your sufferings. One helpful activity is, of course, striving to teach the Cause in spite of personal feelings of shortcomings, thus allowing the healing words of the Cause to flood your mind with their grace and positive power.[592]

*Written on behalf of the Universal House of Justice*

*Concerning Death*

# Concerning Death

O Son of the Supreme! I have made death a messenger of joy to thee. Wherefore dost thou grieve? I made the light to shed on thee its splendour. Why dost thou veil thyself therefrom?[593]

*Bahá'u'lláh*

## The progress of the soul

Know thou of a truth that the soul, after its separation from the body, will continue to progress until it attaineth the presence of God, in a state and condition which neither the revolution of ages and centuries, nor the changes and chances of this world, can alter. It will endure as long as the Kingdom of God, His sovereignty, His dominion and power will endure. It will manifest the signs of God and His attributes, and will reveal His loving kindness and bounty. The movement of My Pen is stilled when it attempteth to befittingly describe the loftiness and glory of so exalted a station. The honour with which the Hand of Mercy will invest the soul is such as no tongue can adequately reveal, nor any other earthly agency describe.[594]

*Bahá'u'lláh*

To consider that after the death of the body the spirit perishes is like imagining that a bird in a cage will be destroyed if the cage is broken, though the bird has nothing to fear from the destruction of the cage. Our body is like the cage, and the spirit is like the bird. We see that without the cage this bird flies in the world of sleep; therefore, if the cage becomes broken, the bird will continue and exist. Its feelings will be even more powerful, its perceptions greater, and its happiness increased. In truth, from hell it reaches a paradise of delights because for the thankful birds there is no paradise greater than freedom from the cage. That is why with utmost joy and happiness the martyrs hasten to the plain of sacrifice.[595]

*'Abdu'l-Bahá*

The progress of man's spirit in the divine world, after the severance of its connection with the body of dust, is through the bounty and grace of the Lord alone, or through the intercession and the sincere prayers of other human souls, or through the charities and important good works which are performed in its name.[596]

*'Abdu'l-Bahá*

When the human soul soareth out of this transient heap of dust and riseth into the world of God, then veils will fall away, and verities will come to light, and all things unknown before will be made clear, and hidden truths be understood.

Consider how a being, in the world of the womb, was deaf of ear and blind of eye, and mute of tongue; how he was bereft of any perceptions at all. But once, out of that world of darkness, he passed into this world of light, then his eye saw, his ear heard, his tongue spoke. In the same way, once he hath hastened away from this mortal place into the Kingdom of God, then he will be born in the spirit; then the eye of his perception will open, the ear of his soul will hearken, and all the truths of which he was ignorant before will be made plain and clear.[597]

*'Abdu'l-Bahá*

## Our spiritual connection with those who have passed on

As we have power to pray for these souls here, so likewise we shall possess the same power in the other world, which is the Kingdom of God. Are not all the people in that world the creatures of God? Therefore, in that world also they can make progress. As here they can receive light by their supplications, there also they can plead for forgiveness and receive light through entreaties and supplications. Thus as souls in this world, through the help of the supplications, the entreaties and the prayers of the holy ones, can acquire development, so is it the same after death.[598]

*'Abdu'l-Bahá*

Why shouldst thou be sad and heartbroken? This separation is temporal; this remoteness and sorrow is counted only by days. Thou shalt find him in the Kingdom of God and thou wilt attain to the everlasting union. Physical companionship is ephemeral, but heavenly association is eternal. Whenever thou rememberest the eternal and never ending union, thou wilt be comforted and blissful.[599]

*'Abdu'l-Bahá*

## On the death of a child

I have been greatly affected by the death of Mr Sandy Kinney. What a lovely child he was. On my behalf say to Mr and Mrs Kinney: 'Do not grieve, and do not lament. That tender and lovely shrub has been transferred from this world to the rose-garden of the Kingdom and that longing dove has flown to the divine nest. That candle has been extinguished in this nether world that it may be rekindled in the Supreme Concourse. Ye shall assuredly meet him face to face in the world of mysteries at the assemblage of Light.'[600]

*'Abdu'l-Bahá*

Be not sorrowful on account of the departure of thy good son. He hath indeed departed from this narrow and gloomy world which is darkened by unlimited sorrow, unto the Kingdom which is spacious, illumined, joyous and beautiful. God delivered him from this dark well and promoted him unto the Supreme Height! He gave him wings whereby he soared to the heaven of happiness. Verily this is the great mercy from Him who is precious and forgiving.[601]

'Abdu'l-Bahá

The death of that beloved youth and his separation from you have caused the utmost sorrow and grief; for he winged his flight in the flower of his age and the bloom of his youth to the heavenly nest. But he hath been freed from this sorrow-stricken shelter and hath turned his face toward the everlasting nest of the Kingdom, and, being delivered from a dark and narrow world, hath hastened to the sanctified realm of light; therein lieth the consolation of our hearts.

The inscrutable divine wisdom underlieth such heart-rending occurrences. It is as if a kind gardener transferreth a fresh and tender shrub from a confined place to a wide open area. This transfer is not the cause of the withering, the lessening or the destruction of that shrub; nay, on the contrary, it maketh it to grow and thrive, acquire freshness and delicacy, become green and bear fruit. This hidden secret is well known to the gardener, but those souls who are unaware of this bounty suppose that the gardener, in his anger and wrath, hath uprooted the shrub. Yet to those who are aware, this concealed fact is manifest, and this predestined decree is considered a bounty. Do not feel grieved or disconsolate, therefore, at the ascension of that bird of faithfulness; nay, under all circumstances pray for that youth, supplicating for him forgiveness and the elevation of his station.[602]

'Abdu'l-Bahá

## The wings of the soul

Be not grieved at the calamity which hath unexpectedly come upon thee and for the misfortune which heavily weigheth upon thee. It behooveth one like thee to endure every trial, to be pleased with the decree and to commit all thy affairs to God, so that thou mayest be a calm, approved and pleasing soul before God. Know thou, that thy beloved son hath soared, with the wing of soul, up to the loftiest height which is never-ending in the Kingdom of God. Rejoice at this great prosperity which the chosen ones were longingly asking from the Holy and Exalted Threshold (of God). Truly, I say unto thee, wert thou informed of the position in which is thy son, thy face would be illuminated by the lights of happiness and thou wouldst thank thy forgiving Lord therefor and thou wouldst long for ascending to that praiseworthy position.[603]

*'Abdu'l-Bahá*

As to those souls who are born into this life as ethereal and radiant entities and yet, on account of their handicaps and trials, are deprived of great and real advantages, and leave the world without having lived to the full – certainly this is a cause for grieving. This is the reason why the universal Manifestations of God unveil Their countenances to man, and endure every calamity and sore affliction, and lay down Their lives as a ransom; it is to make these very people, the ready ones, the ones who have capacity, to become dawning points of light, and to bestow upon them the life that fadeth never. This is the true sacrifice: the offering of oneself, even as did Christ, as a ransom for the life of the world.[604]

*'Abdu'l-Bahá*

A friend asked: 'How should one look forward to death?'

'Abdu'l-Bahá answered: 'How does one look forward to the goal of any journey? With hope and with expectation. It is even so with the end of this earthly journey. In the next world, man will find himself freed from many of the disabilities under which he now suffers. Those who have passed on through death, have a sphere of their own. It is not removed from ours; their work, the work of the Kingdom, is ours; but it is sanctified from what we call 'time and place'. Time with us is measured by the sun. When there is no more sunrise, and no more sunset, that kind of time does not exist for man. Those who have ascended have different attributes from those who are still on earth, yet there is no real separation.

'In prayer there is a mingling of station, a mingling of condition. Pray for them as they pray for you!'[605]

*'Abdu'l-Bahá*

## They pray for us as we pray for them

If you have a bed of lilies of the valley that you love and tenderly care for, they cannot see you, nor can they understand your care, nevertheless, because of that tender care, they flourish.

So it is with your husband. You cannot see him, but his loving influence surrounds you, cares for you, watches over you. They, who have passed into the Divine Garden, pray for us there, as we pray for them here.[606]

*Attributed to 'Abdu'l-Bahá*

. . . sincere prayer always has its effect, and it has a great influence in the other world. We are never cut off from those who are there. The real and genuine influence is not in this world but in that other.[607]

*Attributed to 'Abdu'l-Bahá*

## Spiritual conversation

'Can a departed soul converse with someone still on earth?'

Answer: 'A conversation can be held, but not as our conversation. There is no doubt that the forces of the higher worlds interplay with the forces of this plane. The heart of man is open to inspiration; this is spiritual communication. As in a dream one talks with a friend while the mouth is silent, so is it in the conversation of the spirit.[608]

*'Abdu'l-Bahá*

# A state of being far nobler and more beautiful

You ask an explanation of what happens to us after we leave this world: This is a question which none of the Prophets have ever answered in detail, for the very simple reason that you cannot convey to a person's mind something entirely different from everything they have ever experienced. 'Abdu'l-Bahá gave the wonderful example of the relation of this life to the next life being like the child in the womb; it develops eyes, ears, hands, feet, a tongue, and yet it has nothing to see or hear, it cannot walk or grasp things or speak; all these faculties it is developing for this world. If you tried to explain to an embryo what this world is like it could never understand – but it understands when it is born, and its faculties can be used. So we cannot picture our state in the next world. All we know is that our consciousness, our personality, endures in some new state, and that that world is as much better than this one as this one is better than the dark womb of our mother was . . .[609]

*Written on behalf of Shoghi Effendi*

Such earnest souls, when they pass out of this life, enter a state of being far nobler and more beautiful than this one. We fear it only because it is unknown to us and we have little faith in the words of the Prophets who bring a true message of certainty from that realm of the spirit. We should face death with joy especially if our life upon this plane of existence has been full of good deeds.[610]

*Written on behalf of Shoghi Effendi*

Concerning your question whether a soul can receive knowledge of the Truth in the world beyond. Such a knowledge is surely possible, and is but a sign of the loving Mercy of the Almighty. We can, through our prayers, help every soul to gradually attain this high station, even if it has failed to reach it in this world. The progress of the soul does not come to an end with death. It rather starts along a new line. Bahá'u'lláh teaches that great and far-reaching possibilities await the soul in the other world. Spiritual progress in that realm is infinite, and no man, while on this earth, can visualize its full power and extent.[611]

*Written on behalf of Shoghi Effendi*

He [Shoghi Effendi] was very sorry to hear of the severe blows you have sustained through the loss of your children. We cannot understand such things; but we can, as Bahá'ís, bow our heads and say God knows the beginning and end of our paths in life, whereas we only see a section at a time and cannot judge clearly or wisely.[612]

*Written on behalf of Shoghi Effendi*

## The blessings of the other world

Bahá'u'lláh says that were we to have the proper vision to see the blessings of the other world we would not bear to endure one more hour of existence upon the earth. The reason why we are deprived of that vision is because otherwise no one would care to remain and the whole fabric of society will be destroyed.

Shoghi Effendi wishes you therefore to think of her blessings and rejoice in her happiness. Should we have true faith in the words of the prophets we would not fear death nor feel despondent over the passing of our loved ones.[613]

*Written on behalf of Shoghi Effendi*

In His Tablets Bahá'u'lláh says that were we able to comprehend the facilities that await us in the world to come, death would lose its sting; nay rather we would welcome it as a gateway to a realm immeasurably higher and nobler than this home of suffering we call our earth. You should therefore think of their blessings and comfort yourself for your momentary separation. In time all of us will join our departed ones and share their joys.[614]

*Written on behalf of Shoghi Effendi*

# Bibliography

'Abdu'l-Bahá. *Paris Talks*. London: Bahá'í Publishing Trust, 1979.
— *The Promulgation of Universal Peace*. Wilmette, Illinois: Bahá'í Publishing Trust, 2nd edn. 1982.
— *The Secret of Divine Civilization*. Wilmette, Illinois: Bahá'í Publishing Trust, 1957.
— *Selections from the Writings of 'Abdu'l-Bahá*. Haifa: Bahá'í World Centre, 1978.
— *Tablets of Abdul-Baha Abbas*. New York: Bahá'í Publishing Committee; vol. 1, 1930; vol. 2, 1940; vol. 3, 1930.
— *The Tablets of the Divine Plan*. Wilmette, Illinois: Bahá'í Publishing Trust, rev. edn. 1977.
The Báb. *Selections from the Writings of the Báb*. Haifa: Bahá'í World Centre, 1976.
*Bahá'í Prayers: A Selections of Prayers revealed by Bahá'u'lláh, the Báb and 'Abdu'l-Bahá*. Wilmette, Illinois: Bahá'í Publishing Trust, 1991.
*Bahá'í World, The.* vol. 18 (1979-83). Haifa: Bahá'í World Centre, 1986.
*Bahá'í World Faith*. Wilmette, Illinois: Bahá'í Publishing Trust, 2nd edn. 1976.
Bahá'u'lláh. *Epistle to the Son of the Wolf*. Wilmette, Illinois: Bahá'í Publishing Trust, 1988.
— *Gleanings from the Writings of Bahá'u'lláh*. Wilmette, Illinois: Bahá'í Publishing Trust, 1983.
— *The Hidden Words*. Wilmette, Illinois: Bahá'í Publishing Trust, 1990.
— *The Kitáb-i-Aqdas*. Haifa: Bahá'í World Centre, 1992.
— *Kitáb-i-Íqán*. Wilmette, Illinois: Bahá'í Publishing Trust, 1989.
— *Prayers and Meditations*. Wilmette, Illinois: Bahá'í Publishing Trust, 1987.
— *The Seven Valleys and the Four Valleys*. Wilmette, Illinois: Bahá'í Publishing Trust, 1991.

— *Tablets of Bahá'u'lláh.* Wilmette, Illinois: Bahá'í Publishing Trust, 1988.

*Bahíyyih Khánum, the Greatest Holy Leaf: A Compilation from Bahá'í Sacred Texts and Writings of the Guardian of the Faith and Bahíyyih Khánum's Own Letters.* Haifa: Bahá'í World Centre, 1982.

Balyuzi, H. M. *Eminent Bahá'ís in the Time of Bahá'u'lláh: with some Historical Background.* Oxford: George Ronald, 1985.

Blomfield, Lady [Sara Louise]. *The Chosen Highway.* Wilmette, Illinois: Bahá'í Publishing Trust, 1967.

*Compilation of Compilations, The.* Prepared by the Universal House of Justice 1963-1990. 2 vols. [Sydney]: Bahá'í Publications Australia, 1991.

*Diary of Juliet Thompson, The.* Los Angeles: Kalimát Press, 1983.

*Divine Art of Living, The: Selections from the Writings of Bahá'u'lláh and 'Abdu'l-Bahá.* Compiled by Mabel Hyde Paine, revised by Anne Marie Scheffer. Wilmette, Illinois: Bahá'í Publishing Trust, 1986.

Esslemont, J. E. *Bahá'u'lláh and the New Era.* London: Bahá'í Publishing Trust, 1974.

Gail, Marzieh. *Summon Up Remembrance.* Oxford: George Ronald, 1987.

*Lights of Guidance: A Bahá'í Reference File.* Compiled by Helen Hornby. New Delhi: Bahá'í Publishing Trust, 2nd edn. 1988.

*Living the Life.* London: Bahá'í Publishing Trust, 1984.

Maxwell, May. *An Early Pilgrimage.* Oxford: George Ronald, 1976.

Moffett, Ruth. *Du'á: On Wings of Prayer.* Happy Camp, California: Naturegraph Publishers, rev. edn. 1984.

Rutstein, Nathan. *Corinne True: Faithful Handmaid of 'Abdu'l-Bahá.* Oxford: George Ronald, 1987.

Shoghi Effendi. *The Advent of Divine Justice.* Wilmette, Illinois: Bahá'í Publishing Trust, 1990.

— *Arohanui: Letters of Shoghi Effendi to New Zealand.* Suva, Fiji: Bahá'í Publishing Trust, 1982.

— *Bahá'í Life.* Compiled by the Universal House of Justice. Wilmette, Illinois: Bahá'í Publishing Trust, 1981.

— *Citadel of Faith: Messages to America 1947-1957.* Wilmette, Illinois: Bahá'í Publishing Trust, 1965.

— *Dawn of a New Day: Messages to India 1923-1957*. New Delhi: Bahá'í Publishing Trust, 1970.
— *Directives from the Guardian*. New Delhi: Bahá'í Publishing Trust, 1973.
— *God Passes By*. Wilmette, Illinois: Bahá'í Publishing Trust, rev. edn. 1974.
— *High Endeavors: Messages to Alaska*. [Anchorage]: National Spiritual Assembly of the Bahá'ís of Alaska, 1976.
— *The Light of Divine Guidance: The Messages from the Guardian of the Bahá'í Faith to the Bahá'ís of Germany and Austria*. vol. 1. Hofheim-Langenhain: Bahá'í-Verlag, 1982.
— *Messages to Canada*. [Toronto]: National Spiritual Assembly of the Bahá'ís of Canada, 1965.
— *The Promised Day is Come*. Wilmette, Illinois: Bahá'í Publishing Trust, rev. edn. 1980.
— *The Unfolding Destiny of the British Bahá'í Community: The Messages of the Guardian of the Bahá'í Faith to the Bahá'ís of the British Isles*. London: Bahá'í Publishing Trust, 1981.
*Star of the West*. Rpt. Oxford: George Ronald, 1984.
*Throne of the Inner Temple, The*. Compiled by Elias Zohoori. Jamaica, 1985.
The Universal House of Justice. *A Wider Horizon: Selected Messages of the Universal House of Justice 1983-1992*. Riviera Beach, Florida: Palabra Publications, 1992.
— *Messages from the Universal House of Justice 1963:1986: The Third Epoch of the Formative Age*. Wilmette, Illinois: Bahá'í Publishing Trust, 1996.

# References

1. Bahá'u'lláh, *Gleanings*, p. 70.
2. ibid. p. 215.
3. 'Abdu'l-Bahá, *Promulgation*, pp. 225-6.
4. From a letter written on behalf of Shoghi Effendi to an individual believer, 14 December 1941. *Lights of Guidance*, no. 2039, p. 601.
5. From a letter written on behalf of Shoghi Effendi. Shoghi Effendi, *Unfolding Destiny*, p. 434.
6. Bahá'u'lláh, *Seven Valleys*, pp. 13-15.
7. 'Abdu'l-Bahá, *Paris Talks*, pp. 50-1.
8. Words attributed to 'Abdu'l-Bahá, quoted in Gail, *Summon Up Remembrance*, pp. 255-6.
9. From a letter written on behalf of Shoghi Effendi to an individual believer, 5 August 1949. *Lights of Guidance*, no. 1014, p. 297.
10. From a letter written on behalf of Shoghi Effendi to an individual believer, 25 February 1945.
11. From a letter written on behalf of the Universal House of Justice to an individual believer, 14 March 1985.
12. Bahá'u'lláh, *Hidden Words*, Arabic 48.
13. From a Tablet of 'Abdu'l-Bahá, quoted in *Star of the West*, vol. 14, no. 2, p. 41.
14. 'Abdu'l-Bahá, *Paris Talks*, p. 51.
15. 'Abdu'l-Bahá, *Tablets*, pp. 303-4.
16. 'Abdu'l-Bahá, *Selections*, p. 182.
17. Words attributed to 'Abdu'l-Bahá in answer to questions asked by Dr Edward Getsinger. *Star of the West*, vol. 6, no. 6, p. 45.
18. Shoghi Effendi, *Bahá'í Administration*, p. 50.
19. From a letter written on behalf of Shoghi Effendi to an individual believer, 14 December 1941. *Lights of Guidance*, no. 2039, p. 601.

20. From a letter written on behalf of Shoghi Effendi to an individual believer, 3 March 1943. *Lights of Guidance*, no. 2049, pp. 603-4.
21. From a letter written on behalf of the Universal House of Justice to an individual believer, 9 January 1977. *Lights of Guidance*, no. 1226, p. 366.
22. From a letter written on behalf of Shoghi Effendi to an individual believer, 6 October 1954. *Living the Life*, pp. 35-6.
23. From a letter written on behalf of Shoghi Effendi to an individual believer, 23 December 1948. Shoghi Effendi, *Unfolding Destiny*, p. 453.
24. From a letter written on behalf of Shoghi Effendi to an individual believer, 22 November 1936. *Compilation*, vol. 2, no. 1282, p. 7.
25. The Báb, *Selections*, p. 215.
26. ibid. p. 165.
27. 'Abdu'l-Bahá, *Selections*, p. 239.
28. 'Abdu'l-Bahá, *Paris Talks*, p. 178.
29. ibid. p. 110.
30. 'Abdu'l-Bahá, *Selections*, p. 81.
31. ibid. p. 200.
32. Bahá'u'lláh, *Hidden Words*, Arabic 50.
33. Bahá'u'lláh, *Gleanings*, p. 209.
34. Bahá'u'lláh, *Prayers and Meditations*, p. 3.
35. The Báb, *Selections*, p. 165.
36. 'Abdu'l-Bahá, *Promulgation*, p. 46.
37. ibid. p. 48.
38. From a letter written on behalf of Shoghi Effendi to an individual believer, 28 April 1936. *Compilation*, vol. 2, no. 1281, p. 7.
39. Letter written on behalf of Shoghi Effendi to an individual believer, 29 May 1935. Shoghi Effendi, *Unfolding Destiny*, p. 434.
40. Letter written on behalf of Shoghi Effendi to an individual believer, 2 January 1932. ibid. p. 429.
41. Memorandum of the Research Department to the Universal House of Justice, 9 November 1994.

REFERENCES

42. Bahá'u'lláh, *Prayers and Meditations*, p. 155.
43. Bahá'u'lláh, *Kitáb-i-Íqán*, pp. 8-9.
44. Bahá'u'lláh, *Prayers and Meditations*, p. 9.
45. Bahá'u'lláh, *Gleanings*, p. 71.
46. Bahá'u'lláh, *Kitáb-i-Íqán*, p. 53.
47. Bahá'u'lláh, *Gleanings*, p. 129.
48. 'Abdu'l-Bahá, *Tablets*, p. 252.
49. 'Abdu'l-Bahá, in *Divine Art of Living*, p. 87.
50. 'Abdu'l-Bahá, *Selections*, pp. 120-1.
51. ibid. pp. 181-2.
52. From a Tablet of 'Abdu'l-Bahá to Mrs Ella Goodall Cooper. *Star of the West*, vol. 2, no. 15, pp. 5-6.
53. 'Abdu'l-Bahá, *Tablets*, p. 471.
54. 'Abdu'l-Bahá, *Paris Talks*, p. 50.
55. 'Abdu'l-Bahá, *Selections*, p. 274.
56. 'Abdu'l-Bahá, *Tablets*, pp. 655-7.
57. 'Abdu'l-Bahá, *Selections*, p. 210.
58. 'Abdu'l-Bahá, ibid., pp. 264-5 (partially retranslated at the Bahá'í World Centre).
59. Shoghi Effendi, *Advent*, pp. 19-20.
60. From a letter written on behalf of Shoghi Effendi to an individual believer, 4 April 1930. *Lights of Divine Guidance*, vol. 2, p. 34.
61. Bahá'u'lláh, *Tablets*, p. 27.
62. ibid. p. 164.
63. Bahá'u'lláh, *Prayers and Meditations*, p. 76.
64. 'Abdu'l-Bahá, *Paris Talks*, pp. 49-50.
65. ibid. 108.
66. 'Abdu'l-Bahá, in *Divine Art of Living*, p. 85.
67. 'Abdu'l-Bahá, *Some Answered Questions*, p. 265.
68. 'Abdu'l-Bahá, *Selections*, pp. 152-3.
69. From a letter written on behalf of Shoghi Effendi to an individual believer, 19 March 1946.
70. From a letter of the Universal House of Justice to an individual believer. *Lights of Guidance*, no. 1209, pp. 359-60.
71. From a letter of the Universal House of Justice to an individual believer. *Lights of Guidance*, no. 1146, pp. 341-2.

72. Letter written on behalf of Shoghi Effendi to an individual believer, 8 April 1948. Shoghi Effendi, *Unfolding Destiny*, pp. 449-50.
73. Letter written on behalf of Shoghi Effendi to an individual believer, 23 June 1948. Shoghi Effendi, *Unfolding Destiny*, p. 451.
74. Bahá'u'lláh, *Gleanings*, p. 72.
75. 'Abdu'l-Bahá, *Paris Talks*, p. 104.
76. 'Abdu'l-Bahá, *Selections*, pp. 234-5.
77. Letter written on behalf of Shoghi Effendi. *Compilation*, vol. 1, no. 285, pp. 146-7.
78. Letter written on behalf of Shoghi Effendi to an individual believer, 31 August 1937. *Compilation*, vol. 1, no. 288, pp. 148-9.
79. 'Abdu'l-Bahá, *Promulgation*, pp. 248-9.
80. ibid. pp. 429-30.
81. Shoghi Effendi, *Bahá'í World*, vol. 18, p. 37.
82. Shoghi Effendi, *Messages to America*, pp. 51-2.
83. Shoghi Effendi, *World Order*, p. 196.
84. Letter of the Universal House of Justice to the Bahá'ís of the World, 26 January 1982. *Compilation*, vol. 1, no. 327, pp. 167-8.
85. Letter of the Universal House of Justice to the Bahá'ís of the World, 2 January 1986. *Compilation*, vol. 1, no. 328, pp. 168-9.
86. 'Abdu'l-Bahá, *Bahá'í World*, vol. 18, p. 29.
87. Words attributed to 'Abdu'l-Bahá, quoted in Gail, *Summon Up Remembrance*, p. 258.
88. Shoghi Effendi, in *Bahá'í World*, vol. 18, p. 37.
89. Shoghi Effendi, *God Passes By*, pp. 61-2.
90. From a letter of the Universal House of Justice to the Iranian believers resident in other countries throughout the world, 10 February 1980. *Compilation*, vol. 1, no. 326, pp. 166-7.
91. Shoghi Effendi, *Bahá'í Administration*, p. 27.
92. Shoghi Effendi, *Dawn of a New Day*, p. 91.
93. ibid. p. 95.
94. From a letter written on behalf of Shoghi Effendi to an individual believer, 26 March 1942.

95. Bahá'u'lláh, in *Compilation*, vol. 1, no. 304, pp. 153-4.
96. Shoghi Effendi, *World Order*, pp. 195-6.
97. Letter written on behalf of Shoghi Effendi to an individual believer, 24 June 1936. *Compilation*, vol. 1, no. 287, p. 148.
98. Shoghi Effendi, *God Passes By*, p. 412.
99. Bahá'u'lláh, *Hidden Words*, Arabic 51.
100. Bahá'u'lláh, *Prayers and Meditations*, p. 239.
101. ibid. pp. 220-1.
102. ibid. p. 132.
103. ibid. p. 78.
104. ibid. p. 219.
105. Bahá'u'lláh, *Epistle*, p. 17.
106. ibid.
107. Bahá'u'lláh, *Prayers and Meditations*, p. 186.
108. 'Abdu'l-Bahá, *Selections*, p. 280.
109. ibid. p. 309.
110. ibid. p. 245.
111. Bahá'u'lláh, *Gleanings*, p. 93.
112. ibid. pp. 245-6.
113. ibid. p. 94.
114. Bahá'u'lláh, *Tablets*, p. 64.
115. Bahá'u'lláh, *Gleanings*, pp. 65-6
116. Bahá'u'lláh, *Hidden Words*, Persian 6.
117. 'Abdu'l-Bahá, quoted in *Compilation*, vol. 1, no. 1020, pp. 460-1.
118. 'Abdu'l-Bahá, *Selections*, p. 163.
119. 'Abdu'l-Bahá, *Secret of Divine Civilization*, pp. 59-60.
120. Shoghi Effendi, *Bahá'í Administration*, p. 60.
121. ibid. p. 61.
122. From a letter written on behalf of Shoghi Effendi to an individual believer, 8 January 1949. *Lights of Guidance*, no. 388, p. 114.
123. From a letter written on behalf of Shoghi Effendi to an individual believer, 14 December 1941. *Compilation*, vol. 2, no. 1295, p. 11.
124. From a letter written on behalf of Shoghi Effendi to an individual believer, 10 December 1947. *Compilation*, vol. 2, no. 1318, pp. 18-19.

125. From a letter written on behalf of the Universal House of Justice to an individual believer, 27 March 1983.
126. Bahá'u'lláh, *Hidden Words*, Persian 56.
127. Bahá'u'lláh, *Tablets*, p. 94.
128. Bahá'u'lláh, *Hidden Words*, Persian 57.
129. Bahá'u'lláh, *Gleanings*, p. 9
130. The Báb, *Selections*, pp. 161-2.
131. 'Abdu'l-Bahá, *Selections*, p. 314.
132. Words attributed to 'Abdu'l-Bahá, from the diary of Ahmad Sohrab. *Star of the West*, vol. 8, no. 2, p. 25.
133. Words attributed to 'Abdu'l-Bahá, in response to questions asked by Dr Edward Getsinger. *Star of the West*, vol. 6, no. 6, p. 44.
134. Shoghi Effendi, *Advent*, pp. 33-4.
135. From a letter written on behalf of Shoghi Effendi to an individual believer, 18 February 1945. *Lights of Guidance*, no. 2037, p. 601.
136. Letter written on behalf of Shoghi Effendi to an individual, 15 August 1957. Shoghi Effendi, *Unfolding Destiny*, p. 462.
137. From a letter written on behalf of Shoghi Effendi, 5 April 1950.
138. Written on behalf of Shoghi Effendi. *Light of Divine Guidance*, vol. 2, p. 84.
139. Letter written on behalf of Shoghi Effendi. *Lights of Guidance*, no. 275, pp. 78-9.
140. From a letter written on behalf of the Universal House of Justice to an individual believer, 2 December 1985.
141. Bahá'u'lláh, *Hidden Words*, Arabic 55.
142. ibid. Arabic 52.
143. ibid. Arabic 56.
144. ibid. Persian 53.
145. ibid. Persian 51.
146. ibid. Persian 55.
147. Bahá'u'lláh, *Tablets*, p. 219.
148. Bahá'u'lláh, *Gleanings*, p. 209.
149. The Báb, *Selections*, p. 192.
150. 'Abdu'l-Bahá, *Selections*, p. 204.
151. ibid. p. 240.

152. Words attributed to 'Abdu'l-Bahá, from the diary of Ahmad Sohrab. *Star of the West*, vol. 8, no. 2, p. 19.
153. Shoghi Effendi, *Citadel*, pp. 124-5.
154. ibid. p. 149.
155. ibid. p. 124.
156. Shoghi Effendi, *Messages to Canada*, p. 65.
157. From a letter written on behalf of Shoghi Effendi translated from the Persian, 21 January 1928. *Compilation*, vol. 2, no. 2085, p. 352.
158. From a letter written on behalf of Shoghi Effendi to an individual believer, 8 December 1935. *Lights of Guidance*, no. 449, pp. 134-5.
159. From a letter written on behalf of Shoghi Effendi to the National Spiritual Assembly of the United States, 19 July 1956. *Lights of Guidance*, no. 440, p. 131.
160. Shoghi Effendi, *Citadel*, pp. 36-7.
161. ibid. pp. 126-7.
162. From a letter written on behalf of Shoghi Effendi to an individual believer, 19 March 1945. *Lights of Guidance*, no. 1842, p. 542.
163. From a letter written on behalf of Shoghi Effendi, 8 May 1948.
164. Letter written on behalf of Shoghi Effendi to an individual believer. Shoghi Effendi, *Unfolding Destiny*, p. 454.
165. From the letter of the Universal House of Justice, Naw-Rúz 1979.
166. Letter of the Universal House of Justice, Riḍván 1990. *Wider Horizon*, p. 79.
167. From a letter written on behalf of the Universal House of Justice to an individual believer, 8 May 1979. *Compilation*, vol. 1, no. 138, pp. 53-4.
168. Bahá'u'lláh, *Gleanings*, p. 129.
169. Bahá'u'lláh, *Prayers and Meditations*, pp. 158-9.
170. 'Abdu'l-Bahá, in *Bahá'í World*, vol. 18, pp. 25-6.
171. 'Abdu'l-Bahá, cited in *Compilation*, vol. 1, no. 269, pp. 136-7.
172. 'Abdu'l-Bahá, cited in Shoghi Effendi, *World Order*, p. 17.
173. 'Abdu'l-Bahá, *Selections*, pp. 238-9.

174. 'Abdu'l-Bahá, *Tablets*, pp. 547-8.
175. 'Abdu'l-Bahá, *Selections*, p. 240.
176. 'Abdu'l-Bahá, *Bahá'í World*, vol. 18, p. 29.
177. Shoghi Effendi, *Advent*, pp. 2-3.
178. Shoghi Effendi, *World Order*, p. 17.
179. Shoghi Effendi, *Advent*, pp. 41-2.
180. From a letter written on behalf of Shoghi Effendi to an individual believer, 22 October 1930. Shoghi Effendi, *Unfolding Destiny*, p. 425.
181. From a letter written on behalf of Shoghi Effendi to an individual believer, 24 May 1927. *Compilation*, vol. 1, no. 348, p. 181.
182. The Universal House of Justice, letter to all National Spiritual Assemblies, 26 November 1974. *Compilation*, vol. 1, no. 292, p. 150.
183. From a memorandum prepared by the Research Department of the Universal House of Justice, *Compilation of Scholarship*, February 1995.
184. Bahá'u'lláh, *Gleanings*, pp. 39-40.
185. 'Abdu'l-Bahá, *Tablets of the Divine Plan*, pp. 53-5.
186. 'Abdu'l-Bahá, from a Tablet to Isabella D. Brittingham. *Lights of Guidance*, no. 438, p. 131.
187. Shoghi Effendi, *Promised Day is Come*, p. 3.
188. ibid. pp. 4-6.
189. Shoghi Effendi, *Bahá'í World*, vol. 18, p. 32.
190. From a letter written on behalf of Shoghi Effendi to an individual believer in reply to a letter dated 14 October 1931. *Lights of Guidance*, no. 447, pp. 133-4.
191. ibid.
192. From a letter written on behalf of Shoghi Effendi to a Bahá'í family, 14 April 1932. *Lights of Guidance*, no. 446, p. 133.
193. From a letter written on behalf of Shoghi Effendi. *Directives of the Guardian*, pp. 11- 12.
194. From a letter written on behalf of Shoghi Effendi to an individual believer, 8 January 1949. Shoghi Effendi. *Unfolding Destiny*, p. 454.

195. From a letter written on behalf of Shoghi Effendi to an individual believer, 20 September 1948. Shoghi Effendi, *Unfolding Destiny*, p. 452.
196. From a letter written on behalf of Shoghi Effendi to the National Spiritual Assembly of the United States, 20 June 1954. *Lights of Guidance*, no. 448, p. 134.
197. Letter of the Universal House of Justice, Riḍván 1992. *Wider Horizon*, pp. 102-3.
198. Letter of the Universal House of Justice to the International Teaching Centre, 20 February 1984.
199. From a letter written on behalf of the Universal House of Justice to an individual believer, 15 June 1987.
200. From a letter written on behalf of the Universal House of Justice to an individual believer, 7 July 1976.
201. From a letter written on behalf of the Universal House of Justice to the Iranian believers resident in various countries throughout the world, 10 February 1980.
202. Bahá'u'lláh, *Gleanings*, p. 234.
203. ibid. p. 251.
204. Bahá'u'lláh, *Bahá'í World Faith*, p. 362.
205. Bahá'u'lláh, *Gleanings*, p. 38.
206. ibid. p. 233.
207. Bahá'u'lláh, *Tablets*, p. 190.
208. Bahá'u'lláh, cited in *Compilation*, vol. 1, no. 334, p. 171.
209. The Báb, *Selections*, p. 18.
210. Bahá'u'lláh, *Epistle*, p. 147.
211. The Báb, *Selections*, p. 123.
212. 'Abdu'l-Bahá, *Selections*, p. 51.
213. ibid. p. 279.
214. Words attributed to 'Abdu'l-Bahá, from the diary of Ahmad Sohrab. *Star of the West*, vol. 8, no. 19, p. 241.
215. 'Abdu'l-Bahá, *Selections*, p. 205.
216. 'Abdu'l-Bahá, *Tablets*, 484.
217. ibid. pp. 673-4.
218. 'Abdu'l-Bahá, *Selections*, p. 64.
219. ibid. p. 79.
220. ibid. pp. 9-10.

221. 'Abdu'l-Bahá, *Tablets*, p. 62.
222. Words attributed to 'Abdu'l-Bahá, quoted in Gail, *Summon Up Remembrance*, p. 254.
223. ibid. p. 255.
224. Words attributed to 'Abdu'l-Bahá, quoted in Maxwell, *Early Pilgrimage*, p. 40.
225. 'Abdu'l-Bahá, in *Divine Art of Living*, p. 65.
226. 'Abdu'l-Bahá, quoted in *Star of the West*, vol. 9, no. 13, p. 141.
227. Shoghi Effendi, *Citadel*, p. 58.
228. 'Abdu'l-Bahá, quoted in *Star of the West*, vol. 8, no. 19, p. 241.
229. Letter written on behalf of Shoghi Effendi, 27 April 1946. Shoghi Effendi, *Dawn of a New Day*, p. 201.
230. From a letter written on behalf of Shoghi Effendi to an individual believer, 4 June 1934. Shoghi Effendi, *Unfolding Destiny*, p. 433.
231. From a letter written on behalf of an individual believer, 22 September 1936. *Compilation*, vol. 2, no. 1705. p. 220.
232. From a letter written on behalf of Shoghi Effendi to an individual believer, 27 March 1938. *Compilation*, vol. 2, no. 1708, p. 221.
233. From a letter written on behalf of Shoghi Effendi to an individual believer, 30 June 1937. *Compilation*, vol. 2, no. 1707, p. 221.
234. From letter written on behalf Shoghi Effendi to an individual believer, dated 12 October 1949. *Compilation*, vol. 2, no. 1716, p. 223.
235. From letter written on behalf of Shoghi Effendi, 6 October 1954. *Compilation*, vol. 1, no. 516, p. 232.
236. From a letter on written on behalf of Shoghi Effendi to an individual believer, 14 February 1925. *Lights of Guidance*, no. 1378, p. 417.
237. From a letter written on behalf of Shoghi Effendi, 9 April 1949. Shoghi Effendi, *Unfolding Destiny*, p. 225.
238. From a letter written on behalf of Shoghi Effendi, 7 January 1934. Shoghi Effendi, *Dawn of a New Day*, p. 196.
239. From a letter written on behalf of Shoghi Effendi, 9 August 1944.

240. From a letter written on behalf of Shoghi Effendi, 11 July 1939.
241. From a letter of the Universal House of Justice to the National Spiritual Assembly of the United States, May 1994.
242. From a letter of the Universal House of Justice, Riḍván 151.
243. Bahá'u'lláh, *Gleanings*, p. 93.
244. Bahá'u'lláh, *Prayers and Meditations*, p. 147.
245. Bahá'u'lláh, *Gleanings*, p. 106.
246. ibid. pp. 245-6.
247. Bahá'u'lláh, *Tablets*, p. 249.
248. Bahá'u'lláh, *Prayers and Meditations*, p. 101.
249 Shoghi Effendi, *Bahá'í Administration*, p. 130.
250. Shoghi Effendi, *Advent*, p. 72.
251. 'Abdu'l-Bahá, *Selections*, p. 242.
252. Tablet of 'Abdu'l-Bahá to Charles Haney, *Star of the West*, vol. 10, no. 19, p. 348.
253. 'Abdu'l-Bahá, *Selections*, pp. 163-4.
254. ibid. pp. 219-20.
255. 'Abdu'l-Bahá, *Secret of Divine Civilization*, pp. 23-4.
256. 'Abdu'l-Bahá, *Selections*, p. 135.
257. Words attributed to 'Abdu'l-Bahá, 3 July 1909. *Diary of Juliet Thompson*, p. 35.
258. Words attributed to 'Abdu'l-Bahá, from the diary of Ahmad Sohrab. *Star of the West*, vol. 13, no. 6, p. 152.
259. Words attributed to 'Abdu'l-Bahá, from the diary of Ahmad Sohrab. *Star of the West*, vol. 8, no. 1, p. 21.
260. Words attributed to 'Abdu'l-Bahá, from the diary of Ahmad Sohrab. *Star of the West*, vol. 13, no. 10, pp. 270-1.
261. Words attributed to 'Abdu'l-Bahá, from the diary of Ahmad Sohrab. *Star of the West*, vol. 8, no. 1, p. 21.
262. Shoghi Effendi, *Citadel of Faith*, p. 85.
263. From a letter of Shoghi Effendi, 12 June 1952. Shoghi Effendi, *Unfolding Destiny*, p. 287.
264. From a letter of Shoghi Effendi, 3 November 1948. Shoghi Effendi, *Citadel of Faith*, p. 58.
265. From a letter written on behalf of Shoghi Effendi. *Bahá'í Life*, p. 6.

266. From a letter written on behalf of Shoghi Effendi, 9 March 1943. Shoghi Effendi, *Unfolding Destiny*, p. 156.
267. From a letter written on behalf of Shoghi Effendi to the Bahá'ís of Kitalya Farm Prison, 26 March 1957. *Compilation*, vol. 2, no. 1338, p. 26.
268. From a letter written on behalf of Shoghi Effendi to the Spiritual Assembly of Atlanta, Georgia, 5 February 1947. *Compilation*, vol. 2, no. 1314, p. 17.
269. From a letter written on behalf of Shoghi Effendi to an individual believer, 28 December 1925. Shoghi Effendi, *Unfolding Destiny*, pp. 421-2.
270. From a letter written on behalf of Shoghi Effendi. *Directives of the Guardian*, p. 87.
271. From a letter of the Universal House of Justice to the National Spiritual Assembly of the United States, May 1994.
272. From a letter of the Universal House of Justice to the Bahá'ís of the East and West, 18 December 1963. *Lights of Guidance*, no. 451, p. 135.
273. Bahá'u'lláh, *Prayers and Meditations*, p. 254.
274. From a Tablet of Bahá'u'lláh translated from the Arabic. *Compilation*, vol. 1, no. 363, p. 188.
275. Bahá'u'lláh, *Gleanings*, p. 295.
276. From a Tablet of Bahá'u'lláh translated from the Arabic. *Compilation*, vol. 1, no. 365, p. 188.
277. From a Tablet of Bahá'u'lláh translated from the Arabic. *Compilation*, vol. 1, no. 364, p. 188.
278. Bahá'u'lláh, quoted in Shoghi Effendi, *God Passes By*, p. 119.
279. 'Abdu'l-Bahá, *Paris Talks*, page 111.
280. 'Abdu'l-Bahá, cited in *Compilation*, vol. 1, no. 308, p. 156.
281. 'Abdu'l-Bahá, *Tablets*, p. 636.
282. From a letter written on behalf of Shoghi Effendi to an individual believer, 8 December 1935. *Compilation*, vol. 2, no. 1762, p. 238.
283. From a letter written on behalf of Shoghi Effendi to an individual believer, 27 January 1945. *Compilation*, vol. 1, no. 811, p. 382.

REFERENCES

284. From a letter written on behalf of Shoghi Effendi to an individual believer. *Lights of Guidance*, no. 955, p. 284.
285. 'Abdu'l-Bahá, *Promulgation*, pp. 246-7.
286. From a letter written on behalf of Shoghi Effendi to an individual believer, 26 October 1938. *Compilation*, vol. 2, no. 1768, p. 239.
287. Letter written on behalf of Shoghi Effendi to an individual believer, 26 October 1938. *Compilation*, vol. 2, no. 1768, p. 240.
288. 'Abdu'l-Bahá, in *Bahá'í World Faith*, p. 368.
289. From a letter written on behalf of Shoghi Effendi to an individual believer, 30 June 1938. *Lights of Guidance*, no. 1510, p. 461.
290. Words attributed to Shoghi Effendi in the pilgrim notes of Ruth Moffett, in Moffett, *Du'á*, pp. 27-8.
291. 'Abdu'l-Bahá, *Paris Talks*, p. 175.
292. 'Abdu'l-Bahá, *Tablets*, pp. 629-30.
293. From a Tablet of 'Abdu'l-Bahá translated from the Persian. *Compilation*, vol. 1, no. 1025, p. 461.
294. 'Abdu'l-Bahá, cited in *Lights of Guidance*, no. 892, p. 266.
295. Cablegram of Shoghi Effendi, 21 June 1932. Shoghi Effendi, *Messages to America*, p. 1.
296. Letter written on behalf of Shoghi Effendi, 11 March 1933. *Compilation*, vol. 1, no. 471, p. 218.
297. From a letter of Shoghi Effendi to the Bahá'ís of Adhirbayján, 13 January 1923. *Compilation*, vol. 1, no. 427, p. 204.
298. Letter written on behalf of Shoghi Effendi to an individual believer, 28 April 1955. *Compilation*, vol. 1, no. 518, p. 232.
299. Letter written on behalf of Shoghi Effendi to an individual believer, 27 August 1951. *Compilation*, vol. 1, no. 515, p. 231.
300. From a letter written on behalf of Shoghi Effendi, 15 August 1945. *Compilation*, vol. 1, no. 498, p. 227.
301. Bahá'u'lláh, *Gleanings*, pp. 86-7.
302. Bahá'u'lláh, *Tablets*, p. 51.
303. Bahá'u'lláh, *Gleanings*, p. 338.
304. Bahá'u'lláh, *Hidden Words*, Persian 31.

305. Bahá'u'lláh, *Gleanings*, pp. 337-8.
306. Bahá'u'lláh, *Prayers and Meditations*, p. 240.
307. Bahá'u'lláh, *Tablets*, p. 155.
308. From a Tablet of Bahá'u'lláh translated from the Arabic, in 'Extracts from the Bahá'í writings and letters of the Guardian and the Universal House of Justice on suffering and tests'.
309. Bahá'u'lláh, *Gleanings*, p. 133.
310. 'Abdu'l-Bahá, *Some Answered Questions*, p. 244.
311. Tablet of 'Abdu'l-Bahá to Mr and Mrs Rabb. *Star of the West*, vol. 14, no. 6, p. 168.
312. Words attributed to 'Abdu'l-Bahá in the diary of Ahmad Sohrab. *Star of the West*, vol. 8, no. 2, p. 17.
313. The Báb, *Selections*, p. 217.
314. 'Abdu'l-Bahá, *Tablets*, p. 86.
315. ibid. p. 455.
316. ibid. p. 456.
317. From a letter written by Shoghi Effendi to an individual believer, 7 June 1928.
318. From a letter written on behalf of Shoghi Effendi to an individual believer, 28 April 1936. *Compilation*, vol. 2, no. 1281. p. 7.
319. From a letter written on behalf of Shoghi Effendi to an individual believer, 10 December 1947. *Compilation*, vol. 2, no. 1318, p. 19.
320. Bahá'u'lláh, *Gleanings*, pp. 289-90.
321. ibid. pp. 325-6.
322. 'Abdu'l-Bahá, *Selections*, pp. 17-18.
323. 'Abdu'l-Bahá, *Tablets*, p. 552.
324. 'Abdu'l-Bahá, *Selections*, pp. 9-10.
325. 'Abdu'l-Bahá, *Tablets*, p. 325.
326. Words attributed to 'Abdu'l-Bahá in answer to questions asked by Dr Edward Getsinger. *Star of the West*, vol. 6, no. 6, p. 45.
327. 'Abdu'l-Bahá, *Selections*, p. 220.
328. ibid. p. 274.
329. ibid. p. 295.
330. Tablet of 'Abdu'l-Bahá to Juliet Thompson. *Star of the West*, vol. 2, nos. 7 and 8, p. 13.

REFERENCES

331. Words attributed to 'Abdu'l-Bahá, from the diary of Ahmad Sohrab. *Star of the West*, vol. 8, no. 16, p. 218.
332. From a Tablet of 'Abdu'l-Bahá, quoted in *Star of the West*, vol. 8, no. 17, p. 227.
333. From a Tablet of 'Abdu'l-Bahá, quoted in *Star of the West*, vol. 8, no. 17, p. 228.
334. From a Tablet of 'Abdu'l-Bahá to Charles Haney, May 1911. *Star of the West*, vol. 10, no. 19, p. 348.
335. Words attributed to 'Abdu'l-Bahá, from the diary of Ahmad Sohrab. *Star of the West*, vol. 8, no. 6, p. 66.
336. Words attributed to 'Abdu'l-Bahá, quoted in *Diary of Juliet Thompson*, p. 21.
337. Words attributed to 'Abdu'l-Bahá spoken to Lua Getsinger, in the diary of Ahmad Sohrab. *Star of the West*, vol. 4, no. 12, p. 208.
338. Shoghi Effendi, *Advent*, p. 72.
339. Bahá'u'lláh, *Gleanings*, pp. 328-9.
340. ibid. p. 276.
341. ibid. pp. 275-6.
342. 'Abdu'l-Bahá, *Selections*, p. 200.
343. ibid. pp. 177-8.
344. 'Abdu'l-Bahá, *Tablets*, pp. 557-8.
345. 'Abdu'l-Bahá, *Selections*, pp. 220-1.
346. ibid. pp. 236.
347. 'Abdu'l-Bahá, *Paris Talks*, p. 99.
348. 'Abdu'l-Bahá, *Selections*, p. 192.
349. ibid. p. 12.
350. 'Abdu'l-Bahá, *Paris Talks*, pp. 178-9.
351. From a letter written on behalf of Shoghi Effendi to an individual believer, 10 February 1951. Shoghi Effendi, *Unfolding Destiny*, pp. 459-60.
352. From a letter of the Universal House of Justice to the National Spiritual Assembly of the United States, May 1994.
353. Bahá'u'lláh, *Gleanings*, p. 5.
354. ibid. pp. 308-9.
355. ibid. p. 289.
356. Shoghi Effendi, *Bahá'í Administration*, p. 132.

357. From a letter written on behalf of Shoghi Effendi to an individual believer, 23 April 1956. *Compilation*, vol. 2, no. 1335, p. 25.

358. From a letter written on behalf of Shoghi Effendi. *Directives of the Guardian*, p. 78.

359. Letter written on behalf of Shoghi Effendi to two believers, 23 February 1939. *Compilation*, vol. 2, no. 1769, p. 240.

360. From a letter written on behalf of Shoghi Effendi to an individual believer in 1949. *Lights of Guidance*, no. 283, p. 81.

361. From a letter written on behalf of Shoghi Effendi, 11 April 1949. *Compilation*, vol. 1, no. 508, p. 229.

362. Letter written on behalf of Shoghi Effendi. *Compilation*, vol. 1, no. 512, pp. 230-1.

363. From a letter written on behalf of Shoghi Effendi to an individual believer, 24 February 1950. *Compilation*, vol. 2, no. 1325, pp. 21-2.

364. Letter of the Universal House of Justice to the Bahá'ís of the World, Riḍván 1966. *Lights of Guidance*, no. 441, pp. 131-2.

365. Letter of the Universal House of Justice to all National Spiritual Assemblies, 13 July 1972. *Lights of Guidance*, no. 1795, p. 528.

366. From a letter of the Universal House of Justice to the National Spiritual Assembly of the United States, 7 September 1965. *Lights of Guidance*, no. 1144, p. 341.

367. From a letter of the Universal House of Justice to an individual believer, 3 March 1987.

368. From a letter of the Universal House of Justice to an individual believer, excerpts from letter to all National Spiritual Assemblies, 6 February 1973. *Lights of Guidance*, no. 1209, p. 360.

369. Bahá'u'lláh, *Hidden Words*, Arabic 52.

370. Bahá'u'lláh, *Compilation*, vol. 1, no. 1020, p. 460.

371. Bahá'u'lláh, *Tablets*, p. 175.

372. Bahá'u'lláh, quoted in Balyuzi, *Eminent Bahá'ís*, p. 22.

373. Bahá'u'lláh, *Gleanings*, p. 129.

374. ibid.

375. ibid. p. 290.
376. Bahá'u'lláh, *Tablets*, p. 138.
377. Bahá'u'lláh, *Gleanings*, p. 120.
378. From a letter written on behalf of Shoghi Effendi to an individual believer, 30 October 1951. *Lights of Guidance*, no. 2046, p. 603.
379. Bahá'u'lláh, *Kitáb-i-Aqdas*, para. 43.
380. Bahá'u'lláh, *Tablets*, p. 156.
381. Bahá'u'lláh, *Gleanings*, p. 329.
382. The Báb, *Selections*, p. 161.
383. 'Abdu'l-Bahá, *Tablets*, p. 266.
384. ibid. p. 457.
385. From a letter written on behalf of Shoghi Effendi. Shoghi Effendi, *Dawn of a New Day*, p. 12.
386. 'Abdu'l-Bahá, *Bahá'í World Faith*, pp. 395-6.
387. From a letter written on behalf of Shoghi Effendi to an individual believer, 18 April 1940. Shoghi Effendi, *Unfolding Destiny*, p. 437.
388. From a letter written on behalf of Shoghi Effendi. Shoghi Effendi, *Dawn of a New Day*, pp. 96-7.
389. From a letter written on behalf of Shoghi Effendi. Shoghi Effendi, *Light of Divine Guidance*, vol. 1, p. 96.
390. 'Abdu'l-Bahá, in *Divine Art of Living*, p. 90.
391. From a Tablet of 'Abdu'l-Bahá to Corinne True, quoted in Rutstein, *Corinne True*, p. 90.
392. 'Abdu'l-Bahá, *Tablets*, p. 51.
393. From a Tablet of 'Abdu'l-Bahá translated from the Persian. *Compilation*, vol. 1, no. 306, p. 154.
394. From a letter written on behalf of Shoghi Effendi to the Spiritual Assembly of Manchester, 20 July 1932. Shoghi Effendi, *Unfolding Destiny*, p. 405.
395. 'Abdu'l-Bahá, *Promulgation*, p. 54.
396. 'Abdu'l-Bahá, in *Bahíyyih Khánum*, p. 7.
397. Words attributed to 'Abdu'l-Bahá. *Star of the West*, vol. 12, no. 18, p. 280.
398. From a letter written on behalf of Shoghi Effendi to an individual believer, 31 May 1933.
399. Bahá'u'lláh, *Hidden Words*, Arabic 35.

400. Bahá'u'lláh, *Gleanings*, pp. 81-2.
401. ibid. p. 149.
402. The Báb, *Selections*, p. 103.
403. ibid. p. 210.
404. From a Tablet of 'Abdu'l-Bahá to Ruth Klos. *Star of the West*, vol. 10, no. 17, p. 319.
405. 'Abdu'l-Bahá, in *Bahá'í Prayers*, p. 152.
406. 'Abdu'l-Bahá, *Paris Talks*, p. 29.
407. 'Abdu'l-Bahá, *Selections*, p. 127.
408. 'Abdu'l-Bahá, *Paris Talks*, p. 108.
409. ibid. pp. 109-10.
410. Words attributed to 'Abdu'l-Bahá, from the diary of Ahmad Sohrab. *Star of the West*, vol. 8, no. 2, p. 21.
411. 'Abdu'l-Bahá, cited in *Compilation*, vol. 1, no. 795, p. 376.
412. Words attributed to 'Abdu'l-Bahá, quoted in *The Diary of Juliet Thompson*, pp. 24-5.
413. Shoghi Effendi, *Advent*, pp. 20-1.
414. From a letter written on behalf of Shoghi Effendi to an individual believer, 26 December 1935. *Lights of Guidance*, no. 1870, p. 550.
415. From a letter written on behalf of Shoghi Effendi to an individual believer, 3 October 1943. *Lights of Guidance*, no. 701, p. 209.
416. From a letter written on behalf of Shoghi Effendi to an individual believer, 17 October 1944. Shoghi Effendi, *Unfolding Destiny*, p. 440.
417. From a letter of Shoghi Effendi to the Spiritual Assembly of Tehran, 30 October 1924. *Lights of Guidance*, no. 457, pp. 136-7.
418. From a letter written on behalf of Shoghi Effendi to an individual believer, 8 January 1949. *Lights of Guidance*, no. 388, p. 114.
419. Letter written on behalf of Shoghi Effendi to an individual believer, 22 November 1941. *Compilation*, vol. 2, no. 1770, p. 240.
420. Letter written on behalf of Shoghi Effendi to the Youth Session, Louhelen School, 25 August 1944. *Compilation*, vol. 1, no. 809, p. 381.

421. From a letter written on behalf of Shoghi Effendi to an individual believer, 8 January 1949. Shoghi Effendi, *Unfolding Destiny*, p. 453.

422. From a letter written on behalf of Shoghi Effendi to an individual believer, 3 March 1955. Shoghi Effendi, *Unfolding Destiny*, p. 461.

423. From a letter written on behalf of Shoghi Effendi to an individual believer, 6 September 1946. *Compilation*, vol. 1, no. 159, p. 61.

424. From a letter written on behalf of Shoghi Effendi to an individual believer, 3 February 1937. Shoghi Effendi, *Unfolding Destiny*, p. 436.

425. From a letter written on behalf of Shoghi Effendi to the Spiritual Assembly of Bristol, 22 September 1948. Shoghi Effendi, *Unfolding Destiny*, p. 392.

426. From a letter written on behalf of Shoghi Effendi to an individual believer, 5 July 1947. *Lights of Guidance*, no. 246, p. 70.

427. Words attributed to 'Abdu'l-Bahá. *Star of the West*, vol. 9, no. 8, p. 96.

428. From a letter written on behalf of Shoghi Effendi. Shoghi Effendi, *Light of Divine Guidance*, vol. 1, pp. 69-70.

429. 'Abdu'l-Bahá, quoted in *Star of the West*, vol. 14, p. 165.

430. From a letter written on behalf of Shoghi Effendi. *Lights of Guidance*, no. 396, p. 116.

431. Letter of the Universal House of Justice, Riḍván 1995.

432. From a letter written on behalf of Shoghi Effendi to an individual believer, 22 October 1949. Shoghi Effendi, *Unfolding Destiny*, p. 457.

433. 'Abdu'l-Bahá, quoted in Esslemont, *New Era*, p. 108.

434. From a letter written on behalf of Shoghi Effendi to an individual believer, 14 July 1945. *Lights of Guidance*, no. 95, pp. 115-16.

435. From a letter written on behalf of Shoghi Effendi, 8 May 1947. Shoghi Effendi, *Unfolding Destiny*, p. 199.

436. From a letter written on behalf of Shoghi Effendi. *High Endeavors*, p. 68.

437. Written on behalf of Shoghi Effendi. *Lights of Guidance*, no. 701, p. 237.

438. From a letter written on behalf of Shoghi Effendi to an individual believer, 15 October 1952. *Lights of Guidance*, no. 381, p. 112.
439. From letter written on behalf of Shoghi Effendi to an individual believer, 11 August 1957. *Lights of Guidance*, no. 1766, p. 519.
440. From a letter written on behalf of Shoghi Effendi to an individual believer, 22 October 1949. Shoghi Effendi, *Unfolding Destiny*, p. 456.
441. From a letter written on behalf of the Shoghi Effendi to an individual believer, 23 November 1947. *Compilation*, vol. 1, no. 1976, p. 482.
442. From a letter written on behalf of Shoghi Effendi to an individual believer, 5 April 1942. *Compilation*, vol. 1, no. 808, p. 381.
443. From a letter written on behalf of Shoghi Effendi to the Bahá'í Youth of Bombay, 6 June 1941. *Compilation*, vol. 1, no. 492, p. 225.
444. From a letter written on behalf of Shoghi Effendi, 27 March 1945. Shoghi Effendi, *Unfolding Destiny*, p. 172.
445. Letter of the Universal House of Justice, Riḍván 1972.
446. From a letter written on behalf of the Universal House of Justice, 6 August 1989. *Compilation*, vol. 2, no. 2347, p. 459.
447. Letter of the Universal House of Justice, Riḍván 1989.
448. Bahá'u'lláh, *Hidden Words*, Arabic 27.
449. Bahá'u'lláh, *Hidden Words*, Persian 66.
450. ibid.
451. Bahá'u'lláh, *Kitáb-i-Aqdas*, para. 19.
452. Bahá'u'lláh, *Kitáb-i-Íqán*, p. 193.
453. Tablet of 'Abdu'l-Bahá to Dr M. G. Skinner, 12 August 1913. *Lights of Guidance*, no. 312, p. 91.
454. 'Abdu'l-Bahá, *Selections*, pp. 230-1.
455. 'Abdu'l-Bahá, *Promulgation*, p. 453.
456. 'Abdu'l-Bahá, *Will and Testament*, p. 13.
457. From a letter written on behalf of Shoghi Effendi to an individual believer, 12 May 1925. *Lights of Guidance*, no. 306, p. 88.

458. Letter of the Universal House of Justice to the National

Spiritual Assembly of the United States, 21 September

459. From a letter written on behalf of the Universal House of

Justice to an individual believer, 23 September 1975. *Lights

of Guidance*, no. 311, p. 91.

460. Bahá'u'lláh, *Gleanings*, p. 9.

461. 'Abdu'l-Bahá, *Tablets of the Divine Plan*, p. 53.

462. 'Abdu'l-Bahá, *Selections*, p. 210.

463. From a letter written on behalf of Shoghi Effendi to an

individual believer, 24 February 1950. *Compilation*, vol. 2,

no. 1325, pp. 21-2.

464. 'Abdu'l-Bahá, *Paris Talks*, pp. 147-8.

465. From a letter written on behalf of Shoghi Effendi to an

individual believer, 5 April 1956. *Messages from the Universal

House of Justice*, pp. 499-500.

466. From a letter written on behalf of Shoghi Effendi to an

individual believer, 16 February 1951. *Compilation*, vol. 2,

no. 1330, p. 23.

467. Bahá'u'lláh, *Epistle*, p. 55.

468. From a letter written on behalf of Shoghi Effendi to an

individual believer, 18 December 1945. *Compilation*, vol. 2,

no. 1308, p. 15.

469. 'Abdu'l-Bahá, *Promulgation*, p. 453.

470. Words attributed to 'Abdu'l-Bahá. Source unknown.

471. From a letter of the Universal House of Justice, 17 July

1979. *Compilation*, vol. 2, no. 2339, p. 455.

472. From a letter written on behalf of Shoghi Effendi to an

individual believer during the year 1949. *Lights of Guidance*,

no. 1801, pp. 529-30.

473. From a letter written on behalf of Shoghi Effendi. Shoghi

Effendi, *Light of Divine Guidance*, vol. 1, p. 152.

474. From a letter written on behalf of Shoghi Effendi to an

individual believer, 27 January 1947. Shoghi Effendi,

*Unfolding Destiny*, p. 442.

475. From a letter written on behalf of Shoghi Effendi to an

individual believer, 26 May 1946. *Compilation*, vol. 1,

no. 814, p. 383.

476. From a letter written on behalf of Shoghi Effendi to an individual believer, 27 February 1943. *Compilation*, vol. 2, no. 1289, p. 9.
477. From a letter written on behalf of Shoghi Effendi to an individual believer, 30 June 1923. *Lights of Guidance*, no. 2048, p. 603.
478. From a letter written on behalf of Shoghi Effendi to an individual believer, 17 October 1944. *Compilation*, vol. 2, no. 1301, p. 13.
479. 'Abdu'l-Bahá, *Selections*, p. 203.
480. 'Abdu'l-Bahá, *Promulgation*, p. 244.
481. Words attributed to 'Abdu'l-Bahá, *Star of the West*, Vol. 8, no. 19, p. 4.
482. Letter of the Universal House of Justice to an individual believer, 24 July 1973.
483. From a letter written on behalf of Shoghi Effendi to an individual believer, 12 May 1925. *Compilation*, vol. 2, no. 1272, pp. 3-4.
484. From a letter written on behalf of Shoghi Effendi to an individual believer, 26 October 1943. *Lights of Guidance*, no. 291, p. 83.
485. From a letter written on behalf of Shoghi Effendi to an individual believer, 19 September 1948. *Lights of Guidance*, no. 397, p. 116.
486. From a letter written on behalf of Shoghi Effendi to an individual believer, 15 August 1957. Shoghi Effendi, *Unfolding Destiny*, p. 462.
487. 'Abdu'l-Bahá, *Selections*, p. 24.
488. 'Abdu'l-Bahá, *Tablets*, p. 436.
489. Words attributed to 'Abdu'l-Bahá, quoted in Gail, *Summon Up Remembrance*, p. 258.
490. From letter written on behalf of Shoghi Effendi to an individual believer, 4 October 1950. *Lights of Guidance*, no. 1341, p. 403.
491. Shoghi Effendi, *Advent*, pp. 39-41.
492. From a letter written on behalf of Shoghi Effendi, in *Messages to Canada*, p. 12.

493. From a letter written on behalf of Shoghi Effendi to an individual believer, 26 October 1943. *Dawn of a New Day,* p. 106.
494. From a letter written on behalf of Shoghi Effendi to the National Spiritual Assembly of Germany and Austria, 30 June 1949. *Lights of Guidance,* no. 2045, pp. 602-3.
495. From a letter written on behalf of Shoghi Effendi to an individual believer, 6 December 1935. *Lights of Guidance,* no. 1381, p. 418.
496. The Universal House of Justice, September 1964. *Messages from the Universal House of Justice,* p. 43.
497. Bahá'u'lláh, *Kitáb-i-Aqdas,* para. 35.
498. Bahá'u'lláh, *Prayers and Meditations,* p. 171.
499. 'Abdu'l-Bahá, *Selections,* pp. 264-5.
500. ibid. pp. 267-8.
501. ibid. p. 268.
502. Shoghi Effendi, *Citadel,* p. 131.
503. Shoghi Effendi, *Advent,* p. 16.
504. Shoghi Effendi, *Citadel,* p. 83.
505. From a letter written on behalf of Shoghi Effendi to an individual believer, 25 November 1956. *Compilation,* vol. 2, no. 1337, p. 26.
506. From a letter written on behalf of Shoghi Effendi to an individual believer, 3 August 1932. *Compilation,* vol. 2, no. 1276, p. 5.
507. From a letter written on behalf of Shoghi Effendi to an individual believer, 22 August 1957. *Compilation,* vol. 2, no. 2011. p. 325.
508. Letter written on behalf of Shoghi Effendi to an individual believer, 19 October 1941. Shoghi Effendi, *Unfolding Destiny,* p. 438.
509. From letter written on behalf of Shoghi Effendi to an individual believer, 6 October 1954. *Lights of Guidance,* no. 406, p. 118.
510. From letter written on behalf of Shoghi Effendi to an individual believer, 12 July 1952. *Lights of Guidance,* no. 405, p. 118.

511. From a letter written on behalf of Shoghi Effendi to an individual believer, 14 October 1942.
512. From a letter written on behalf of Shoghi Effendi. *Light of Divine Guidance*: vol. 1, p. 45.
513. From a letter written on behalf of Shoghi Effendi to an individual believer, 19 October 1941. Shoghi Effendi, *Unfolding Destiny*, p. 438.
514. From a letter of the Universal House of Justice to the Bahá'í youth of the world, 8 May 1985. *Lights of Guidance*, no. 2153, p. 637.
515. Letter of the Universal House of Justice to the National Spiritual Assembly of the United States, May 1994.
516. From a letter written on behalf of the Universal House of Justice to an individual believer, 7 July 1976. *Lights of Guidance*, no. 415, p. 123.
517. Bahá'u'lláh, *Gleanings*, p. 313.
518. Bahá'u'lláh, in *Bahá'í Prayers*, p. 211.
519. Bahá'u'lláh, *Gleanings*, p. 119.
520. ibid. pp. 119-20.
521. Bahá'u'lláh, *Prayers and Meditations*, pp. 108-9.
522. ibid. pp. 146-7.
523. ibid. pp. 155-6.
524. Bahá'u'lláh, *Epistle*, p. 94.
525. Bahá'u'lláh, *Prayers and Meditations*, p. 302.
526. ibid. pp. 170-1.
527. Bahá'u'lláh, *Gleanings*, p. 296.
528. 'Abdu'l-Bahá, *Selections*, p. 56.
529. ibid. pp. 262-3.
530. Words attributed to 'Abdu'l-Bahá, quoted in Gail, *Summon Up Remembrance*, p. 242.
531. From a letter of Shoghi Effendi, 25 August 1926. *Arohanui*, p. 21.
532. Statement of the Universal House of Justice on the occasion of the Centenary Commemoration of the Ascension of Bahá'u'lláh at Bahjí, 29 May 1992.
533. Bahá'u'lláh, *Tablets*, p. 168.
534. From a Tablet of Bahá'u'lláh translated from the Arabic. *Compilation*, vol. 1, no. 167, p. 93.

535. From a Tablet of Bahá'u'lláh translated from the Persian. *Compilation*, vol. 1, no. 168, p. 93.
536. From a Tablet of 'Abdu'l-Bahá translated from the Persian. *Compilation*, vol. 1, no. 185, pp. 98-9.
537. From a Tablet of 'Abdu'l-Bahá translated from the Persian. *Compilation*, vol. 1, no. 183, p. 98.
538. From a Tablet of 'Abdu'l-Bahá translated from the Persian. *Compilation*, vol. 1, no. 179, pp. 96-7.
539. Cited in a letter of Shoghi Effendi to the National Spiritual Assembly of Persia, 15 February 1922. *Compilation*, vol. 1, no. 182, p. 97.
540. Letter written on behalf of Shoghi Effendi, 12 November 1930. *Compilation*, vol. 1, no. 194, p. 103.
541. From a letter written on behalf of Shoghi Effendi, 16 June 1932. *Compilation*, vol. 1, no. 195, p. 103.
542. From a letter of Shoghi Effendi, 14 February 1945. *Compilation*, vol. 1, no. 202, p. 106.
543. From a letter written on behalf of Shoghi Effendi to an individual believer, 12 March 1934. *Lights of Guidance*, no. 927, p. 276.
544. From a letter written on behalf of Shoghi Effendi to the National Spiritual Assembly of the British Isles, 15 June 1950. *Lights of Guidance*, no. 957, pp. 284-5.
545. From a letter of the Universal House of Justice to National Spiritual Assemblies, 6 February 1973. *Messages from the Universal House of Justice*, pp. 111-12.
546. From a letter written on behalf of the Universal House of Justice, 17 July 1989. *Compilation*, vol. 2, no. 2346, p. 459.
547. From a letter written on behalf of the Universal House of Justice. *Compilation*, vol. 2, no. 2339, p. 455.
548. From a letter written on behalf of the Universal House of Justice. *Compilation*, vol. 1, no. 210, p. 109.
549. Bahá'u'lláh, *Hidden Words*, Arabic 31.
550. Bahá'u'lláh, *Gleanings*, p. 130.
551. ibid. p. 204.
552. ibid. p. 236.
553. ibid. pp. 308-9.
554. Bahá'u'lláh, *Tablets*, pp. 24-5.

555. ibid. p. 219-20.
556. Bahá'u'lláh, *Epistle*, p. 55.
557. Bahá'u'lláh, *Gleanings*, pp. 310-11.
558. 'Abdu'l-Bahá, *Promulgation*, p. 176.
559. Bahá'u'lláh, *Tablets*, p. 63.
560. ibid. p. 93.
561. ibid. p. 121.
562. ibid. p. 222.
563. ibid. p. 125.
564. Bahá'u'lláh, *Gleanings*, p. 126.
565. Bahá'u'lláh, *Seven Valleys*, p. 58.
566. From a letter written on behalf of Shoghi Effendi. *Lights of Guidance*, no. 794, p. 238.
567. Letter written on behalf of Shoghi Effendi to an individual believer, 1 September 1933. *Arohanui*, pp. 32-3.
568. From a letter written on behalf of Shoghi Effendi. *Lights of Guidance*, no. 790, p. 237.
569. Bahá'u'lláh, *Prayers and Meditations*, pp. 262-3.
570. ibid. p. 78.
571. Bahá'u'lláh, *Gleanings*, pp. 153-4.
572. Bahá'u'lláh, in *Bahá'í Prayers*, p. 98.
573. 'Abdu'l-Bahá, *Selections*, p. 151.
574. From a Tablet of 'Abdu'l-Bahá to Alberta Hall. *Star of the West*, vol. 9, no. 15, p. 173.
575. Words attributed to 'Abdu'l-Bahá, from the diary of Ahmad Sohrab. *Star of the West*, vol. 8, no. 18, p. 231.
576. 'Abdu'l-Bahá, *Paris Talks*, p. 19.
577. 'Abdu'l-Bahá, *Selections*, pp. 151-2.
578. From a letter written on behalf of Shoghi Effendi to an individual believer, 16 February 1935. *Lights of Guidance*, no. 928. p. 276.
579. From a letter written on behalf of Shoghi Effendi to an individual believer, 23 May 1935. *Compilation*, vol. 1, no. 1059, p. 477.
580. 'Abdu'l-Bahá, *Selections*, pp. 161-2.
581. ibid. p. 156.
582. ibid.

583. 'Abdu'l-Bahá, *Promulgation*, p. 204.
584. Words attributed to 'Abdu'l-Bahá, in *Throne of the Inner Temple*, p. 23.
585. From a letter written on behalf of Shoghi Effendi to an individual believer, 5 September 1949. *Lights of Guidance*, no. 978, p. 289.
586. From a letter written on behalf of Shoghi Effendi to an individual believer, 12 January 1957. *Lights of Guidance*, no. 956, p. 284.
587. From a letter written on behalf of Shoghi Effendi to an individual believer, 12 April 1948. *Lights of Guidance*, no. 948, p. 281.
588. From a letter written on behalf of Shoghi Effendi to an individual believer, 27 September 1947. Shoghi Effendi, *Unfolding Destiny*, p. 446.
589. From a letter written on behalf of Shoghi Effendi to an individual believer, 29 May 1935. Shoghi Effendi, *Unfolding Destiny*, p. 434.
590. From a letter written on behalf of Shoghi Effendi to an individual believer, 23 July 1953. *Lights of Guidance*, no. 943, p. 280.
591. From a letter written on behalf of the Universal House of Justice to an individual believer, 23 July 1984. *Lights of Guidance*, no. 954, pp. 283-4.
592. From a letter written on behalf of the Universal House of Justice to an individual believer, 15 June 1982. *Lights of Guidance*, no. 955, p. 284.
593. Bahá'u'lláh, *Hidden Words*, Arabic 32.
594. Bahá'u'lláh, *Gleanings*, pp. 155-6.
595. 'Abdu'l-Bahá, *Some Answered Questions*, p. 228.
596. ibid. p. 240.
597. 'Abdu'l-Bahá, *Selections*, p. 177.
598. 'Abdu'l-Bahá, *Some Answered Questions*, p. 232.
599. 'Abdu'l-Bahá, *Tablets*, p. 99.
600. From a Tablet of 'Abdu'l-Bahá to Charles Mason Remey. *Star of the West*, vol. 11, no. 15, p. 260.
601. 'Abdu'l-Bahá, *Tablets*, p. 51.
602. 'Abdu'l-Bahá, *Selections*, pp. 199-200.
603. 'Abdu'l-Bahá, *Tablets*, p. 86.

604. 'Abdu'l-Bahá, *Selections*, pp. 64-5.
605. 'Abdu'l-Bahá, quoted in *'Abdu'l-Bahá in London*, pp. 95-6.
606. Words attributed to 'Abdu'l-Bahá, quoted in Blomfield, *Chosen Highway*, p. 215.
607. Words attributed to 'Abdu'l-Bahá, quoted in Esslemont, *Bahá'u'lláh and the New Era*, p. 179.
608. 'Abdu'l-Bahá, *Paris Talks*, p. 179.
609. From a letter written on behalf of Shoghi Effendi to an individual believer, 3 October 1943. *Lights of Guidance*, no. 701, pp. 208-9.
610. From a letter written on behalf of Shoghi Effendi to an individual believer, 31 December 1932. *Lights of Guidance*, no. 697, p. 208.
611. From a letter written on behalf of Shoghi Effendi to an individual believer, 22 May 1935. *Lights of Guidance*, no. 683, pp. 204-5.
612. From a letter written on behalf of Shoghi Effendi to an individual believer, 19 September 1951.
613. From a letter written on behalf of Shoghi Effendi to an individual believer, 22 October 1932. *Lights of Guidance*, no. 696, pp. 207-8.
614. From a letter written on behalf of Shoghi Effendi to an individual believer, 13 January 1932. *Lights of Guidance*, no. 695, p. 207.

# Index

Universal House of Justice, 8

virtues, ix-xi, 13, 42, 98, 134,
    157, 200, 214, 217, 238
volition, *see* free will
war, 46, 47, 96, 115-16, 120,
    121, 123-4
weakness, 14-15, 78, 219-20
wealth, 93-5, 146, 171
West, the, 107, 111
wisdom, 21, 60-1
work, 87, 101, 147-8, 199
world, physical, x, 21-3, 27,
    91-102, 149-51, 183, 184,
    187-8, 201, 235, 254
World Order, New, 42, 121,
    137, 148, 150
worthiness, 212

Yaḥyá, Mírzá, 30, 188
youth, 224, 254

# The Arc of Ascent
*The Purpose of Physical Reality II*

by John S. Hatcher

John Hatcher examines the relationship between individual spiritual development and the progress of the global society in its mission to carry forward and 'ever-advancing civilization'.

*In this book Hatcher demonstrated how it is the divinely-ordained institutions of Bahá'u'lláh that give form to spiritual truths and function as channels through which God's long-awaited Kingdom can be established on this earth. Just as the physical human form is a vehicle through which the spiritual qualities are perfected and manifested, so these institutions are the vehicles through which God's Kingdom finds expression in social order on this earth.*
May Khadem, M.D., Assistant Professor, Northwestern University Medical School

*Professor Hatcher's profound statement about the Bahá'í Faith, written in the context of the great literature of the West, of which he is a master, wins the respect and esteem of religious people of all faiths. He writes with sincerity and elegance, a rare combination in the literature of religious philosophy and piety. Much is to be learned from him.*
Jacob Neusner, Distinguished Research Professor of Religious Studies, University of Florida

*. . . a masterly exposition on the evolution of the human spirit, employing literature, philosophy, theology, psychology and history to demonstrate the ultimate purpose of an all-loving Creator.*
Dr Duane K. Troxel, Associate Professor, University of Colorado at Denver

*Softcover only*
*400 pages*

*21.6 x 13.8 cm*
*ISBN 0-85398-371-2*

# Divine Therapy
*Pearls of Wisdom from the Bahá'í Writings*

compiled by Annamarie Honnold

*To all who seek inner peace and joy.*

*Every divine Manifestation is the very life of the world, and the skilled physician of each ailing soul.*　　　　　'Abdu'l-Bahá

We live in an 'age of anxiety'. The loss of serious interest in religion has deprived people of the help of ministers, priests and rabbis. 'Nowadays people go to the psycho-therapist rather than to the clergyman', wrote Carl Jung.

To the Bahá'í, 'All true healing comes from God. There are two causes for sickness, one is material, the other spiritual. If the sickness is of the body a material remedy is needed, if of the soul, a spiritual remedy.'

Psychiatry tells us to accept ourselves, religion tells us how to do so. This collection of quotations from the Bahá'í Sacred Writings offers vital help for emotional and spiritual healing. Grouped in three main sections, 'Coping with Stress', 'Orientation to the Divine' and 'Developing Helpful Attitudes', these 'pearls of wisdom' from the extensive literature of the Bahá'í Faith concentrate on common problems and their solutions, and will be of comfort and value to many.

*Softcover only*
*224 pages*
*21 x 13.8 cm*
*ISBN 0-85398-237-6*

# Dimensions in Spirituality

*Reflections on the Meaning of Spiritual Life and Transformation in Light of the Bahá'í Faith*

by J. A. McLean

Faced with the spiritual bankruptcy of contemporary society, increasing numbers of searching, thoughtful people are turning to various forms of spirituality to discover authentic selfhood, deeper meaning, and real and lasting happiness in their lives.

J. A. McLean offers the reader personal reflections and analysis of the writings of the Bahá'í Faith, combined with insights gleaned from spiritual psychology, philosophical theology and the world's religions in order to map out dimensions in spirituality. The author offers to the contemporary seeker insights into the search for truth, the meaning of prophetic faith and belief, prayer and meditation, finding meaning in adversity, the meaning of spirituality and transformation, the place of divine and human love in spiritual life, and the dynamics of spiritual growth.

*Softcover only*
*336 pages*
*23.2 x 15.3 cm*
*ISBN 0-85398-376-3*

# Reflections
*Verses from the Bahá'í Teachings*

Compiled by Akwasi O. Osei

*One hour's reflections is preferable to seventy years of pious worship.*
Bahá'u'lláh

A rich offering of verses taken from the Bahá'í writings, beautifully presented, to help us reflect on:

- The Meaning of Life

- The Mystery of Love

- Peace

- Virtue

- The Value of Deeds

- Religion

as well as

- The New World envisaged by Bahá'u'lláh

'a charming and refreshing collection of glittering jewels'
United Kingdom Bahá'í Review Panel.

*Softcover only*
*128 pages*
*19.2 x 12.9 cm*
*ISBN 0-85398-386-0*